HV 8699 .U5 H363 2001
Hamm, Theodore, 1966-
Rebel and a cause :
Caryl Chessman and the p
32355002858264

DATE DUE

THEODORE HAMM

Rebel and a Cause

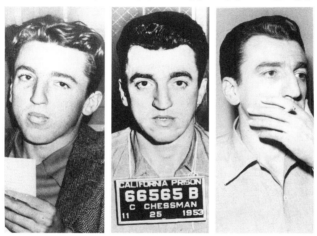

Caryl Chessman and the Politics of the
Death Penalty in Postwar California,
1948–1974

UNIVERSITY OF CALIFORNIA PRESS
BERKELEY   LOS ANGELES   LONDON

Photos on title page courtesy of AP/WIDE WORLD PHOTOS

University of California Press
Berkeley and Los Angeles, California

University of California Press, Ltd.
London, England

© 2001 by
The Regents of the University of California

Library of Congress Cataloging-in-Publication Data

Hamm, Theodore, 1966–
   Rebel and a cause : Caryl Chessman and the
politics of the death penalty in postwar California,
1948–1974 / Theodore Hamm.
       p.   cm.
   Includes bibliographical references and index.
   ISBN 0-520-22427-2 (alk. paper)—ISBN 0-520-
22428-0 (pbk. : alk. paper)
   1. Chessman, Caryl, 1921–1960.   2. Capital
punishment—California—History—20th century.
3. Death row inmates—California.   I. Title.
HV8699.U5 H363   2001
364.66'09749'09045—dc21

                                    2001027614

Printed in the United States of America
08 07 06 05 04 03 02 01
10 9 8 7 6 5 4 3 2 1

The paper used in this publication meets the mini-
mum requirements of ANSI/NISO Z39.48–1992
(R 1997) (*Permanence of Paper*).

For Mom and Jill

Contents

Acknowledgments

When this study first took shape in the mid-1990s, I was fortunate to spend an afternoon with Rosalie T. Asher, Chessman's attorney for nearly eleven years. While Rosalie is sure to disagree with some of my conclusions, I sincerely thank her for inspiring me to pursue the case.

I was lucky to have not one but two exemplary Ph.D. advisers at the University of California, Davis. It was from Michael L. Smith that I first learned the ins and outs of California history, and every step of the way he has brought his customary wit, generosity, and razor-sharp intellect to this project. Meanwhile, it was in the first-year seminar I took with Clarence Walker that I first learned the rules of the game. Ever since, Clarence has been a first-rate critic as well as a very good friend. Also at Davis, I give special thanks to Jay Mechling, Wilson Smith, Karen Halttunen, Ted W. Margadant, David Brody, Ruth Rosen, Cathy Kudlick, and to the late gentlemen-scholars Paul Goodman and C. Roland Marchand. I also am grateful to the entire department for honoring me with the Reed-Smith fellowship in 1994–95. The history department office there would not survive without the work of Debbie Lyon, Eteica Spencer, and Charlotte Honeywell, and I owe them a note of thanks as well.

A chance library recall first put me in contact with Paula Fass at Berkeley, and she immediately made me feel like a colleague. Especially for this, but no less for her perceptive insights, I am most appreciative. I also benefited greatly from my participation in the California Studies Group, and for this I particularly credit Dick Walker. The Center for Chinese

Studies at Berkeley might be an odd fit with my résumé, but my work stint there was extremely rewarding. Before leaving the Bay Area, I also had the wonderful opportunity to teach in the college program at San Quentin. Started by Professor Naomi Janowitz, the program is now run by my good friend Sean McPhetridge. To these two folks, as well as to the incomparable Vern Griffith, I am deeply in dept. Space prevents me from acknowledging all of my students in the San Quentin Project, so I'll only single out those with whom I worked most, namely Doug Mickey, Pete Edelbacher, Steven Ainsworth, Prentice Snow, and Armenia Cudjo, capable scholars all.

In these days of academic downsizing, I was doubly fortunate to serve as visiting assistant professor at the University of Massachusetts, Amherst, in the spring of 1998. I can't say enough about the support provided by Mary Wilson, Kathy Peiss, David Glassberg, Bruce Laurie, and the rest of the faculty and staff there. The graduate students in my "Race, Politics and Culture since 1930" seminar, in particular Leo Maley and Jeff Balfour, also helped make the semester extremely worthwhile. Since moving to New York, I have had the great pleasure of getting to know Danny Walkowitz, and I have benefited repeatedly from his constant support and always trenchant scholarly advice. My undergraduate advisor at Rutgers, Michael Rockland, has returned to become a trusted mentor at a different stage, and to him, too, I am extremely grateful. To Leslie Fishbein and the rest of the American studies department at Rutgers, and to Betts Brown and the entire metropolitan studies program at NYU, I say thanks for keeping me intellectually as well as financially afloat.

Innumerable libraries made this study possible. Most prominently, I am grateful to the library staff at Davis; the Bancroft Library; the California State Library; the California State Archives; Swarthmore College; the Southern California Library for Social Studies and Research; the Schomburg Center for Research in Black Culture; and the Tamiment Library at NYU. Similarly, I owe a note of appreciation to Tony Platt, who graciously allowed me to make use of his personal library of criminology texts. At UC Press, I am indebted to Monica McCormick for making this project happen, and to Jean McAneny for bringing it to press. Special thanks to Evan Camfield, for his first-rate job copyediting the manuscript. Quite literally, I owe my life to the medical staff at San Francisco General Hospital, who rescued me from a near-fatal bacterial infection in the winter of 1993. In terms of giving life to this particular study, though, I must emphasize my appreciation to the infinite array of people who took time—at cocktail parties, in locker rooms, and everywhere in between—to share their own remembrances of the Chessman case.

I saved my friends for next to last, but I trust that this will not be considered any sort of slight. From the first day of graduate school orientation, Drew Wood and I knew we would be pals forever. Time and again, both he and Monica Barczak have been there when I needed them, and when we just wanted to fire up the bbq. John Logan and I have also been tight since we started at Davis together, and in him and Adriana Craciun I am fortunate to have good friends across the Atlantic. Randolph Lewis and Circe Sturm, meantime, have brought down-home goodness into my life. Among other Davis comrades, Brad Schrager, Carl-Petter Sjovold, Dave Hendricks, and Amy Patterson top the list. Elsewhere, much respect goes to Tamara Falicov, and not only for tracking down all of the eclectic Chessman paraphernalia I now own. I can't thank all my pals in SF, but I will say that Monique Ramos and Mikey Taluc introduced me to most of them. Then there's all my chums at *The Brooklyn Rail,* who keep the words flowing. Between my antipodes have been the likes of Al Reeder and Maddie Soglin; Rayman Nedzel; J. Scott Burgeson; Alberto Gutierrez; Victoria Young and Jonas Salganik; and, of course, Jason Jones.

Ask anyone who has visited the Corona or Upland Public Libraries over the past few years and they are likely to tell you how they were assisted by the kindest, most helpful reference librarians they'd ever met. I am proud as well as grateful that such people are my dad, Bob, and stepmom, Yoga. As a scholar I could do worse than to have such tireless research assistants, and as a son I could hardly ask for more loving parents. To my in-laws and fellow *peregrinos,* Bill and Dorothy DeVoti, I can only express my amazement at how giving, supportive, and unusually tolerant of an underemployed son-in-law they have been. And it is to them, and Angie, as well as to a few angels above, that I owe thanks for the greatest present of all, namely Emily. Companion in both word and deed, and for life, she has truly been a gift sent directly from Providence.

TH
Brooklyn, New York 2000

Introduction

Today it is easy to forget that it was the Caryl Chessman case
in California in the late 1950s, more than any other criminal
case in the past generation, that stirred the national debate
over capital punishment. . . . If one were to approach the current national death penalty controversy by studying the political and legal struggle in one state, one could hardly do better
than to focus on California.

> Hugo Adam Bedau, The Courts, the Constitution,
> and Capital Punishment (1977)

Beginning in the mid-1950s, capital punishment faced renewed opposition in American society. Within a decade, states from Oregon to New
York eliminated the death penalty, the overall rate of executions slowed
considerably, and public opinion against capital punishment reached an
all-time high. Like their Jacksonian and Progressive predecessors, the
postwar generation of activists saw the death penalty as contradicting
what they viewed as the core principle of punishment: reforming the prisoner. This notion, known since the Progressive Era as the rehabilitative
ideal, fundamentally shaped the anti–death penalty sentiment witnessed
among growing numbers of American citizens during the late 1950s. This
study seeks to explain why the political and legal successes scored by
this most recent abolitionist campaign ultimately faced a powerful coun-
tertrend in public opinion, which by the late 1960s had turned dramatically in support of capital punishment.[1]

To assess postwar death penalty abolitionism, the following chapters focus primarily on the popular controversy surrounding the 1960
execution of Caryl Chessman. The Chessman case was interpreted by
liberal intellectuals, prison reformers, and activists as uniquely representative of the period's larger movement against capital punishment.[2]
Sentenced to death by a Los Angeles jury for sexually assaulting two
women on local lovers' lanes in 1948, Chessman received numerous

stays of execution as higher courts determined whether he received a fair right to appeal his original conviction. Rather than strictly legal considerations, however, it was Chessman's status as a prolific death row author that generated his widespread notoriety. For the vocal, often quite influential supporters who rallied to his defense, Chessman's written efforts seemed to clearly illustrate his therapeutic reform. Bay Area college student activists endorsed this view, and in their protests began to define the perspective that analysts would soon characterize as distinctly New Left. Chessman's May 1960 execution, in turn, sparked significant popular outcry, both outside the gates of San Quentin and at U.S. embassies around the world. Writing a decade later, the historian William O'Neill identified "the fight to save Caryl Chessman [as] the most important attack on capital punishment in American history."[3]

The following chapters mark an initial attempt both to place the Chessman debate in its historical context and to assess the larger movement against the death penalty during the late 1950s. As Maurice Isserman recently observed, the catalytic impact of Chessman's case on early New Left organizing has not received critical scrutiny;[4] nor, for that matter, has any attention been given to the manner in which the death penalty became instrumental in the California New Right's rise to power, a point first evidenced during the Chessman debate. Previous studies such as William Kunstler's *Beyond a Reasonable Doubt?* (1961) and Frank J. Parker's *Caryl Chessman: The Red Light Bandit* (1975), in fact, focused almost exclusively on the question of Chessman's guilt or innocence. Examining the trial, court records, and legal machinations of the case, these authors reached opposite conclusions about Chessman's guilt. As a result, the question of whether Chessman indeed committed the crimes for which he was executed will not be central here.[5] Rather, the historical issues of why so many postwar citizens embraced Chessman's cause—or, by contrast, viewed his execution as justified—form the core of this study. In many respects a debate over the larger therapeutic principles of postwar penology, these opposing views fundamentally shaped California politics of the early 1960s. From late 1959 forward, the early incarnations of both the New Left and New Right in the state would make extensive use of the Chessman controversy in their respective criticisms of the liberal administration of Governor Edmund G. (Pat) Brown (1958–1966).

An Overview

Carol (he began to use the spelling "Caryl" in his teens) Whittier Chessman was born in St. Joseph, Michigan, on May 27, 1921, the only child of Hallie and Serl Chessman, a Baptist couple. Later that year they moved to Glendale, California, near Pasadena. There Whittier "Serl" Chessman, a direct descendant of the poet John Greenleaf Whittier, worked at a variety of jobs, most notably his own Venetian blind business; by the late 1930s that venture failed, and the elder Chessman twice tried to commit suicide, both times unsuccessfully. Hallie Chessman, meanwhile, was left paralyzed after a 1929 automobile accident, a condition that caused her increased difficulty in raising her son, who was stricken with encephalitis at an early age. As Caryl later recounted, during adolescence he began to steal groceries and other goods in order to help his family make ends meet during the lean Depression years.[6]

In July 1937, Chessman was sent to Preston Industrial School for stealing a car, marking the first of his many visits to the state's disciplinary institutions; ultimately, Chessman would be confined for all but three of the next twenty-three years. Released the following April, Chessman was back at Preston in May, again convicted of automobile theft. In October 1939, Chessman got caught taking another car, and now was placed in Los Angeles County road camp. There he met other members of what became the "Boy Bandit Gang," all of whom were nabbed by L.A. authorities in April 1941 after a wild flurry of robberies and shootouts with police. For his efforts as self-proclaimed ringleader of the gang, Chessman was sentenced to San Quentin and then transferred to Chino, from which he escaped in October 1943. Arrested for robbery the next month in Glendale, Chessman returned north under a sentence of five years to life. After spending the majority of this stretch at Folsom State Prison, Chessman came home to Glendale in December 1947.[7]

Between January 3 and January 23, 1948, a rash of robberies occurred throughout the greater L.A. region, from Pasadena to Redondo Beach, including burglaries of two clothing stores, three muggings, and one car theft. During the same period, a pair of nonlethal sexual assaults were committed against Regina Johnson and Mary Alice Meza on two separate lovers' lanes, one in Flintridge Hills and the other on Mulholland Drive. Because the assailant approached the victims' cars flashing a red spotlight, imitating a police car, he became known as the "red light bandit." The red light bandit coerced both women to perform oral sex at gunpoint; he also unsuccessfully attempted to force intercourse on Meza.

On January 23, in the wake of a five-mile chase down Vermont Avenue, Caryl Chessman and an accomplice, David Knowles, were brought to the Hollywood police station, where they were held on suspicion of the various robberies as well as the sex crimes. In 1948, the accused were not yet legally entitled to have an attorney present, and after a seventy-two-hour interrogation, Chessman admitted to all charges, saying that he alone committed the sexual assaults. He would later claim that his confession had been beaten out of him by police. Both victims proceeded to positively identify Chessman as the red light bandit. Accordingly, in late January 1948, Chessman was formally charged with eighteen counts, including robbery, sexual assault, and kidnapping. Because the red light crimes involved moving the female victims from their cars, under Section 209 of the California penal code, better known as the "Little Lindbergh Law," they constituted "kidnapping with bodily harm," a capital offense. When Chessman stood trial in Los Angeles Superior Court in May 1948, he thus faced a prosecution determined to send him to the gas chamber for crimes that did not include murder.[8]

With the bravado he would display repeatedly over the next twelve years, Chessman represented himself in court. Indeed, he refused the services of the local public defender, assuring the initial judge that he was "a good enough lawyer." In so doing, he took on virtually alone the formidable tandem of Deputy District Attorney J. Miller Leavy and Judge Charles W. Fricke, both of whom had a strong track record of winning capital convictions. Both, moreover, would remain prominent and viscerally hostile spokesmen against clemency for Chessman.

The jury of eleven women and one man sentenced Chessman to death. But on June 23, 1948, two days before Chessman was scheduled to appear before Fricke for official sentencing, the original court reporter, Ernest Perry, died suddenly. Immediately, Chessman moved for a new trial based on what he predicted would be an inaccurate transcription of the original proceedings. Fricke denied Chessman's motion, but this issue would become the sticking point disputed in the higher courts over the next twelve years. Chessman's contention of inaccuracy would be strengthened by Fricke's appointment in July 1948 of the new court reporter: Stanley Fraser, an alleged alcoholic and Leavy's uncle by marriage. In October of that same year, the Executive Committee of the Los Angeles Superior Court Reporters' Association described Perry's original court shorthand as "completely undecipherable." Fricke, though, approved Fraser's first transcription in 1949, setting off a continuous battle between Chessman, now on death row at San Quentin, and the state, federal, and eventually U.S. Supreme courts. After the California Supreme Court accepted Fraser's transcript and affirmed Chessman's sentence, it appeared as though the execution would be carried out in March 1952. In late February of that year, however, state Supreme Court Justice Jesse W. Carter announced the first of what would eventually number eight stays of execution granted to Chessman, nearly all of which stemmed from the questionable accuracy of the trial transcript.[9]

While the contest between Chessman and the higher courts took place largely outside the public eye, the publication of Chessman's autobiographical work *Cell 2455 Death Row* in early May 1954 moved the case to center stage. Hailed by critics, Chessman's book instantly called attention to the author's impending execution, now set for May 14, 1954. On May 13, Marin County Superior Judge Thomas Keating signed another stay so that Chessman's writ of habeas corpus asking for a new trial (because of the transcript question) could be considered. Keating's action sparked a firestorm of controversy, prompting California Attorney General Pat Brown—not yet an outspoken opponent of capital punishment—to ask the state's highest judicial body to overturn it. The California Supreme Court indeed nixed the habeas corpus appeal a month later, but the conflict only intensified that summer. Scheduled to be part of a triple execution set for July 30, 1954, Chessman again received a last-minute reprieve, this time after one of his legal team tracked down Justice Carter, who was camping in the Sierras. Carter again stayed the execution, calling the transcript wholly unreliable and sending Chessman's writ of habeas corpus to the U.S. Supreme Court. Brown, in turn, moved unsuccessfully to block the two other executions set for that July 30, angrily stating, "There is no reason why a man who can write a book should have an advantage these two apparently friendless people do not have." Brown's hostile actions at this stage anticipated what ultimately would be his most clear-cut position regarding the Chessman case. Over the objections of Keating, Carter, and later Supreme Court Justice William O. Douglas, the higher courts repeatedly though narrowly rejected Chessman's appeals, and against his larger abolitionist scruples the future governor pledged to enact the death penalty while it remained California law.[10]

The transcript issue continued to be debated back and forth in the higher courts for the next five years. But when Brown assumed the governor's office in early 1959, his stance on the Chessman case seemed anything but certain. As attorney general, he had become the leading spokesman for the movement to abolish the death penalty in California.

Inexorably, the fate of that effort became entwined with the ongoing Chessman controversy. By late 1959, two more judicial stays had been granted, the legitimacy of the transcript had been affirmed after two separate hearings and no fewer than two thousand corrections, and Chessman had managed to have two more books smuggled out of San Quentin for publication. Because of the legal wrangling, Chessman had established a national record for longevity on death row, causing the American Civil Liberties Union and others to argue that his tenure now amounted to "cruel and unusual punishment." In preparation for a clemency hearing to be held between Brown and Chessman's attorneys in mid-October 1959, the governor's clemency secretary, Cecil Poole, expressed what would become the administration's overall view of the legal issues raised by the case. "Legally," Poole wrote, "the issue has not been Chessman's guilt or innocence." Instead, the controversy sprang from the higher courts' increasing concern with "procedural due process" during the postwar era. Though inseparable in theory, these views were held in abeyance by Poole, Brown, and other prominent officials involved in the case. Absolutely certain of the prisoner's guilt, Brown during the clemency meeting focused directly on the issue of rehabilitation, in the process showing his clear belief in the ideal even as he strongly disputed whether Chessman himself exemplified it.[11]

In late 1959 Chessman would again be spared from execution, this time because of a stay granted by U.S. Supreme Court Justice Douglas, who called for a review of lower court rulings. Shortly thereafter, though, the full Supreme Court declined to hear the case, and Chessman's new execution date was set for February 19, 1960. By mid-February of that year the controversy occupied front-page headlines, and voices in opposition to Chessman's death sentence emerged from across the state, the nation, and, increasingly, the world. Warned by the State Department about the possibility of disruptive protests over the Chessman affair during President Eisenhower's concurrent trip to South America, Governor Brown announced his most controversial decision. On February 18, the day before the scheduled execution, Brown gave Chessman a sixty-day reprieve while simultaneously declaring that he would bring a bill recommending abolition of the death penalty before the state legislature. That bill never left committee, but the impact on Brown's political career was nevertheless devastating; even though he would allow Chessman's execution to proceed—in the midst of even more public outcry—in May 1960, the California right, led by the Los Angeles press and soon by Richard Nixon, charged that Brown had "wavered" in his handling of the case. Meanwhile, for death penalty abolitionists, within whose ranks could be counted some of the most vocal activists of the early New Left, Brown's ultimate betrayal in allowing Chessman to go to the gas chamber likewise would not soon be forgotten.[12]

The Issues

Throughout the Chessman case two competing narratives vied for public acceptance. Beginning with his 1948 trial, Los Angeles prosecutors and local media portrayed Chessman as a violent, menacing "sex fiend." In the particularly heated climate of postwar Los Angeles, the extreme sentence Chessman received fit with a larger official backlash against a perceived increase in sexual transgression, violent and otherwise, which observers linked to the wartime growth of the city. Although few other executions would result, state politicians frequently proposed similar usage of the Little Lindbergh Law in order to combat the postwar sex crime "wave" apparently engulfing the city and state. The popular psychiatric linkage between so-called "sexual psychopaths" and homosexual behavior (first developed by Army psychiatrists during World War II) would also play a part in the Chessman debate. Chessman's detractors further stressed the impact of this psychopathic behavior on the plight of his two female victims, one of whom—Mary Alice Meza—remained institutionalized (for schizophrenia) after 1949. As the Southern California press stoked public support for his 1960 execution, the sexual conflicts of the early postwar period continued to inform the popular narrative against Chessman.[13]

A different set of professional "experts" would shape popular opinion in defense of Chessman. In the wake of the 1954 release of *Cell 2455 Death Row,* leading criminologists and literary critics endorsed Chessman's claims that he had been reformed. During this period, politicians, prison officials, criminologists, psychiatrists, and a wide range of other professional observers all espoused belief in the postwar prison as a site of rehabilitation. As California's national importance grew in the aftermath of World War II, the state's criminal justice system advertised itself as the leader in implementing the "new penology." Influential criminologists like Harry Elmer Barnes and Negley K. Teeters, along with liberal intellectuals like Max Lerner and Elizabeth Hardwick, viewed Chessman's writings as particularly illustrative of the new penology's connections between reading, writing, and individual reform. By contrast, San Quentin psychiatrists and wardens, as well as Governors Warren, Knight, and Brown, saw Chessman as a fundamentally defiant, unchanged criminal psychopath. However contradictory, these opposing views of Chessman's specific individual character generated extensive public debate about the larger therapeutic premise of the postwar criminal justice system itself.[14]

As it provided a unique forum for public discussion of the modern reform ideal, the Chessman controversy also marked a clear departure in twentieth-century protest against capital punishment. The most notable anti–death penalty campaigns witnessed since the Progressive Era (around the cases of Tom Mooney, Sacco and Vanzetti, the Scottsboro Boys, and the Rosenbergs) had been led by leftist organizations, especially labor unions and the Communist Party. Just prior to Cell 2455's 1954 publication, California Governor Goodwin Knight (1953–1958) had responded to a popular campaign by granting clemency to Wesley Robert Wells, an African American prisoner, whose defense was led by the Communist-affiliated Civil Rights Congress, in tandem with left labor unions and the black press. Wells's supporters critiqued his death sentence (for throwing an ashtray at a prison guard) as an example of "prison Jim Crow." The Chessman defense, by contrast, rising to prominence at the end of the Red Scare, had few direct ties to an existing left. Rather, Chessman launched his public appeal in the name of ascendant notions of behavioral expertise. Like the several thousand self-defined "ordinary" citizens who wrote to Governors Knight and Brown about the case, Chessman himself argued against the death penalty in the name of individual contribution and therapeutic rehabilitation. Common to abolitionist discourse by the late 1950s, these ideals nevertheless stood in sharp contrast to the critique of racial and class discrimination articulated by the Wells defense. Equally important was a parallel tactical transition: with middle-class professionals now steering the debate, a focus on state policymaking replaced grassroots political organizing as the preferred abolitionist strategy against the death penalty. Driven by liberal criminologists, attorneys, lobbying organizations, and sympathetic public officials, from the mid-1950s onward California abolitionism was characterized first by legislative then by legal campaigns.

The evident tension between liberal death penalty abolitionism and the New Right's eventual political response ultimately casts doubt on one of the prevailing postwar assumptions held by anti–death penalty criminologists, lawyers, and activist organizations alike—namely, that the death penalty can and should be abolished regardless of public opinion on the issue. As most carefully defined by the criminologists/legal scholars Franklin Zimring and Gordon Hawkins, this approach urges the United States to follow the example of other Western industrial nations, where previously overwhelming support for the death penalty declined precipitously in the wake of official abolition during the 1950s. For Zimring and Hawkins, the impetus for a comparable United States effort will come mainly from the Supreme Court, but also from the work of "brave governors" who follow the advice of "opinion-leading elites." "Minority opposition to the death penalty can be a political problem if it emanates from people who count," they write. California's experience during the Brown-Reagan years, however, illustrates the perils of ignoring broader public opinion.[15]

Voicing many of the same criticisms as the period's leading specialists, Governor Brown publicly pushed for abolition and became the figurehead of the liberal approach. It was this position that rendered his stance in the Chessman case so controversial. Despite solid majority support for capital punishment, the spark generated by the 1960 Chessman protests had caused a number of key participants to call for a grassroots campaign aimed at a popular referendum on the issue. Such a course was never taken, causing left participants to criticize the "distrust of the people" evident among liberal politicians and lobbying organizations like the Friends Committee on Legislation. Indeed, seduced by their unique access to the postwar state, liberal abolitionists effectively allowed the New Right to capture the popular death penalty debate unimpeded by popular political resistance.[16]

Initially relentless in his legislative efforts against capital punishment, by 1963 Brown had switched to an executive strategy, staying virtually every execution in order to help create a logjam in the higher courts. Richard Nixon made the death penalty fundamental to his (unsuccessful) 1962 gubernatorial campaign against Brown. After the 1965 Watts conflict, "law and order" formed a central component of Ronald Reagan's "white backlash" campaign for governor. Early in his administration (1966–1974), Reagan defined his pro–death penalty stance in opposition to black militance; over his first six years in office, moreover, Reagan continually clashed with the NAACP's Legal Defense Fund, which targeted California's racially biased use of the death penalty. By the late 1960s, the federal courts began to respond positively to the NAACP-led legal campaign. In response, the New Right steadily mobilized public support for restoration, and later expansion, of the death penalty. When the U.S. Supreme Court abolished the death penalty in 1972, two-thirds of California voters endorsed Proposition 17, a

Reagan-sponsored ballot initiative calling for restoration of the state's death penalty. Simultaneously antitherapeutic and antitechnocratic, Reagan's pro–death penalty politics were instrumental in helping the California New Right build an enduring popular consensus against the Great Society liberalism of the Pat Brown years.

In examining the growth, then the splintering, of middle class opposition to the death penalty, this study is comprised of five chapters. As chapter one demonstrates, earlier abolitionist movements coexisted with comparable efforts at prison reform. After a survey of the Jacksonian and Progressive Era movements, this chapter connects the Chessman controversy to the spread of the "new," therapeutic principles of postwar penology. Chapter two introduces the popular narrative that developed against Chessman, which argued that he was a dangerous product of the sex crime "wave" besetting postwar Los Angeles. Relying on popular psychiatric theories, newspaper columnists and hostile public officials stridently declared Chessman to be an unreformable sexual psychopath, a menacing condition these critics sensationalized by making frequent reference to the plight of his female victims. As examined in chapter three, Chessman responded to this portrayal by trying literally to write his way off death row. Because Chessman's books seemed to manifest vividly postwar notions of writing and rehabilitation, criminologists and liberal intellectuals helped initiate the popular campaign on his behalf.

Chapter four contrasts the Wells defense with Chessman's, paying particular attention to the shift from left to liberal death penalty protest during the mid-1950s. As illustrated by the letters they wrote to Governors Knight and especially Brown, thousands of self-identified "ordinary citizens" felt inspired enough by the Chessman case to argue strenuously against the death penalty in the name of therapeutic penology; in so doing, they showed the ways in which "new class" abolitionist ideals resonated with a growing sector of the postwar "new middle class." Lastly, chapter five traces the impact of the Chessman controversy on the politics of criminal justice in California during the 1960s. While Chessman's case sparked mobilization from the New Left and especially the New Right, by the end of the 1960s both the NAACP and the Black Panther Party moved questions of racial bias, rather than the rehabilitative ideal, to the center of criminal justice debate. Well into the following, explosive decade, both the New Left and the New Right in California thus kept the Chessman controversy alive in order to challenge the liberal ideals the case had most dramatically raised.

CHAPTER ONE

The Antithesis of Reform

The death penalty is the antithesis of the rehabilitative,
non-punitive, non-vindictive orientation of twentieth century
penology.

> *Donal E. J. MacNamara, president of the*
> *American League to Abolish Capital*
> *Punishment (1961)*

[If] Chessman is executed . . . I predict that this will touch off
a vast movement in the United States against capital punishment, which may not be such a bad thing either!

> *James Simmons of Hayward to Governor*
> *Goodwin Knight, July 10, 1954*

Movements against the death penalty have occurred cyclically throughout the course of American history. In the wake of the American Revolution, prominent public officials began to criticize capital punishment,
viewing it as antithetical to the new nation's republican ideals. By the
1840s, growing protest from a variety of influential quarters enabled
a number of state legislatures to end public executions, and a handful
of states eliminated capital punishment altogether. Public opposition to
the death penalty faded from prominence until the Progressive Era,
when it reemerged among reform-oriented prison administrators and
like-minded politicians, resulting in the abolition of the death penalty by
voter referendum in a handful of states. The post–World War II period
saw renewed popular campaigns against the death penalty, which proved
successful in a handful of states.[1]

The same three periods with substantial anti–death penalty campaigns—the 1840s, 1910s, and 1950s—also witnessed reform movements aimed at transforming the character of punishment itself. Each of
the struggles against capital punishment occurred during periods when
the goal of reforming the prisoner aroused great concern among public
officials and their predominantly liberal, mainly middle class constituencies. As Donal E. J. MacNamara's statement above illustrates, prison

activists have frequently recognized the link between opposition to the death penalty and a broader conception of criminal justice. Historiographically, however, movements either directed against capital punishment or on behalf of prison reform have been treated separately. Studies of the former have tended to emphasize the intellectual and cultural roots of opposition to the death penalty, thus underestimating the link between prison management and popular views of criminal justice.[2] Works addressing prison reform, conversely, have tended to overlook the ways in which the death penalty has sparked broader debate about the nature of American punishment itself.[3] In short, the reciprocal impact of the two movements on one another has not been fully assessed.

The repeated link between campaigns targeting prison improvement with those opposing the death penalty raises the fundamental question: why reform prisoners? Why have so many past efforts to change the nature of imprisonment been based on this notion, and why has this ideal become prominent in some periods rather than others? A number of common features of the 1840s, 1910s, and the 1950s suggest some key contributing factors. All three of these periods saw a rapid expansion of the middle class, in terms of both economics and, more important, public influence. From this expansion emerged vocal ranks of citizens who sought to establish their identity as a class, a fact best illustrated by their broad participation in various reform movements. Each period also witnessed a growing concern with national self-identification, or American values, though the meaning of such values would alter considerably. These features indeed form a common backdrop, but alone they cannot explain why the issues of prison reform and the death penalty only intermittently galvanized significant public outcry.

Instead, the issues raised by public debates over punishment illuminated a set of middle class values specific to each era. In the Jacksonian period, reformers looked to the disciplinary regimen of industrial capitalism as the appropriate means of reforming prisoners and other deviants.[4] Progressive Era activists, by contrast, sought to make prison more like the outside community, indicating a widespread confidence among professional specialists in the ability of schools, recreational activities, and other institutions to foster reform.[5] Postwar observers shared many of the assumptions of their Progressive predecessors, differing only in their level of success. Between 1945 and 1965, for example, the California prison system typified the Progressive ideal of modeling prison after life in the outside community, this time under the modern variant of reform, namely rehabilitation.[6] In general, these disciplinary efforts expressed a public confidence in the ability of American institutions to return the outcast to the community. Each movement, however, diminished markedly when confronted with broader social and political conflict, whether brought on by the Civil War, the aftermath of World War I, or the 1960s. This pattern suggests that a decrease in popular outcry against the death penalty often corresponded with a wider diminution in public confidence in the general ameliorative capacities of American institutions.

The shifting approaches to punishment during these three reform-oriented eras reflected historic changes in popular explanations of criminal behavior. No longer the innate sinner of the colonial era, by the nineteenth century the criminal came to be viewed as either the product of a faulty environment or, more dramatically, as a "monster" existing outside of community norms. Influenced strongly by the new sociology of the Chicago School, Progressives targeted the eradication of slum life and created institutions designed to instill middle class habits in the deviant. Postwar penologists and other specialists identified both environment and, increasingly, the psychological character of criminals as crucial, and they designed a prisoner's therapeutic regimen of rehabilitation accordingly. In each era, punishment contradicting the prevailing ideals —whether isolation (in the Progressive Era) or the death penalty (at all other times)—provoked severe objection from those most actively attending to these issues.

The public debate over Caryl Chessman's execution illustrated the specific influences shaping popular opposition to the death penalty in the postwar period. Chessman had been defined by the courts, prison psychiatrists, and the press as a sex criminal, and his case thus generated considerable discussion over the causes and impact of such criminal behavior. Yet while on death row Chessman became a prolific writer, proving to many experts and ordinary citizens that he fit the postwar model of the rehabilitated prisoner. Liberal intellectuals and ordinary citizens thus rallied behind Chessman, viewing his execution as a contradiction of the ideals of postwar American criminal justice. Indeed, in the course of the Chessman protests, the stream of influences comprising the postwar anti–death penalty movement—from reaction to the horrors of World War II to the spread of behavioral science—came visibly to the surface.

Locating the roots of the arguments against Chessman's 1960 execution requires a return to the initial debates over imprisonment itself. How has belief in the ideal of prison as a site of individual reform influenced public activism against the death penalty? In what ways can movements based around such principles be characterized as distinctly middle class? The answers to these questions shed considerable light on the closely related issue of why identifiable campaigns against capital punishment have arisen only in certain periods during American history. An initial survey of the historic links between prison reform and larger popular sentiment against the death penalty thus helps place the mid-twentieth century struggle in perspective. That the Chessman controversy originated in California is no coincidence, for this was the state where the modern rehabilitative ideal was most actively implemented and contested. In challenging the California prison system to conform to its stated goal, the Chessman campaign starkly outlined the particular set of issues facing postwar opponents of the death penalty.

The Jacksonian Era

Rhetorically, the ideal of reform has provided historic legitimation of the prison itself. By the mid-1790s, the earliest prisons established at Philadelphia and Newgate (New York) revealed the basic outlines of what would later become the American penitentiary system. Although not strictly a Quaker effort, the Walnut Street Jail (built in 1794) enacted a regime of solitary confinement reflecting the Quakerite emphasis on the "inner light," or individual acceptance of God's truth. By day Walnut Street prisoners worked at small craft production and by night they read the Bible, at all times within the confines of their cells. Conversely, under the supervision of Quaker merchant Thomas Eddy, Newgate—erected in 1796—encouraged both religious worship and inculcation of "habits of industry and society." According to W. David Lewis, "To Eddy's mind, the reformation of the offender was the chief end of punishment." By the 1820s, New York's so-called Auburn system merged Eddy's industrial program with elements of what was now termed the Pennsylvania system, combining industrial labor by day with solitary confinement by night, all under the rule of silence.[7]

That the establishment of the early prisons was accompanied by wholesale revisions in the two state's criminal codes, whereby prison replaced execution as punishment for a wide variety of offenses, illustrated the degree to which early reformers recognized the contradiction between capital punishment and the ostensibly reformative mission of imprisonment. "The punishment of death precludes the possibility of the amendment of the criminal by any human means," one critic declared.

In the early republic, historian Louis Masur argues, opponents of public executions prioritized both humanitarian objections to violence and republican concerns about the importance of virtue in making their arguments. According to Masur, early reformers like Benjamin Rush "feared in public executions the onset of a destructive cycle. The State hanged criminals to control disorder. Executions, however, by brutalizing and demoralizing spectators, generated more crime, resulting in additional executions." Humanitarian reformers focused on the dangerous impact of violence on those who witnessed it, while republican theorists emphasized the role of individual virtue in maintaining public order. Observers like Rush found the raucous nature of crowd behavior at public executions quite threatening, in that it suggested that the public enjoyed the spectacle of violence, thereby lessening the didactic impact of the gallows.[8]

The new types of punishment implemented during the early republic reflected a changing cultural explanation for the origins of criminal behavior. During the colonial period, the criminal offender was seen as a sinner before God, but one with whom the community shared a collective responsibility. As revealed by colonial execution sermons, the presence of crime indicated a powerful sense of communal guilt while offering little hope of amelioration. By the late eighteenth century, however, ideas rooted in Lockeian psychology gained increasing acceptance. Locke's tabula rasa had suggested that criminal behavior was not predestined, but instead learned by experience. Accordingly, in the Pennsylvania system prisoners would be kept separate in order to prevent the prison from becoming a breeding ground of criminal activity. By contrast, the Auburn system allowed for prisoners to interact, albeit silently, so that they might adopt a new industrial regimen. In both cases, the gallows—though still frequently used—was increasingly considered problematic, for it implied that the new institutions failed in their efforts to alter the character of the deviant.[9]

The 1830s saw the rise of prison reform societies, groups comprised of middle class citizens dedicated to both the efficient management of penitentiaries and to improving the lot of prisoners. Headed by Louis Dwight, the Boston Prison Discipline Society became a strong advocate of the Auburn system. In terms similar to those later used by Michel Foucault in describing the "panoptic" effect of prisons, Dwight explained how the Auburn system of discipline offered "a principle of very extensive application to families, schools, academies, colleges, factories, mechanics' shops." The New York Prison Discipline Society, formed in

1844, aimed "not at the infliction of retributive pain on the prisoner, but at his reformation." Though not as confident in the promise of the Auburn system as its Boston counterpart, the New York society accepted the principle of industrial labor while focusing more on ending harsh physical punishments. With the passage of an antiflogging bill by the New York legislature in 1847, the reformers had succeeded in removing one symbol of punishment they found both distasteful and counterproductive.[10]

During the Jacksonian period, popular debate about capital punishment similarly centered on removing what public officials saw as the troubling spectacle of public executions. Yet, ironically, after public executions were eliminated in the mid-1830s, organized activism aimed at eliminating the death penalty as a whole increased dramatically. Created in the mid-1840s, the New York and Massachusetts Societies for the Abolition of Capital Punishment tended to argue against the death penalty from a Whig perspective. "Many Whigs," according to Masur, "saw the gallows as an impediment to the kind of society they dreamed of fashioning: industrious, self-disciplined, and culturally homogenous. The execution of a citizen was a confession that the Whig ideal did not always work." Such ideals would suffuse antebellum debate, as Whigs and other engaged citizens saw it as their responsibility to create a society where industriousness and self-discipline prevailed. In 1849 Wendell Phillips argued vociferously against the death penalty, claiming it was the responsibility of the "favorable community," or the "moral and intellectual elite of the state," to reform the outcast. Led by other notable figures like William Cullen Bryant and Horace Greeley, the era's anti–death penalty organizations consisted of thousands of middle class citizens, many of whom actively participated in a variety of other ongoing reform campaigns.[11]

The overlapping efforts for improved prison discipline and against capital punishment must be understood precisely in relation to these other reform movements. Indeed, the prison drives were similar in composition to abolitionist, temperance, antiprostitution, and various evangelical campaigns during the antebellum era. The activists were part of the period's rapidly expanding middle class, while their subjects were those whose lives existed outside of the demands of industrial capitalism. Participation in such public organizing campaigns allowed a vocal faction of citizens to define who they were as a class by involving themselves in changing the lives of people whose values they considered inappropriate. In terms of prison issues, the reformers tended to see themselves as the "moral and intellectual elite" most capable of bringing the deviant back to the community, which they would do by "kindness, not coercion." To adjust to their newfound place in the market economy, Jacksonian prison activists actively spread the new gospel of industrial discipline. Their watchdog efforts, in turn, enabled capital punishment foes to view the sentence of life imprisonment as an acceptable alternative. This "out of sight, out of mind" line of thinking confirms David Brion Davis's argument concerning the underlying motivation behind antebellum objections to capital punishment: "escaping communal guilt." In their work, antebellum activists implicitly defined the meaning of a middle class movement against the death penalty: It would be led by a vocal core of civic-minded professionals who sought to insure that the punishments their society enacted were neither violent nor cruel, and that the institutions they helped manage could effectively reform even those whom society deemed to be its most wayward criminals.[12]

By the mid-1850s, however, popular opposition to capital punishment had subsided. Legislatures in three states (Michigan, Rhode Island, and Wisconsin) abolished the death penalty between 1847 and 1853. Yet these legislative successes were not backed by the support of a widespread popular movement; by the early 1850s membership in anti–death penalty and prison reform organizations had dwindled considerably. Understandably, the attention of middle class reformers and ordinary citizens had now turned to the more pressing issue of slavery. For abolitionists, the peculiar institution's brutality implied communal guilt, whereas the expansion of the northern market economy strengthened a regime based principally on industrial self-discipline. Within a decade, as Davis argues, the mass killing produced by the sectional conflict would make the question of individual executions seem quite small indeed.[13]

The Progressive Era

Prison reform did not again become a subject of popular debate until the Progressive Era. Prior to the 1890s, neither the brutality of Southern convict leasing nor the poor conditions of northern prisons caused significant protest. Historians of the period attribute the lack of general concern to the composition of the prison populations; the plight of neither emancipated African Americans nor immigrants to the industrial north elicited popular sympathy during the latter decades of the nineteenth century. Nonetheless, a few voices of prison innovation did emerge during the period, and their ideas would help lay the groundwork for the Progressive Era reform movement.[14]

In the early 1870s, Enoch Wines, Franklin Sanborn, and Zebulon Brockway launched the National Congress of Penitentiary and Reformatory Discipline. In its Declaration of Principles, the Congress sounded a familiar theme: the "reformation of criminals, not the infliction of vindictive suffering." Although such a goal in principle was no different from that of Jacksonian reformers, the statement then advocated a fundamentally new practice for its realization. A prisoner's "proof of reformation," the Congress said, would now hold the key to his release. During the 1880s, Brockway attempted to implement this goal at the Elmira Reformatory in New York. In praising Brockway's efforts, *The North American Review* called Elmira a "great industrial and educational establishment," where the inmate was ready "to work out his own salvation." The notion that a prisoner should "prove his reformation," in turn, would sustain the key penal innovations of the Progressive Era, namely the indeterminate sentence, probation and parole.[15]

Between 1900 and 1920, a diverse coalition rallied behind the cause of prison reform. Most northern and western states would indeed pass legislation during this period in support of the indeterminate sentence, probation, and parole. According to David Rothman, these changes reflected the thinking of "concerned citizens, settlement house workers, psychologists, and psychiatrists . . . directors of charitable societies, judges, district attorneys, wardens and superintendents." Each group's rationale may have been different, but on one fundamental point they could agree: the uniform discipline of the Jacksonian period needed to be replaced by an individualized model of treatment. Yet, paradoxically, each prisoner's specific program would be carried out in the more communal atmosphere of the rehabilitative prison. As they held both ideas simultaneously, Progressive reformers further evinced a notable certainty regarding the ability of correctional institutions to successfully alter the behavior of their subjects.[16]

In emphasizing individual treatment, the Progressive prison combined the growing insights of both sociology and psychiatry. As targeted by settlement house activists, or as analyzed by the fieldworkers of the Chicago School, the detrimental impact of life in the so-called slums became a catch-all explanation for problems such as crime. According to Rothman, Progressives nevertheless treated the issues faced by their subjects in individual terms; the road to a well-ordered lifestyle, in short, differed according to each person's circumstances. Similarly, the emerging field of psychiatric analysis understood the problem of criminal behavior in individualized terms. This discourse, which became increasingly prominent from the 1920s onward, located the sources of deviance in the mental composition of each subject. Although these two interpretations—slum environment versus individual deficiency—seem quite different, Progressives held them in awkward balance. Together these two views led to the development of the classification system of prisoners, whereby the initial diagnosis of a prisoner's chances for rehabilitation determined the course of his particular therapeutic program.[17]

Despite the growing emphasis on individualized treatment, Progressives tried to make daily prison affairs more closely resemble life in the outside community. Innovators like Sing Sing warden Thomas Mott Osborne attempted to introduce vocational classes, organized recreation, and entertainment into the prison. Such programs, Osborne stated, were designed to make inmates "not good *prisoners,* but good *citizens.*" Although not widely realized until the post–World War II period, Osborne's ideas shared a similar intellectual basis with the shift toward indeterminate sentencing and parole. As Jonathan Simon maintains, Progressives, unlike their Jacksonian predecessors, held a fundamental confidence in the ability of early twentieth century industrial society to provide social stability. In the minds of earlier activists, Simon argues, penitentiaries were "designed to replace the chaos of the industrial community with rigorous techniques of training and control." For Progressives, however, prisons "now loomed as chaotic communities of the corrupt cut off from the organizing forces of the industrial community." The reformed prisoner, Progressives believed, was not simply a disciplined worker but a full-fledged participant in modern American society.[18]

Indeed, the buoyant outlook of Progressives toward the promise of American life sustained the new methods of prison discipline. Progressives, according to Rothman, "had no fundamental quarrel with the American economic and social system . . . and were equally convinced of the supreme desirability of a middle-class lifestyle in cultural as well as material terms." This disposition inspired many of the reform efforts of the period, from settlement house work to the prison reform movement. Just as they had confidence in the superiority of their own worldview, middle class reformers believed in their own abilities as managerial experts to guide various institutions. Wardens, parole board members, psychiatrists, and other professional specialists gained tremendous authority with the shift toward indeterminate sentencing and parole. It was they who would judge whether a prisoner had proved his reformation, a change which provoked little controversy. Officials of the era justified their innovations because they saw themselves as trained experts, and in a broader sense as humanitarians. As California's head of parole wrote to the State Board of Prison Directors in 1917: "From a humanitarian standpoint . . . men who [have] committed crimes have a far better chance to recover their self-respect and become useful members of the community outside of prison walls." Active on a variety of fronts, Progressives updated Wendell Phillips's earlier stated call for the "favorable community" to take responsibility for the wayward deviants in its midst.[19]

The movement against the death penalty during the Progressive Era was small and short-lived, but it nonetheless revealed important ties to the prison reform effort. Between 1910 and 1920, a number of states— including Minnesota, Oregon, and Missouri—abolished capital punishment. The size and western location of the states illustrated the failure of the movement to gain significant national success, but the process in Oregon and Missouri clarified the connection between prison reform, opposition to the death penalty, and broader political and social change. Between 1911 and 1915, Oregon's Governor Oswald West led the state's efforts to ban all executions. Invoking the theme of institutional progress, West called the death penalty a representative of the "old barbarous system" of criminal justice. The Oregon state legislature responded by repealing capital punishment in 1915. After spirited debate, Missouri's state legislature followed suit two years later. In analyzing the Missouri directive, Ellen Guillot connected abolitionist sentiment to "the movement for the reform of prison life and for the reformation of individual criminals [which] was at that time nation-wide." According to Guillot, "the basic idea" that death penalty opponents presented to the legislature "was that capital punishment forestalled the possibility of reformation."[20]

Yet in the immediate aftermath of World War I, both states restored the death penalty. Oregon's new governor, James Withycombe, called for its return in order to combat "I.W.W.ism and other forms of disloyalty." Withycombe's successor, Ben W. Olcott, declared that since 1919 "a wave of crime has swept over the country." In response, Oregon voters brought back the death penalty by popular referendum in 1920. A pair of well-publicized murders of police officers, both by prisoners on parole, caused a similar increase in public support for capital punishment in Missouri. In 1919, the state legislature allowed for the return of executions and simultaneously enacted restrictions on parole. Thus, where Progressives had ardently tried to sell the public on their innovative methods of institutional reform, various public officials countered by using the events of the post–World War I period to expand the definition of criminal behavior. Against the backdrop of labor activism and political radicalism, the goal of rehabilitating criminals gave way to the need to punish all those who challenged the authority of the state.[21]

In a recent analysis John Galliher, Gregory Ray, and Brent Cook identify a number of characteristics common to the various movements to abolish the death penalty (and to the movements to reinstate it) during the Progressive Era. In the ten states that ended capital punishment during the period, influential politicians usually led the effort. Governor George Hunt of Arizona, for example, told the state's first legislature in 1912, "I subscribe to the belief that the murderer may be punished far more effectively through the medium of an awakened consciousness than by the breaking of his neck." Such widespread belief in prison as the appropriate site of regeneration was shaken by the well-publicized claims of unrepentant murderers in a number of states. In several separate instances, according to Galliher, "A convicted murderer publicly acknowledged that he might not have committed the crime had the threat of the death penalty existed." Leading public officials may have supported Progressive ideas of prison rehabilitation, but upon hearing such frightening claims from the prisoners themselves, voters quickly soured. Moreover, in states like Colorado, Arizona, and Tennessee, a rash of race-based lynchings followed upon the abolition of the death penalty, sparking fears of "mob violence" among public officials. As Galliher's study reveals, racial politics greatly influenced patterns of reinstatement during the early 1920s. Of the ten states that banned executions, only the two with the most homogenous populations (Minnesota and North Dakota) did not bring the punishment back by the 1930s. Post–World War I radicalism thus merged with the threat posed by the period's black migrations in stoking public sentiment in favor of the death penalty. Under attack from both inside and outside prison, popular support for abolition—as well as for the larger Progressive reform ideal—faded by the early 1920s.[22]

The New Penology

During the 1920s and 1930s there was little public interest in ameliorating the conditions of prison life. The Great Depression produced severe overcrowding inside prisons, making reform experiments—such as

the Norfolk (Mass.) Prison Colony—difficult to sustain. Prison administrators rarely voiced support for penal innovation, and the institutions
generally came to be seen as brutal human warehouses devoid of any direct economic utility. Despite the sensational controversies generated by
the execution of Sacco and Vanzetti in 1927 and the death sentence col-
lectively received by the Scottsboro Boys in the 1930s (discussed in chapter two), the period also lacked a sustained movement against the death
penalty as a whole. The overall rate of executions in the United States
reached its height (at least until the current period) during the Depression, and a 1936 Gallup Poll recorded 68 percent death penalty support
nationwide. Two decades later, however, an identifiable movement to
ban capital punishment again surfaced. As the rate of executions reached
a thirty-year low, the voices raised in favor of abolition came from a wide
spectrum of American citizens. In a variety of ways, the experience of
World War II sparked renewed interest in prison reform and helped re-
vive middle class opposition to the death penalty.[23]

The public drive for prison reform made its strongest impact in the
state most dramatically transformed by the war, namely California. In
the late 1930s a number of press scandals exposing the severity of punishment in California prisons, including several at the federal penitentiary at Alcatraz, awakened public interest in prison affairs. Yet it was
not until late 1943, in the wake of another media controversy, that Governor Earl Warren launched a massive overhaul of the state's prison
system. Sensational outcry about the "yacht bandit," a Folsom Prison
convict named Lloyd Sampsell, provided the final catalyst for Warren's
reform drive. San Francisco newspapers discovered that Sampsell, with
the complicity of prison guards, had been a regular weekend visitor on
his girlfriend's yacht in San Francisco Bay. Aside from helping to rectify
widespread corruption and public perception of lax treatment of prisoners, the Sampsell affair enabled prison administrators to promote
their real goal in overhauling the state's prison system: an end to "idleness." In explaining the intent of the Prison Reorganization Act of 1944,
Richard McGee, the director of the state's newly created Department of
Corrections, stated, "there is too much idleness at Folsom . . . it is my
belief [that] inmates should be occupied with industrial production or
agriculture." While amending seemingly lax prison conditions made for
good press, it was the wartime need for prison labor that truly catalyzed
California's embrace of the new rehabilitative penology.[24]

The Reorganization Act implemented many of the reforms that Progressives had long advocated. The key to "good penal administration," McGee declared, was the presence of "professionalized personnel." Although McGee referred to prison guards, his position lent support to the other trained specialists, like psychiatrists and social workers, whose strength had grown over the previous two decades. The Act also initiated full usage of the indeterminate sentence, thus solidifying the process whereby a prisoner's "proof of reformation" determined his date of release. Furthermore, the legislation stipulated which wardens would remain at their jobs. Two who stayed, Chino's Kenyon J. Scudder and San Quentin's Clinton T. Duffy, became vocal advocates of the "new penology," meaning a renewed emphasis on rehabilitation. Duffy would soon acquire a public reputation as both a prison innovator and an opponent of the death penalty, and his efforts exemplified the triumph of Progressive prison reform ideas in the postwar period.[25]

Throughout the 1940s Clinton Duffy helped establish San Quentin's standing as the most experimental modern prison. Surprisingly, Duffy even became a national celebrity of sorts, serving as the inspiration for no less than two Hollywood portrayals of sympathetic prison wardens. Profiled in national magazines throughout the early postwar period, Duffy solidified his name as a leading prison reformer with the publication of *The San Quentin Story* in 1950. Extensively excerpted in *The Saturday Evening Post,* Duffy's book described how the prison had been transformed from a "bloody battleground" to a "huge, modern laboratory." Accordingly, the warden highlighted all of the changes he had instituted in the previous decade: clean uniforms, "work for every man," a larger library, a nationally syndicated radio program, and the first prison chapter of Alcoholics' Anonymous. Duffy, in short, adhered to the Progressive ideal of making prison life more like the outside community. The death penalty, he maintained, strongly contradicted this larger goal of "rehabilitative treatment." After leaving San Quentin in the early 1950s to head the state's parole board, Duffy became a vocal proponent of abolition. Boldly declaring "The rich are never executed; only the poor end up on death row," the former warden eventually wrote a book detailing his experiences with condemned men and women. Exceptional only in terms of influence, Duffy's views illustrated the evident contradiction between Progressive penology and the persistence of the state's ultimate punishment.[26]

The emphasis on rehabilitation promoted by administrators like Duffy matched the dominant arguments made by criminologists during the postwar period. Formerly a branch of sociology, criminology became its own independent discipline in the late 1940s after the University of California first established a separate department of criminology and other universities quickly followed suit. During this formative era the challenge of making contemporary prisons adopt the rehabilitative approach was posed most forcefully by the Temple University criminologists Harry Elmer Barnes and Negley K. Teeters. Their book *New Horizons in Criminology* (1951) became a standard text in the field, and in it Barnes and Teeters offered nearly one thousand pages of "modern" diagnosis, treatment, and analysis of the "American Crime Problem." Foremost among the authors' many goals was that "the ideal of rehabilitative treatment must be substituted for retributive punishment," a process best achieved by the widespread introduction of the indeterminate sentence. In general, Barnes and Teeters echoed the programming ideas of their Progressive predecessors, like vocational training, education classes, and the introduction of recreation and entertainment into the prison. Given the use of *New Horizons in Criminology* as a training manual in the state's correctional system, it is thus not surprising that San Quentin and other California prisons closely resembled the model put forth by Barnes and Teeters.[27]

Throughout the postwar period, California indeed prided itself on being a "modern laboratory" of prison reform. As the metaphor suggests, a certain scientific expertise provided the foundation of the state's new penological initiatives. In the state's expanding, interlocking network of military bases, aerospace factories, and research universities, a significant body of knowledge about techniques of behavioral modification steadily emerged. Psychiatrists who screened recruits during the war gained in public influence, and various new types of personnel engineering initiated on military bases were now applied throughout the public and, increasingly, private sectors. Not coincidentally, the same state which saw the most dramatic rise of the postwar military industrial complex would also become the most prominent laboratory of prison reform. Even if the technocratic ideas of postwar penology would gain only a limited base of popular support in the state, California provided the seedbed that enabled those arguments to become prominent across the country. Nationally, the abolition movement would also cast its ideas in terms of scientific expertise, progress, and rehabilitation. To bolster familiar arguments about both the detrimental impact of violence and the need to reform prisoners, the anti–death penalty movement of the 1950s increasingly adopted the mantle of behavioral science.[28]

The Postwar Abolitionist Campaign

The position statements of older abolitionist organizations like the American League to Abolish Capital Punishment illustrated the increased prominence of social and behavioral scientific expertise in postwar death penalty debate. Warden Duffy, noted psychiatrist Karl Menninger, and influential criminologist Thorsten Sellin joined various religious and political leaders on the League's board of directors. In 1960 the separate but closely related New York Council to Abolish the Death Penalty issued a pamphlet intended to answer common questions on the death penalty. Titled "Abolish the Death Penalty," the booklet in its introduction demonstrated the influence of social and behavioral science, asserting that "research both here and aboard has proven that capital punishment is no deterrent to crime." In response to the question "How does the death penalty fit into the modern concept of correctional methods?" the Council wrote, "It doesn't. Capital punishment is exclusively a punitive and vindictive measure, running completely contrary to modern concepts of rehabilitation and treatment of offenders." Emphasizing questions of the death penalty's practical application far more than its ethical foundation, the New York Council mounted an abolitionist argument which rested on the theoretically value-free neutrality of scientific inquiry.[29]

That behaviorist terminology suffused postwar abolitionist discourse can be seen even more dramatically in the position statements of the Friends' Social Service Committee. In its "Statement on Capital Punishment," also published in 1960, the committee outlined a set of criticisms consistent with longstanding Quaker opposition, while at the same time appealing to modern research methods. The statement began, "As Friends, who hold that there is that of God in every man, we believe that even the most degraded can be salvaged by love and faith, wisdom and compassion." Yet, a few paragraphs later, the pamphlet turned from the "moral factor" underlying Quaker abolitionism to the "human situation, since it is the basis of behavior." "We know," the committee continued, "that conduct has roots in personality, and that it is conditioned by psychic elements and environment." Pointing to "new light shed by psychology, psychiatry, and the social sciences," the Friends said the death penalty was no deterrent for those suffering from "mentality and personality deviations," a group which comprised a "large proportion" of those committing the most serious crimes. As Elizabeth and Jay Mechling have written, other forms of Quaker protest during the period increasingly moved away from moral and religious objections to criticisms made "from within the central, secular, scientific values of the society." As they voiced behavioral scientific arguments for abolition, the Friends, like the American League to Abolish Capital Punishment, reinforced the Progressive belief in the abilities of professional experts to successfully manage the problem of social deviance.[30]

Yet the specific discourse most often appealed to by the Friends and other abolitionists, namely psychiatry, offered no one theory providing a consistent rationale for eliminating the death penalty. Psychiatric explanations of criminal behavior had a powerful impact on popular debate over sex crime during the 1950s; yet in stoking fears of the intractable menace known as the "sexual psychopath," popular psychiatric theory seemed fundamentally to contradict the goal of rehabilitative treatment espoused by death penalty foes. Nonetheless, whether they proposed quarantining sex offenders or less dramatic programs of therapeutic treatment, psychiatrists attempted to make their voices heard in public policy. This goal of public influence may have united psychiatrists across the political spectrum, but, like the other professions shaping postwar criminal justice policy, psychiatry contained clear divisions within its ranks concerning how to explain and counteract the problem of criminal behavior.

In "Verdict Guilty—Now What?" an article published in *Harper's* in 1959, leading liberal psychiatrist Karl Menninger repeatedly appealed to "scientific methods" in arguing for wholesale reform of the prison system. The "offender," he believed, tended to be "a persistently perverse, lonely, and resentful individual." Given this fact, "the sensible, scientific question is: What kind of treatment could be instituted that would . . . be most likely to deter him?" Menninger outlined a step-by-step program, beginning with indefinite detention, wherein "all the skill and knowledge of modern behavioral science would be used to examine his personality assets." After a "diagnostic grasp of the offender's personality, those in charge can decide whether there is a chance that he can be redirected into a mutually satisfactory adaptation to the world." For those deemed capable, Menninger recommended education, industrial training, and psychotherapy. Citing the California correctional system as the leader in implementing the new techniques, he argued for a nationwide expansion of both the indeterminate sentence and the use of diagnostic detention centers. Finally, the death penalty clearly undermined the overall goal of Menninger's behavioral approach. "In its place," he

concluded, "should go a quiet, dignified, therapeutic program for the rehabilitation of the disorganized one."[31]

What united death penalty opponents was their faith in the ability
of scientific expertise to combat the problem of crime. Yet what distinguished postwar explanations regarding the origins of deviance from
earlier analyses was their near-complete emphasis on the individual
roots of such behavior. Where Progressives looked to both environmen-
tal and psychiatric explanations, for their followers only the latter held
weight. Throughout the 1950s, however, Progressive ideas of individualized treatment for the first time gained widespread acceptance among
wide sectors of the professional middle class. For those working in the
growing fields of mental health expertise and social scientific research,
the death penalty appeared to be a policy that was both needlessly harm-
ful and methodologically unsound. In his 1964 summary of the major
sources of opposition to capital punishment, Hugo Adam Bedau thus
observed, "Psychiatrists, penologists, and possibly social scientists and
social workers generally, as well as higher government officials, tend to
oppose the death penalty at this time." The degree to which this set of
actors represented an early formation of what political theorists later
termed a "New Class" social movement will be considered in chapter
four. Important here is what these groups proposed as an alternative to
the death penalty—namely, confinement in institutions guided by trained
experts, or people not unlike themselves.[32]

In general, postwar abolitionists understood their work in terms of a
renewed humanitarian campaign in which professional specialists played
a vital role. In analyzing the secular versus the religious arguments about
capital punishment, Bedau wondered in 1964 "how much . . . must one
rely on humanitarian convictions and scientifically grounded hypothe-
ses" to counter the "strictly theological" perspective. Elsewhere, Charles
Milligan, a Protestant minister, sought to join a "responsible Christian
social ethic" with "the humane and the pragmatic criteria" supporting
abolition. Both death penalty opponents and their detractors tended
to use "humane" and "humanitarian" interchangeably in characterizing
the abolitionist point of view. A pervasive belief among abolitionists in
the capacity of mental health professionals to guide programs of institutional rehabilitation comprised only one aspect of postwar objections
to cruel forms of punishment, however.[33]

The horrific experience of World War II would also reawaken longstanding humanitarian arguments about the detrimental impact of vio-

lence and the sanctity of human life. These criticisms necessarily differed from those of the Jacksonians, though, primarily because the newer generation no longer directly confronted the question of public executions. As Bedau wrote, "The adage, 'out of sight, out of mind,' goes some distance toward explaining why . . . the opponents of the death penalty are not as evangelical as were reformers in the last century." Yet the issue of state-sanctioned violence indeed galvanized death penalty foes, who now questioned the broader ethical right of the state to kill. Capital punishment, argued the *Christian Century,* "indelibly stains all the people and institutions of society with the blood of murder." In their oft-cited work *The Offenders: The Case Against Legal Vengeance* (1957), Giles Playfair and Derick Sington summarized their basic argument by stating "all punishment by killing is wrong." Governor Brown, meanwhile, criticized "the recurrent spectacle of publicly sanctioned killing [which] has cheapened human life and dignity without the redeeming grace which comes from justice meted out swiftly, evenly, humanely." Postwar abolitionists, in short, tended to view themselves as unwilling members of a public in whose name people were being put to death.[34]

Such outrage expressed against executions was in many ways connected to a larger critique of state-sanctioned violence during the Cold War era. The horrors of World War II, and in particular the postwar arms race, made the issue of the state's destructive capacity especially pressing for many onlookers. In their aforementioned pamphlet against capital punishment, the Friends Committee wrote, "We speak at this time because we are in the midst of unrest and upheaval when the outlook of religion and the influence of the spirit are profoundly needed by mankind." Directly linking opposition to the death penalty to the arms race, *The Nation* surmised that "it is in part because a defense strategy has been accepted which is based on mass destruction that a section of the public is anxious to reaffirm its belief in the sacredness of human life." The opening sentence of Fred Cook's article in the same issue of *The Nation* was far from uncommon: "Capital punishment today faces fierce attack in many areas of a world in which the atom has posed a new threat and placed a new premium on human life." In defending executions, literary critic Jacques Barzun took issue with this particular argument. "The propaganda for abolition," Barzun maintained, "speaks in hushed tones about the sanctity of human life. . . . But most of the abolitionists belong to nations that . . . quite sensibly arm themselves to the teeth. . . . The West today does not seem to be the time or place to invoke the absolute sanctity of human life." Rather than resignation, death penalty foes viewed the contradiction between the arms race and the sanctity of human life with indignation, making abolitionism only one part of a larger struggle against postwar state violence.[35]

The experience of World War II also gave new meaning to the familiar argument opposing the death penalty on the grounds that the innocent are sometimes executed. The United States bore no small share of the responsibility for the millions of innocent civilians killed worldwide during the war. Yet after the war part of America's national mission involved protection of personal freedoms; unlike its totalitarian rival, America declared itself a nation where the rights of the individual took primacy over the power of the state. In his foreword to Jerome and Barbara Frank's *Not Guilty* (1957), a book which detailed past executions where the condemned turned out to be innocent, Supreme Court Justice William O. Douglas offered the rationale for America's postwar justice system. "We are a civilized people," Douglas declared, "and our law rejects the use of torture. . . . We believe that it is better for ten guilty people to be set free than for one innocent man to be unjustly imprisoned." Hugo Adam Bedau, editor of *The Death Penalty in America* (1964), devoted an entire section to the issue of wrongful executions. Although the actual number of executions in which concrete evidence later proved the innocence of the executed was fairly small, the question rightly continued to haunt many activists. In the past, Bedau argued elsewhere, such revelations had catalyzed abolition in a number of states.[36]

No similar correlation could be made between wrongful execution and state eradication in the postwar era, but this argument for innocence would assume great prominence throughout the Rosenberg and later the Chessman controversies, illustrating its power to animate both left and liberal activism against the death penalty. Notably, even though the conflict between state violence and the deeper "innocence" of the people seemed a more momentous question in postwar Europe, public discussion of the issue took place more forcefully in America during the 1950s. In Europe, conversely, official state elimination of capital punishment would largely precede popular debate over the issue. As American abolitionists began to reckon with the legacy of World War II, criminologists and concerned public officials simultaneously began to place their views in accordance with this worldwide trend against capital punishment that was evidenced most dramatically on the Continent. The Holocaust, in other words, cast its shadow well beyond European borders.[37]

American abolitionist concerns for the protection of innocence and the sanctity of human life were dependent on a wider belief in the ability of prisons to fulfill their rehabilitative mission. Few death penalty opponents proposed sentences other than life imprisonment, although some advocated leaving open the possibility of parole. As Bedau summarized the general abolitionist position, "Incarceration of all convicted capital offenders is a practical alternative to the death penalty, one which could be adopted tomorrow across the land without any administrative upheavals or expenses." Sara Ehrmann, the executive director of the American League to Abolish Capital Punishment, rejected the death penalty on the grounds that innocent prisoners had been executed, and she buttressed her argument by quoting prison wardens about the viability of life imprisonment. Similarly, Fred Cook began his argument in *The Nation* by highlighting "the shocking possibility that the innocent may be doomed to death," but he finished with a story revealing another "vital element" of the issue. Cook wrote of a former cold-blooded killer, who, while in prison during the war, became an "eager and heroic" volunteer, giving his body to medical research. In short, at the core of the arguments against the death penalty was a steadfast belief in the reformative potential of the modern American prison.[38]

Indeed, so dominant was the ideal of rehabilitation among postwar activists that the nation's top law enforcement official felt obliged to respond in his defense of the death penalty. In a series of short articles written for law enforcement publications in the early 1960s, J. Edgar Hoover questioned the reformative capacity of condemned prisoners. After first clarifying that "nothing is so precious in our country as the life of a human being," Hoover expressed his doubts about "the chances of rehabilitating Jack Gilbert Graham, who placed a bomb in his own mother's luggage and blasted her and forty-three other innocent victims into oblivion." "The proponents of 'rehabilitation' for all murderers," Hoover later wrote, "quote those passages of the Bible which they believe support their lavender-and-old-lace world where evil is neither recognized nor allowed." Hoover's statements indicated how death penalty proponents tended to characterize the opposition in gendered terms (a theme addressed in chapter four); what his comments also illustrated, however, was the prominence of the reform question for analysts on both sides of the issue.[39]

As in previous eras, during the 1950s public protest against executions also translated into advocacy of penal reform. Like their Jackson-

ian and Progressive predecessors, postwar critics viewed the death penalty as the antithesis of a prison system intent on restoring the individual to the community. As Playfair and Sington declared, "Abolition
should be fought for not . . . merely as an end in itself, but rather as the
first essential step in a program of penal reform." Writing in *Commonweal,* Father Robert Hovda proposed that "hope of correction . . .
should be a wellspring for a total reform of penal institutions as well as
for this particular cause." Espoused by criminologists, prison administrators, psychiatrists, and a variety of public officials, the terms of the
new penology left a clear imprint on the anti–death penalty debate.
With the experts, the activists shared an unmistakable confidence in the
regenerative possibilities of institutional therapy. Yet expression of such
a view was not confined simply to social scientific analyses and politically oriented publications. During the late 1950s a number of preemi-
nent intellectuals spoke out against the death penalty, and the issue increasingly cropped up in popular media portrayals. As seen in both high
intellectual and popular culture, the terms of the new penology clearly
reached out to a wider audience.[40]

Critiquing Death

First published in America by *The Evergreen Review* in 1957, Albert
Camus's "Reflections on the Guillotine" stressed the horror and irrevo-
cability of capital punishment. Camus began with an anecdote about
how his father had watched an execution in 1914, only to become sick-
ened by what he saw. If such an action "causes vomiting on the part of
the respectable citizen it is supposed to protect," Camus wondered,
"how can anyone maintain that it is likely . . . to bring more peace and
order into the community?" State-sponsored death, according to Camus, disturbed "peace and order" precisely because it implicated the
community, by which he primarily meant middle class citizens, in the act
of murder. After detailing the gory process of death, Camus asked, "Is
there any assurance that none of those executed is remediable? Can it
even be asserted that none of them is innocent?" Of the former question,
Camus stressed how "the chance we all have of making amends" was
foreclosed when society acted as an "absolute judge." The prisoner, he
urged, should remain in prison "at hard labor," thereby alleviating
middle class complicity in this "revolting butchery," this act reminiscent
of a "barbarous period." Indeed, Camus's primary goal seemed to be

not therapeutic reform but removal of the stain of murder from the middle class conscience.[41]

Television programs also emphasized middle class complicity, while at the same time adding a number of other current American arguments against the death penalty. A 1958 *Omnibus* feature hosted by Joseph Welch, the government lawyer who helped defeat Joseph McCarthy, mixed historical fact and expert interviews with a fictional account of a prisoner on death row. The story recounted the plight of Joseph Grimes (Ed Asner), a "typical murderer" (he had no criminal record until murdering his wife in a drunken rage) who now faced the gas chamber. Grimes's life on death row, said Welch in his narration, was "darkly shrouded, [and] removed from our lives," yet "we want to know" how he got there. "Modern psychology," Welch assured viewers, "works hand in hand with enlightened penology" in explaining the causes and cures for crime. The program dealt at length with the historic methods of execution, placing the gas chamber—for which Grimes waited interminably—in the context of horrors of World War II. In conclusion Welch called the death penalty premeditated murder, further saying it refuted the "Christian" injunction, "No man is evil beyond redemption." Popular audiences thus confronted an argument against the death penalty that merged behavioral and social scientific expertise with national and religious values, all centered around the plight of a representative prisoner.[42]

A host of Hollywood films likewise made statements against the death penalty by dramatizing the story of a single, archetypal criminal. Nicholas Ray's *Knock on Any Door* (1949) tells the story of Nick "Pretty Boy" Romano (John Derek), who stands accused of murdering a police officer. Romano is defended by Andy Morton (Humphrey Bogart), who feels guilty because he let Romano's father go to prison, where he eventually died. Through courtroom flashbacks, Morton describes Romano's subsequent descent from good kid to delinquent. In characterizing one of the institutions where Nick was sent, Morton says "There are reformatories with modern methods where delinquents are looked upon as individuals, with individual problems." Nick, however, was sent to a "brutal reformatory," which did nothing but make him want to "get even" upon release. In his closing statement Morton thus declares, "Nick Romano is guilty, but so are we . . . we are scandalized by environment and we call it crime; we denounce crime and yet we disclaim any responsibility for it." In calling for both eradication of the slums and "individual treatment" of the delinquent, the film voiced traditional Progressive ideals. Bogart's final, detailed description of the process of death by electrocution, however, made *Knock on Any Door* an early example of postwar abolitionist sentiment.[43]

Robert Wise's *I Want to Live!* (1958) similarly narrated the descent of a single prisoner, although this time the condemned figure was neither fictional nor typical. The film dramatized the case of Barbara Graham, a former B-girl (a bar employee who enticed men to buy her drinks) and gangster's moll. Graham had been executed at San Quentin in 1955 for the murder of an elderly widow, but the film maintained she was innocent; false testimony from her male comrades, combined with the hostility of the Los Angeles tabloid press and courts, conspired to send her to the gas chamber. In the first half of the film Graham (played by Susan Hayward) is a mixture of streetwise party girl and aspiring homemaker, yet her association with unsavory hoodlums prevents her from realizing her domestic ambitions. Once convicted, though, Graham wins the favor of Carl Palmberg, a "psychologist and a criminologist" who asserts her innocence. As she travels to San Quentin, a television news reporter characterizes her as "not the same woman she was before going to prison." Although innocent, Graham, with the benefit of both scientific expertise and solitary confinement, thus sheds all traces of her delinquent past. After promoting arguments about innocence and the possibilities for reformation, *I Want to Live!* then drives home its criticism of the death penalty in the final scenes, when Graham endures a protracted wait before going to the gas chamber.[44]

Appealing to contemporary social and behavioral science, Cold War national values, and uniquely postwar concerns about state-sanctioned violence, popular abolitionist discussion helped solidify the experts' argument that life in prison was a better alternative. Elimination of the death penalty would remove public complicity in the act of murder, help avoid the "shocking" possibility that innocent prisoners might be executed, and allow those formerly on death row to "make amends" in prison. When they advocated life imprisonment, however, neither specialists, intellectuals, nor engaged ordinary citizens felt they were sending the previously condemned to a life of unremitting cruelty. Prison reformers declared the goal of the "modern" prison to be rehabilitative treatment, thus promising a punishment alternative designed to foster individual recovery. Advocating reform rather than elimination of the deviant, the principles of penology steadily began to resonate among vocal sectors of the postwar citizenry.

Chessman as Symbol

According to numerous onlookers, the case of Caryl Chessman became singularly representative of the larger movement against the death penalty during the postwar period. As a postmortem editorial in the *New York Herald Tribune* argued, "Chessman succeeded in making himself a world-wide symbol of the fight against the death penalty." Over the many years of the case, in fact, analysts saw Chessman in precisely this way, a point evidenced by the titles of popular magazine articles: "Of Death and One Man," "Far More than Chessman," "How Many More Chessmans?" and "Chessman's Challenge." *The Nation,* a consistent advocate on Chessman's behalf, explained how "aroused world opinion, plus intense local interest and agitation, had made Chessman the symbol of the movement to abolish capital punishment." With approval from the national Friends Committee, Norman Cousins wrote in the *Saturday Review,* "The fact that other men are now under death sentence does not weaken the case for saving Chessman. He has become the ultimate symbol of a long-deferred question." Toward the end of the Chessman affair, similarly dramatic commentary filled press columns and headlines across Europe and Latin America. Across the United States, newspapers editorialized both for and against execution, pro-Chessman committees formed from California to New York, and the governor's office in Sacramento received thousands of letters and telegrams every day.[45]

When Chessman's case first emerged onto the national stage in 1954, though, a recognizable movement against the death penalty had not yet taken shape. To be sure, over the course of the preceding half-decade the Civil Rights Congress and other far-left organizations had waged highly visible efforts on behalf of Willie McGee, the Trenton Six, the Martinsville Seven, and the Rosenbergs; but these were single-issue drives not aimed at wiping out all executions. The initial activism surrounding Chessman appeared to be moving toward this goal, however. In identifying the beginnings of a national movement in 1956, *The Nation* wrote that "in California . . . the case of Caryl Chessman, the writer, and the execution of Gloria [sic] Graham have aroused widespread sentiment in favor of abolishing capital punishment." As the Chessman affair began to heat up late in the decade, analysts measured the relationship between the particular case and the larger issue. In March 1960, Harris Survey pollsters began, "The case of Caryl Chessman, the convicted kidnapper sentenced to die May 2, has renewed a worldwide debate: *should capi-*

tal punishment be abolished?" Moreover, this popular linkage became further solidified in the aftermath of Chessman's 1960 execution. A number of books published about the death penalty in the early 1960s began with extensive analysis of the entire controversy. In *Capital Punishment: A World View* (1961), James Avery Joyce viewed the Chessman protests as illustrative of far more than the "humanitarian campaigns" against the death penalty. "This book opens," Joyce wrote, "with the Chessman story . . . not only because of what happened to him, but because of what is happening to us all." However melodramatic, Joyce's statement nevertheless reflected the quite common popular association between Chessman's case and the broader abolitionist movement itself.[46]

Although they launched a wide array of arguments on Chessman's behalf, his supporters unanimously agreed on one key point: to execute him contradicted the ideal of rehabilitation. Whether they viewed him as innocent, disputed legal aspects of the case, or simply opposed the death penalty on principle, pro-Chessman commentators always returned to the issue of individual reform. "California sentenced a young thug," said the *New York Herald Tribune*, but "it killed a man who learned law, and probably citizenship, the hard way." "The Chessman killed by the state was not the Chessman who had committed the crime," a *Nation* editorial stated. "However heinous his crimes and certain his guilt," echoed the *Christian Century*, "it can now be admitted without sentimentalizing his case that the maturing Chessman has risen above the level of his punishment." Notably, many of those who rallied behind Chessman did not believe him to be innocent. Yet even those who did dispute his guilt, like the Friends Committee, still emphasized his apparent character transformation. After asserting the "strong likelihood that Chessman is *completely innocent* of the 'red light crimes'!" a flier distributed by the Southern California Friends stressed how Chessman "has done much to rehabilitate himself . . . and, if his life is spared . . . the process of rehabilitation will continue."[47]

In the minds of liberal criminologists, popular commentators, and anti–death penalty activists, Caryl Chessman indeed seemed to manifest vividly the postwar ideal of the rehabilitated prisoner. As a writer on death row, Chessman appeared to be a model citizen of the modern industrial community. He was quite evidently literate and, according to his books, ready to contribute to scientific understanding of criminal behavior. In turn, prominent criminologists like Harry Elmer Barnes and Negley Teeters became extremely active on Chessman's behalf. Each wrote numerous letters to the governors of California about the case, and, in the fourth edition of their *New Horizons in Criminology* they noted, "Efforts are being made to save him from the California gas chamber in the name of science, if not humanity." Writing in *The Saturday Review* a year after the execution, Barnes maintained that since Chessman had shown such signs of "regeneration," his execution contradicted the "principles of contemporary correctional philosophy and practice—principles which have, perhaps, been most highly developed and most proudly paraded in the state of California." Chessman's apparent reform while in prison, the criminologists said, provided convincing evidence of the therapeutic promise of the new penology.[48]

Yet for both his supporters and detractors, Chessman's convictions for crimes specifically involving sex played a fundamental role in generating the symbolic dimension of the case. Chessman's courtroom conviction and subsequent diagnosis by psychiatrists as a sex criminal carried powerful connotations during the postwar period. The psychiatric discourse of sex crime, and of criminality itself, strongly influenced the arguments made against Chessman, rendering problematic his claim to be reformed. Precisely because it involved lurid assaults, however, Chessman's case compelled wide public debate over the causes of threatening sexual behavior. While such popular fascination helped spark interest in the controversy, it also made Chessman a problematic symbol for the anti–death penalty movement. An anti-Chessman editorial in the *Dallas Morning News* best captured the dilemma, stating, "Opponents of the death penalty, resting their case on Chessman, picked a precarious basis. This man stands convicted of particularly revolting crimes."[49]

Popular understanding of both sex crime and rehabilitation in postwar America thus shaped public discussion of the Chessman case. As they debated Chessman's cause, specialists from several different professional sectors helped outline the abolitionist critique that prevailed by the late 1950s. In their defense of Chessman, these increasingly vocal opponents of the death penalty implicitly identified their conception of the model reformed prisoner. That Chessman was white, literate, and heterosexual was no coincidence, for these categories were inextricably linked to both the popular embrace and institutional practice of the postwar rehabilitative ideal. Like their Jacksonian and Progressive forebears, reformers of the period strongly opposed what they perceived to be the contradiction between capital punishment and the therapeutic institutions they helped design and oversee. In a 1955 letter to Governor

Knight, the Northern California Friends Committee succinctly captured the crux of the Chessman controversy, as well as the core idea sustaining middle class abolitionist sentiment from the antebellum era forward. "Chessman's crimes may have been repulsive," the letter concluded, "but moral rehabilitation may be in process. The State cuts off all possibility of this process when it imposes the death penalty." [50]

CHAPTER TWO

The Sex Crimes of the Red Light Bandit

(1948–1954)

The photograph on the cover of *Time*'s issue of May 8, 1960, showed Caryl Chessman looking pensive as he contemplated the open gas chamber behind him. A few months earlier another *Time* feature story had recapped the events of the previous twelve years, a period in which Chessman had become a worldwide symbol of opposition to the death penalty. The controversy stirred by Chessman had been compared to that of Sacco and Vanzetti, Leopold and Loeb, and even Sir Walter Raleigh; in France "arguments raged as if the Dreyfus case had come alive again." Yet Chessman's sentence had no apparent political motivation, nor did his crimes include murder; racism or any kind of explicit prejudice, moreover, could not explain why he had arrived on death row. A photo caption beside the *Time* article called him simply "kidnaper Chessman." Kidnapping, however, was only the technical charge used to sentence Chessman to the death penalty. In both the courtroom and subsequent popular discussion, Chessman faced the gas chamber for the crimes of the red light bandit, a rapist who stalked the lovers' lanes of postwar Los Angeles.[1]

During the postwar period, longstanding stereotypes of the violent sex criminal were both contested and revised. From the 1930s onward, activists like Jesse Daniel Aames and groups such as the Communist Party and the NAACP waged constant public challenges to the Southern stereotype of black men as rapists. Simultaneously, a popular discourse about sex crimes emerged in which the sexual assailants who provided evidence of a "wave of sex crimes" sweeping the nation were almost always white. Found in popular magazines and journals, this discussion helped define a new menace to America's women and children. That threat appeared in the form of the stalker who preyed on the nuclear family, the core institution of the postwar era. Not seen as motivated by racial or biological disposition, sex criminals and their dangerous behaviors now became the subject of exhaustive, and often alarmist, psychiatric inquiry.

Postwar psychiatrists defined Chessman and other convicted sex criminals as "psychopaths," a term with imprecise meaning but clear connotations during the era. Prevalent throughout the discourse of the "psychopath," and in wider psychiatric discussion of sex crime, was the fear of male homosexuality. The expanding terrain of open sexual practice on the World War II home front worried a variety of public officials, and apparent crises like the postwar sex crime "wave" brought psychiatrists to the forefront of official reaction against a wide range of illicit sexual behaviors. Legal and psychiatric "experts" now linked homosexuality to the most dangerous forms of sex crime, from pedophilia to sex-murder. In Chessman's case this implicit connection was encouraged by the fact that the red light bandit's sexual assaults involved oral sex; that he further attempted to rape one of the victims was rarely mentioned. The oral assaults were deemed "atrocious and unprintable" by California Governor Goodwin Knight, and such indirect reference to them became a common feature in press accounts of the case. Powerful, if never directly stated, popular associations regarding these "fiendish" crimes would remain at the center of the prosecution's ultimately successful case. In defending Chessman, though, several influential observers would explain sex crimes by drawing on the same vocabulary of postwar psychiatry. The major contention of Chessman's supporters, in fact, was simply that he did not fit the established "mold" of the sex criminal, an objection which itself reinforced the definition.

The case against Chessman originated in a local climate particularly hostile to all forms of sexual transgression. Among its many other effects, the boom in internal migration to the Los Angeles area during World War II helped foster an open sexual atmosphere, and for a brief moment the city's traditional Victorian values seemed threatened. A handful of notable sex crime cases—the Black Dahlia in 1947, Chessman the following year, and child slayer Fred Stroble in 1949—caused local newspapers, the courts, and various politicians to campaign for more stringent anti–sex crime legislation, including expanded use of the same Little Lindbergh Law used to sentence Chessman. As his case gained national fame, the Southern California press continued to rally public opinion against Chessman, stridently emphasizing the plight of his victims as the main reason his crimes deserved the death penalty. Initially forged in the contested sexual milieu of postwar Los Angeles, the anti-Chessman narrative remained solidly intact by the time of his 1960 execution.

A national debate over sex crimes thus merged with a powerful set of local fears in creating the pro–death penalty case against Chessman. He was a psychopath, said the psychiatrists, and his condition was incurable. Via the courts the people had spoken, and his sentence of death would show the society's intolerance for such behavior. In the minds of the anti-Chessman forces, the biggest obstacle would not be the courts but the willingness of Governor Brown and liberals like him to sympathize with a dangerous criminal. Not executing him, in this view, meant allowing a wide range of illicit sexual behaviors to go unpunished. Fundamentally antitherapeutic, the standpoint articulated by Chessman's foes would eventually become a cornerstone of the early California New Right politics that began to take shape by the late 1950s. From the trial in 1948 to execution twelve years later, the Chessman controversy thus generated impassioned debate over not merely the fate of one man, but instead the sexual behavior of all men and women in the aftermath of World War II.

Twentieth-Century Sexual Danger

A pervasive fear of violent sexual behavior by emancipated African Americans helped solidify gender relations in the New South. Bound by a distinct sense of honor, white men justified public lynching of black men as necessary to protect the "purity" and "virtue" of Southern womanhood. So powerful was this rationale, according to Fitzhugh Brundage, that it was offered regardless of the precipitating event. "Ignoring statistics that showed that sexual offenses did not spark most lynchings," Brundage writes, "white southerners maintained that rape was the key to lynching." While the actual cause may have been a social assault, like organizing sharecroppers or failure to repay debt, African American crime was more often treated as a sexual affront. As Nancy Maclean argues, the "unspeakable crime" of rape thus served as a metaphor for the South's fear of black emancipation, women's entry into the workforce, and the coming of Northern industry; in other words, the metaphor stemmed from the decline of an agrarian, patriarchal way of life. The extralegal punishment of lynching reinforced, in far more dramatic fashion, the legal punishment of death for a black man who raped a white woman.[2]

The lynching of Leo Frank in 1915 dramatized the popular association between Jews and sexual deviance. Unlike nearly all other southern lynchings, of the two suspects in the (alleged) rape and murder of thirteen-year-old Mary Phagan, it was the white employer rather than the black worker who faced lynch mob hysteria. Frank was a Jew, and thus also belonged to a group seen as lusting after gentile women. Throughout the trial and aftermath, Frank's "lascivious" nature was sensationalized—there were innuendoes about contacts with prostitutes, and of his alleged homosexuality. Frank's lynching, Maclean maintains, occurred against the backdrop of changing Southern economic, political, and gender relations; the Knights of Mary Phagan, in other words, launched a desperate and violent cry for the restoration of an agrarian form of patriarchal relations. There was no question for his accusers that the "Jew Pervert," as Tom Watson called him, had raped young Mary Phagan.[3]

The Leopold-Loeb case of 1924 helped introduce a new "explanation" for sex crime: homosexuality. Nathan Leopold and Richard Loeb, two University of Chicago students from influential local families, devised what they believed to be the "perfect crime"—the kidnap and murder of thirteen-year-old Bobby Franks. Once caught, the local press seized upon the lurid details of the case and speculated wildly about the motivations of the "unlikely killers." According to Paula Fass, "rumors about the mutilation of the body as the site of perverse practices started almost immediately after the discovery of the unclothed child." As a result, the press "alluded to perversions (a code word for homosexuality) between Leopold and Loeb" as a possible motive. Though initially only implicit, this dimension of the case, Fass demonstrates, solidified over the next thirty years, reflecting increased cultural anxieties over the presence of homosexuality in American society.[4]

While the case of the Scottsboro Boys reaffirmed the potency of the New South's stereotype of the black rapist, it also indicated that such characterizations would now face both popular and legal challenge. In early 1931 nine black youths, eight of whom were in their teens, were falsely accused of gang-raping two women aboard a train near Scottsboro, Alabama. The incident caused a local sensation, and the National Guard was called in to prevent lynch mobs from storming the courtroom. After eight of the youths, including one who was thirteen, were sentenced to death, the Communist Party came to their defense. Viewing the boys as "workers" victimized by the "parasite landlords and capitalist classes of the South," the CP rallied national and international support. The strategy of the Party-affiliated International Labor Defense challenged many core aspects of Southern racism, including legal discrimination in courts and the popular equation between black men and rape. By no means the first challenge to the sex criminal stereotype, the Scottsboro defense nonetheless proved to be the most successful, as none of the Boys ultimately received the death penalty.[5]

As evidenced by cases like those of the Martinsville Seven or Willie McGee, the death penalty would continue to be applied to black rapists, real or alleged, well into the 1950s. In both of these instances, the tension evident at Scottsboro between the NAACP's legal methods and the Communist Party's popular campaigning would persist. Ultimately, both strategies would render problematic future attempts to apply the death penalty to blacks accused of rape in the South or elsewhere. The NAACP now clashed with the ILD's successor organization, the Civil Rights Congress, over how best to defend McGee (executed 1951), the Martinsville Seven (all executed 1951), and other black defendants. Where the CRC preferred Scottsboro-style grassroots organizing, the NAACP worked quietly through the courts. Amidst the postwar Red Scare, the NAACP consciously distanced itself from the CRC, which remained closely tied to the Communist Party. Yet the CRC established both popular as well as legal precedents that helped lay the groundwork for the NAACP's courtroom successes over the next two decades, not the least of which was the abolition of the death penalty for rape.[6]

The plight of the so-called Florida Tobacco Roaders perhaps best illustrated the shifting popular representation of sexual danger evident by the late 1950s. In the 1959 case, four white teenagers were convicted of gang-raping a black girl, also in her teens. Beyond the actual charge of rape, *Time* said, "the Southern, segregated state of Florida was being tested in its ability to render equal justice before the law." Indeed, the matter was immediately understood in terms of the issues raised by the Civil Rights Movement. The NAACP claimed that unequal punishment was meted out to blacks and whites in cases of sex crimes—a contention that, despite media fanfare about the "triumph of justice," was perhaps reinforced by the sentence of life imprisonment, rather than the death penalty, given to the teenagers. The trajectory of cases ranging from the Scottsboro Boys to the Florida Tobacco Roaders hardly indicated that the narrative linking black males and rape had been replaced by an equally powerful cultural fear of white sexual violence; but precisely as the figure of black rapist faced popular challenge, the representation of the white stalker did indeed begin to crystallize. Rather than the racialized outsider, the sexual threat now drawing the most public attention came from inside the dominant culture. From the thirties onward, sex crimes committed by white men commanded full attention of the popular press.[7]

Like the myth of the black rapist in the New South, the figure of the white stalker grew amidst a rigid system of gender relations. The domestic ideology of the Cold War era strictly divided gender roles for middle class Americans, designating the male as breadwinner and the female as suburban homemaker. Such stratification seemed a clear expression of the general attitude towards sex that had been developing in American society since the 1920s, which John D'Emilio and Estelle Freedman characterize as "sexual liberalism." Sexual liberalism allowed for erotic behavior, but only within the context of heterosexual, monogamous relationships. Under this notion, "sex need not be confined to marriage, but it was expected to lead in that direction. Homosexual men and women, and young black mothers who failed to marry, violated that requirement, as did the rapist and the prostitute." During the 1940s and 1950s the figure of the white sex criminal came to represent an increased danger to the nuclear family, but unlike his New South predecessor the former's crimes were not attributed to racial or biological predisposition. Instead, the motivations of the white figure would require psychiatric explanation.[8]

The Sexual Psychopath

Discussion of sex crimes in popular magazines and journals of the late 1930s was laden with numerous assumptions reinforcing old stereotypes and creating new ones. According to the emerging discourse, sex crimes were a problem that only psychiatry could solve; after highlighting the prevalence of violent sex offenders throughout the society, nearly every article in the popular press ended with calls for such experts to rescue American society from the scourge. Psychiatrists most often explained sex crime as a disease, or as a yet-unidentified deficiency in the mental "constitution" of the perpetrator. A popular debate about the causes of homosexuality also surfaced during this same period, and, according to John D'Emilio, analysts of the subject submitted many of the same psychiatric diagnoses. Like the homosexual, violent sex criminals such as the rapist and the molester were considered diseased, pathological, and capable of virtually every type of sex crime. The overlap between these two discourses helped create the narrative of the stalker, a figure whose frightening challenge to the nuclear family could be explained by a spurious linkage between his behavior and homosexuality.[9]

In her article on the legal and psychiatric response to the so-called "sexual psychopath," Estelle B. Freedman finds the term coming into usage in magazines and journals during the Depression. Where psychiatrists first used it elastically, applying it to both unemployed men and "hypersexual women," by the late 1930s the term increasingly referred to violent male sexual criminals. Widespread anxieties over the decline in the traditional "breadwinner" role during the Depression, coupled with the expanding influence of psychiatrists in the courts and prisons, brought the threat of the sexual psychopath into public view. The term, Freedman observes, helped "clarify boundaries between normal and abnormal behaviors," such as the one "between heterosexual and homosexual males, labeling the latter as violent child molesters." Sexual psychopath laws during the period, moreover, frequently targeted "male homosexual acts, either with children or adults." According to Freedman, "this fact, and the frequent overlap in use of the terms *sex criminal, pervert, psychopath, and homosexual,* raises the question of whether *psychopath* served in part as a code word for *homosexual* at a time of heightened public consciousness of homosexuality." Chessman's diagnosis as a psychopath would later bring to the surface a connection which, in initial popular debate, remained mostly implicit.[10]

A *Literary Digest* article from 1937 signaled the beginning of the new popular discourse of sexual danger. "Sex Crime Wave Alarms U.S.: Police Grope for Methods to Stem Rising Tide of Perversion," the title read. The article initiated a number of themes—the danger to women posed by rapists, the threat to children from molesters—that would become common in media discussion of the issue. Even though psychiatry had yet to find an answer for, or even a definition of, the sex criminal, it was in this field that the potential for answers lay. In an article in *The Nation* later that same year, Harvard criminologist Sheldon Glueck wrote, "The aggressive sex offender is more a problem for psychopathology than for criminal justice." Until such specialists provided viable solutions, the *Digest* said, the most distressing problem was that the sex criminal could be anyone, even those most considered "normal."[11]

During World War II, psychiatry entered American life in a variety of ways. As Allan Berube demonstrates, military inductees underwent psychiatric testing prior to acceptance. Although many gay GIs fought in the war, openly homosexual draftees were rejected. Military psychiatrists, Berube argues, now defined homosexuality by the *person* rather than by the *act;* as a group homosexuals were "diagnosed" as mentally ill, and often referred to as "sexual psychopaths." On the home front, psychiatrists were called on to help explain the "problems" resulting from the open sexual atmosphere of the wartime period. According to D'Emilio and Freedman, "the war released millions of youth from the social environments that inhibited erotic expression, and threw them into circumstances that opened up new sexual possibilities." For men overseas, as well as women at home, sex outside marriage seemed commonplace; more disturbing for the psychiatric experts, however, was the increase in same-sex behavior the war allowed. As Ellen Herman has recently analyzed, World War II marked the ascent of psychology as an officially sanctioned national "creed." In a variety of realms, therapeutic experts sought to define a healthy "national character." Regarding sexual deviance, and in particular the "homosexual menace," psychiatrists—the most "scientific" of mental health professionals—were now expected to find "cures." [12]

At the height of the war, psychiatrist Robert M. Lindner published *Rebel Without a Cause: The Hypnoanalysis of a Criminal Psychopath.* The book, on which the 1955 Nicholas Ray film was loosely based, outlined the life history of "Harold," whom Lindner diagnosed as a teenage criminal psychopath. In describing the archetypal juvenile delinquent of the period, Lindner treated the criminal and sexual definitions of the psychopath synonymously. Because of his unresolved Oedipal complex, the psychopath, Lindner argued, "cannot wait upon erotic gratification . . . he must rape." "It is undeniable," he continued, "that the universal sexual aims regarded as normal have little place in their style of life. Where there is a sympathetic attachment toward another human it is frequently homoerotic or perverse in some other sense." Equally dangerous, Lindner said, was the psychopath's supposed "hatred for his father," especially because it made him ripe prey for "that Leader [under] whose tinseled aegis license becomes law." In short, the "rebel" had been identified as a sex criminal, and his increasing presence on the home front—according to Lindner—portended nothing less than the coming of fascism. [13]

In the summer of 1946, the case of William Heirens enabled psychiatrists and the popular press both to investigate and to sensationalize the

postwar problem of sex crime. The seventeen-year-old Heirens was convicted of brutally murdering two women in their Chicago homes, and of
sexually assaulting many more. Not since Leopold and Loeb, said *Newsweek,* had Chicago experienced such a "torrid wave" of media coverage,
nor "witnessed such an orgy of sensationalism." Heirens's case created
a puzzle for psychiatric speculation and fodder for tabloid headlines
precisely because of his "normal" veneer. As a "brilliant" young student at the University of Chicago, there seemed little explanation for his
"werewolf"-like brutality. Ominously, Heirens had scrawled the following phrase (in lipstick) on the walls of one of his victims: "for goodness sake, catch me before I kill more. I cannot control myself." Writing
in the *American Mercury* two years later, Frank C. Waldrop stated that
despite his normal physical and intellectual characteristics, Heirens possessed a "deep sexual perversion, unstable and hysterical"; "girls," Waldrop wrote, "never interested him." According to a 1948 *Saturday Evening Post* article, Heirens's numerous "motiveless burglaries" since age
nine, many of which involved women's undergarments, should have
alerted authorities to his condition of "constitutional psychiatric inferi-
ority." Since this diagnosis pointed more toward biological roots, said
the *Post,* it was even more descriptive than the modern term "psychopathic personality." [14]

A 1947 series of *Collier's* reports titled "Terror in Our Cities" emphasized the need for families to protect their children from figures akin
to Heirens. "In alarming numbers," the lead story began, "the little ones
[are] becoming hunted game, stalked by the molester, the sex psychopath and the despoiler." After analyzing a handful of sex crimes in exhaustive detail, the article also made a familiar plea for tougher laws and
early psychiatric treatment. To highlight the danger, *Collier's* warned
how "you and I, our wives, our children and our homes are targets" for
sex criminals. "Police work," it continued, "begins with the Vital Four
—man, wife, child and home." In the postwar epidemic of sex crime, it
was not just children or women but the very ideal of the nuclear family
that seemed under siege.

FBI Director J. Edgar Hoover lent official sanction to the views outlined in the *Collier's* series. "How Safe Is Your Daughter?" asked the
title of Hoover's 1947 cover story in *American Magazine.* According to
the editor's introduction, "Sex offenses have been increasing so rapidly
in recent weeks as to become a nightmare to the mothers of America."
Hoover continued to sound the alarm with frequent references to the

"degenerate sex offenders" on the loose. A photo image on the second page of the article showed three young girls screaming as they ran from a giant hand superimposed above them. The caption quoted Hoover: "The nation's women and children will never be secure . . . so long as degenerates run wild." In the essay Hoover offered ample statistics and anecdotal evidence of the increasing prevalence of rapists and molesters. Placing his views in opposition to those of unnamed "bleeding heart" sympathizers, Hoover argued for expanded medical attention and incarceration for sex offenders.[15]

Hoover continued to raise fears about sex criminals in a 1955 article, again written for *American Magazine,* entitled "How *Safe* Is Your Youngster?" The article declared that "the degenerate offender looms today as a menace to the safety and well-being of every boy and girl in America." Hoover's frightening statistics—for example, "a sex criminal was arrested somewhere every 6.7 minutes"—did not distinguish between rapists and child molesters, although the article focused almost exclusively on the latter category. Blaming the problem on both postwar "social and family upheavals" and the "spirit of abandon and 'anything goes'" prevalent during the war, Hoover again called for tougher law enforcement and more extensive psychiatric treatment. Parents, he said, should be wary of babysitters, and should discourage their children from hitchhiking. In addition, they "should also warn them to avoid so-called lovers' lanes and other secluded trysting places, which are favorite hunting grounds of sex criminals." Long after his initial conviction, Chessman's red light bandit assaults would provide perfect fodder for Los Angeles press dramatizations of Hoover's repeated warnings about the dangers of lovers' lanes.[16]

With Hoover's official sanction, the postwar media sparked fears of a "wave" of sex crimes sweeping across the nation. Whether such an increase actually existed was an open question, however. One 1950 report declared, "There is no evidence that California suffers from a sex crime wave, but from a wave of hysteria regarding the matter." In 1953, the medicine columns of both *Time* and *Newsweek* noted a recent study of the problem by the Langley Porter Clinic of the University of California. Investigators there found no statistical evidence of a "wave" of sex crimes, nor that "stalkers were pervasive." At the outset of his 1954 work *The Sexual Offender and His Offenses,* Benjamin Karpman quoted a number of similar studies refuting the notion of a recent outbreak of sex crimes. The findings cited by Karpman and others indeed paid special attention to the sex crime rate in California, a rapidly growing state where the problems of postwar sexual behavior seemed most politically controversial as well as most thoroughly researched.[17]

As Daniel Bell argued in his 1959 essay "The Myth of Crime Waves," throughout the immediate postwar period public officials regularly manipulated crime statistics in order to serve a variety of purposes. An increase in both incidents and arrests could bolster the reputation of local law enforcement as well as sanction the efforts of authorities to regulate certain types of criminal behavior. A more recent literature on the history of particular "moral panics" relies on the insights of British sociologists Stan Cohen and Stuart Hall, who call attention to the unanimity of opinion which often marks official response to apparent crises. In such instances, Hall (et al.) wrote in *Policing the Crisis* (1978), "'experts' perceive the threat in all but identical terms, and appear to talk 'with one voice' of rates, diagnoses, prognoses and solutions." Whether the fear was of stalkers in the postwar American suburbs or muggers on the streets of London during the 1970s, the resulting crackdown has tended to follow a recognizable pattern. Yet, as Phillip Jenkins suggests in his recent work *Moral Panics* (1998), the very perception of a widespread outbreak in criminal behavior "begins with an event or condition that represents a serious challenge to accepted values." As demonstrated by the experience of Los Angeles in the late 1940s, the precipitating "condition" for the postwar sex crime panic was precisely the liberated sexual climate generated by World War II.[18]

Sex Fiend or Professional Thief?

According to the local press, southern California seemed in constant danger of sexual violence after the war. The particularly gruesome 1947 murder of Elizabeth Short, a white sex worker nicknamed the Black Dahlia, provided a forum for local newspaper columnists, psychiatric experts, and public officials to blame the open atmosphere of World War II for the apparent outbreak of sex crime. Short's murderer was never found, but the press freely speculated on his character. At various times he was believed to be a "Werewolf," a "maladjusted veteran," or a "mannish lesbian. The only common thread tied both the murderer and Short to area nightlife: "The striking brunette," said one account of Short's life, had indeed "cut a gay path through the bright lights of town." Writing in William Randolph Heart's *Herald-Express,* Alice La-Vere—a "noted consulting psychologist"—believed the killer to be a "psychopathic male caught in between impotency and confused sex tendencies." J. Paul de River, head of the Sex Offender's Bureau of the Los Angeles Police Department, saw the culprit as someone who "hate[d] womankind" and who was both a sadist and a masochist. Local observers thus implicated a range of deviant sexual behaviors, whether violent or not, in the murder of the Black Dahlia.[19]

A series of nine unsolved sex murders, covering territory ranging from Long Beach to Santa Monica, took place in Southern California over the next two years. Although there were no attempts to link the red light bandit's 1948 sexual assaults to this pattern of Dahlia-related murders, a climate of fear had become palpable. The amount of local publicity given to the initial Dahlia investigation, wrote the visitor Simone de Beauvoir, made it seem as though "terror glided through the empty streets." In terms of press attention, the work of the red light bandit did not compare. Despite the subsequent analyses of Chessman, his contemporary supporters, and later interpreters, the red light bandit was not initially considered to be a sensational criminal. Local press reports treated his capture as potential resolution of as yet unpublicized crimes. Only one of the several area newspapers, the *Los Angeles Daily News,* provided consistent coverage of Chessman's three-week trial. This fact is somewhat surprising, for as the Dahlia case demonstrated, nothing sold more newspapers in postwar L.A. than sex-related scandal. Nevertheless, when Chessman stood before a jury, he faced members of a local community unusually sensitive to the threat of sex crime in its midst.[20]

"In this case," Deputy District Attorney J. Miller Leavy told prospective jurors, "I do not believe the evidence will show that the defendant has killed or murdered anyone yet." Leavy's statement previewed the prosecution's major contention concerning Chessman's criminal behavior—namely, that he was a career criminal capable of every imaginable offense, including (though not limited to) those of the red light bandit. A story circulating prior to the trial in a local City Hall tabloid called *The Equalizer* supported Leavy's contention. The article linked the charges against Chessman to a host of sordid crimes, including cannibalism and various forms of sodomy. Though veteran Public Defender Al Matthews acted as his legal adviser, Chessman was the only one who spoke for the defense. In quizzing potential jurors, Chessman for his part asked whether they had read *The Equalizer* piece. So damning was the article, in fact, that Chessman moved (unsuccessfully) for a change of venue because of its potential influence on the jury. As both the prosecution's argument and the sensational tabloid story clarified, Chessman stood trial for a set of specific charges that were backed by a powerful and lurid set of associations.[21]

During jury selection both the prosecution and the defense focused on the candidates' views of the death penalty. According to William Kunstler's account of the trial, Leavy's main consideration in choosing jurors seemed to be whether they were willing to apply the death penalty to crimes other than murder. Conversely, Chessman asked them "if they believed in capital punishment, if they thought there was such thing as a criminal type, and if they considered the word of a police officer entitled to more weight than that of a defendant." The twelve citizens ultimately selected came from mostly working class backgrounds; among their occupations were cashier, shipping clerk, dental assistant, and housewife (one married to a machinist, another to a painter). Each side seemed to favor a female jury, and Chessman willingly impaneled four women with teenage daughters and another with a policeman son. Confident in his ability to convince them of his innocence, Chessman readily assented to a jury of eleven women and one man.[22]

Because the sexual assaults against Mary Alice Meza and Regina Johnson were crucial to the prosecution's attempt to convict Chessman of "kidnapping with bodily harm," Leavy spent a good portion of his examination explaining why Chessman's prior criminal record—which did not include sex crimes—nevertheless made him suspect. "The law does not permit us to bring out wholesale the background, everything the defendant did in his life," Leavy said. Even though none of Chessman's earlier offenses had been sexual in nature, Leavy freely drew upon the understanding of sex crime promulgated throughout popular media discussion. "People keep graduating from one thing to another," he suggested, "they get worse; sometimes they get progressively worse . . . There always has to be a first time." To sway the jury to support the death penalty even though no life had been taken, Leavy portrayed Chessman as descending a slippery slope toward greater, more violent malice.[23]

The testimony of the two female victims enabled Leavy to stress the "bodily harm" inflicted by the bandit. Both Johnson, a housewife in her thirties, and the eighteen-year-old Meza identified Chessman in court, and each explained how he had coerced oral sex under the threat of murder. Meza, in particular, detailed her emotional stress, saying she had tearfully begged Chessman to stop, but that after the oral assault he had proceeded to attempt intercourse. In his closing statement, Leavy said the case "calls for but one penalty for what this man has done to little Mary Meza, Mrs. Johnson, and even Mr. Waisler [a victim of a robbery unrelated to the lovers' lane assaults]." In the prosecution's narrative, the Bandit had attacked a defenseless teenage girl and a respectable housewife, not to mention a clothing store proprietor. The sexual assaults against the two females carried the ultimate penalty, and of these Leavy emphasized the plight of Meza. "We know that this girl— that little girl is a virgin," he said in closing. "Isn't it horrible to have a young girl introduced to her sex life by this fiend here?" Since the Meza charges held even more legal weight than those involving Johnson, the prosecution's strategy seemed logical. Yet the melodramatic tone adopted by Leavy set a precedent followed by Chessman's later foes, who likewise made Meza's predicament fundamental to their support for Chessman's death sentence.[24]

To counter the prosecution's case, Chessman immediately rejected the prosecution's charges: "I am not the person who is guilty of these crimes, and most particularly, I am not the red spotlight bandit." However, he then adopted the peculiar strategy of portraying himself as a professional robber. On the stand he matter-of-factly told Leavy, "I have been a thief most of my life." In his defense, moreover, Chessman boasted about his past criminal exploits, at one point admitting to a holdup not included in the eighteen counts. Responding to Leavy's suggestion that he had lost his "guts" because he did not engage in a shootout with police before his capture, Chessman angrily retorted, "Even a hyena, a jackal, when he is trapped in a corner will fight. It was not because I lost my guts. . . . [I]f I did have a knowledge of these crimes I would not have dropped my gun and run." Chessman's claim implied familiarity with at least some of the Bandit's endeavors, but he denied all charges, especially the sexual assaults. "Yes, I have been a thief," he summarized, "I have been in trouble with the police, I have violated many sections of the penal code, but I have never in the past included these offenses here, and have not been guilty of any sexual crime." "My *modus operandi*," he explained, "has always been projected against men rather than women." In protesting his specific innocence while simultaneously asking to be returned to his chosen "profession" as a thief, Chessman indeed put the jury in a bind.[25]

As the jury took the case under deliberation, Judge Charles W. Fricke's official instructions supported the prosecution's contentions regarding Chessman's inevitable path toward sex crime. Known as "San Quentin Fricke," the judge sent more people to death row than any other in California history. Below the general instructions clarifying the credibility of the accused, Fricke wrote by hand, "Defendant has been impeached by his prior convictions, former statements and his own testimony that he has been a thief nearly all his life and has committed robberies not charged." Chessman's criminal past, the judge implied, made all of his denials suspect. Beneath the heading "Bodily Injury—Kidnaping—Defined," Fricke's instructions stated, "The court instructs you that 'bodily harm' is the touching of the person of another against his or her will with physical force in an intentional, hostile, and aggravated manner, or projecting of such force against his or her person." Although the injuries suffered by the clothing store owner could have fit this description, Fricke further clarified bodily harm. "To compel a person a female person to copulate her mouth with the sexual organ of a male person . . . or to either forcibly rape or attempt by the application of force to forcibly rape a female person, is 'bodily harm.' " Quite evidently, Fricke's hostility toward Chessman caused him to advise the jury in a manner intended to bolster the prosecution's case.[26]

The jury showed some initial reluctance to apply the death penalty, however. After a day of deliberation, foreman Clarence Harte (the only male) asked Fricke whether the sentence of "life without parole" allowed Chessman any possibility of release. Fricke said the sentence literally meant there was no chance, but then added, "There is a possibility in all cases that the sentence might be commuted by the governor, or he might be pardoned." Although the impact of Fricke's legally dubious statement remains difficult to determine, the question itself at least indicated the jury's consideration of all possible sentencing options. Upon additional request, Fricke told the jury that if it found Chessman guilty of kidnapping without bodily harm, "the penalty could be a life sentence only." On May 21, 1948, after a day and a half of discussion, a verdict was reached: Chessman was guilty on all counts except one of the lesser robberies. As for the Meza and Johnson kidnapping charges, Foreman Harte stated, "We the jury . . . find that the person named suffered bodily harm and fix the punishment at death."[27]

"Criminal Genius Sentenced to Death," announced a headline in the *Los Angeles Daily News*. Throughout the trial, both Leavy and the defendant himself made frequent reference to Chessman's reportedly "genius"-level I.Q. While his arrogance and defiant stance in court did not win him any favors, it was not Chessman's "smarts" that were put on trial. It will never be fully known why the prosecution seemed so determined to send him to the gas chamber. Only two other people were executed for a sex kidnapping conviction in California; as construed in this case, virtually any sexual assault would have qualified. Chessman's death sentence could be interpreted as a victory for local law enforcement in fighting the sex crime "wave" most dramatized by the Black Dahlia murder, yet the lack of significant media fanfare after the jury's decision somewhat mitigates the weight of this explanation. Their initial motivations aside, the subsequent behavior of participants in the case nonetheless illustrates the degree to which official contempt for Chessman could not be separated from the local campaign against sex crime. As Fricke, Leavy, and local media reports would continue to argue, Chessman had been convicted of "unspeakable" crimes and a jury of his peers had made its decision on the penalty.[28]

Over the next twelve years Fricke and Leavy continued to express their disdain for Chessman. Whether this hostility was directed toward Chessman himself or against sex criminals in general seemed indistinguishable. In a letter to a 1949 state legislative committee investigating sex crime, though, Fricke amplified his views of the latter. A "serious" sex offender, he wrote, "quite frequently has a record of previous misdemeanor sex convictions. . . . [A] competent psychiatric examination would in many of these cases disclose insanity, mental deficiency or abnormality, degeneracy or a definite tendency toward the commission of sex offenses." During Chessman's trial, police psychiatrist J. Paul de River—author of two books graphically cataloguing sex crime—testified that he had examined Chessman but made no observations about the accused's psychiatric condition. Nevertheless, after the case gained public notoriety, prosecutor Leavy—in an effort to implicate Chessman—reportedly showed members of the press photographs of sex crimes culled from de River's collection. In other words, although he did not fit the prevailing psychiatric mold, Leavy placed Chessman into the ranks of the "degenerate" criminals, as Judge Fricke had called sex offenders. Fricke and Leavy, moreover, would publicly campaign against Chessman until his execution in 1960.[29]

The State Responds

"Death Penalty Urged for Child Molesters," a *Los Angeles Times* headline declared in the wake of Governor Warren's one-day conference on sex crime held in December 1949. According to the *Times* report, Warren told the Sacramento meeting that "special consideration" should be given to "ways of halting attacks on little children." A handful of unrelated sex murders committed against children—most sensationally by seventy-year-old Fred Stroble—had taken place in different parts of the state in the preceding few months, thus prompting the special conference. After Warren's opening address, the participating group, comprised mainly of law enforcement officials and prison psychiatrists, adopted two resolutions initiated by Los Angeles District Attorney William Simpson. The first made it easier to obtain a first-degree murder conviction in lethal sexual attacks against children under 14, while the second called for greater use of the Little Lindbergh Law. As the *Times* summarized, "Sex crimes against children [would] be placed under the provisions of the State Antikidnapping Law, making possible the death penalty or life imprisonment without parole." Moreover, "this penal provision [would] apply to forcible attack." Among other measures, the penalty for sodomy would also be increased to twenty years. At least a few experts sought to diminish public fears of a sex crime wave, however. "There hasn't been as great an increase in sex crimes as . . . the public believes," said a Department of Corrections official. With Governor Warren's implicit sanction, members of the state's law enforcement community nevertheless turned the event into their own public forum, issuing strident calls for more severe punishment of sex criminals.[30]

In Los Angeles, meanwhile, a three-day hearing convened by the state Assembly Committee to Investigate Sex Crimes met the same week, and there a greater range of views captured press attention. During the first day's meeting a group of ten psychiatrists unanimously stressed the need for more money for training and research, their belief that "sex offenders should be locked up for indefinite periods," and their "vehement" opposition to "either castration or the death penalty for sex offenders against small girls" (no mention was made of punishments for assailants of boys). While all ten considered sex crimes to be a manifestation of mental illness, some specifically explained them "as the result of sexual imbalances—usually a dominance of the feminine in a masculine creature." After returning from Sacramento on the second day of the hearings, District Attorney Simpson adopted a stance diametrically opposed to the psychiatrists, however. "I don't take the view of the psychiatrists that they're sick people," Simpson said of sex offenders. Instead, sex criminals were "mad dogs—and should be disposed of the same way."[31]

Based on testimony given at these and subsequent hearings, the state Assembly's 1950 *Preliminary Report of the Subcommittee on Sex Crimes* proved to be a mix of psychiatric and law enforcement views. Defining sex crime as "any crime which has some connection with sex," the report began by classifying specific types of offenses. Alfred Kinsey had told a legislative hearing that "sex offenders are in actuality psychiatric cases," and the report concurred. According to Kinsey, sex criminals were best "treated under much the same procedures as cases of insanity are treated under the laws of particular states." As the report detailed, a clear set of labels, both psychiatric and legal, specified the crimes considered to be sex offenses in California. Sodomy and fellatio, for example, constituted separate crimes; the former referred to "relations between man and man," and in California, unlike other states, it specifically meant anal intercourse. While common forms of sexual assault like rape and child molestation merited full attention, the chapter listing sex offenses included only a one-sentence statement about kidnapping: "This crime is likewise sometimes motivated by the sexual desires of the perpetrator." Regarding a particular sex criminal type, the subcommittee wanted to wait for "more accurate tests." "A primary purpose for studying *past sex offenders*," the chapter concluded, ". . . is to obtain means and tests for diagnosing *potential future sex offenders*." [32]

Whether the current rate of sex crimes constituted a "wave" also assumed the report's full attention. In contrasting "Incidence" to "Prosecution," the Subcommittee again borrowed from Kinsey, whose 1948 study had famously declared that 95 percent of the male population had committed legally punishable sex offenses in their adult lifetimes. As a percentage of crimes targeted by local law enforcement, though, the numbers were much lower—in 1948, only 4 percent of arrests in Los Angeles were for sex offenses. However broad the discrepancy, public perception of a crisis seemed readily apparent. In declaring how "available statistics indicate there is no epidemic of sex crimes sweeping across the country and engulfing the citizens of California," the Subcommittee took exception with the popular view. "The 'wave' of sex crimes is no more than the chance occurrence of one or two heinous crimes which received wholesale newspaper publicity," it concluded. If the figures ran contrary to popular opinion, sensational media coverage, along with declarations by influential public officials, apparently fanned the flames. As the report noted, the February 1950 FBI *Bulletin* publicized J. Edgar Hoover's warnings of a 50 percent increase in "vicious attacks on women and children" since 1940. In calling for more sober discussion, the Subcommittee nevertheless conspicuously expanded the notion of who was at risk of sexual assault. Sex crime's "victims are young and old, male and female. There is no group in society that is not affected upon occasion." A problem, if not a "wave," sex crimes required a careful plan of action. [33]

The Assembly report's demographic breakdown of those convicted of sex crimes further affected its proposed solutions. "The crime of lewd and lascivious conduct with children is predominantly a white man's offense." Moreover, "the same high trend of white men was evident in other sex offenses except in commitments for rape, where the proportion was relatively low." The "Mexican group" was responsible for more than a quarter of all commitments to prison for rape, whereas the "Negro group" held a low proportion of all offenses. Accordingly, first among the Subcommittee's proposed remedies was the expanded use of "sexual psychopath legislation." Beginning in 1949, upon conviction for sexual offenses, if the court found evidence of "mental disease or disorder," or saw the subject as "affected in a form predisposing him to the commission of sexual offenses," a psychopath could be sentenced to a mental hospital. Meanwhile, increased attention to the problem by parents, schools, religious organizations, and "mental hygiene" societies would also help, as would appropriate—in other words, not sensational—media coverage. In terms of penalties, however, the legislature viewed the general solution to this largely "white man's offense" to be psychiatric confinement.[34]

But in its concluding section the report proposed an additional, more punitive measure. Even though "the present penalties are . . . as severe as those of any state in the United States . . . [and] there are modern studies indicating additional severity is not a solution. . . . There may be exceptions to this rule." Specifically, "It may be advisable to change the law relating to punishment of certain types of offenses by adding the 'Little Lindbergh Act.' This would provide a greater penalty for certain violations where the victim has suffered great bodily harm. The jury would be allowed to recommend that the death penalty or life imprisonment be imposed upon the defendant." Prior to Chessman, only one prisoner had been sent to death row for sex kidnapping convictions. Yet Thomas Dugger had gone to the gas chamber in 1936, fourteen years before, making his case an unlikely example for the legislature to follow. Although the specific crimes were not clearly identified, the Little Lindbergh Act indeed yielded the ability to "provide a greater penalty for certain violations."[35]

If the red light bandit's assaults showed how coerced fellatio could become a capital offense, the next application of the Lindbergh statute even more vividly reflected an official concern with nonreproductive sex crimes: John Richard Jensen was executed in 1955 for raping and burying alive a male Marine officer, who managed to survive. Despite the subcommittee's suggestion, however, sex kidnapping was by no means a charge meted out with any frequency. Nine death sentences were given under Section 209 between 1950 and 1967, and only Jensen's was carried out. In 1959, precisely as Chessman's case commanded the national spotlight, Governor Brown commuted the sentences of two sex kidnappers on the grounds that, however "sordid and outrageous," their assaults (which included rape) were not "kidnaping in the true sense of the word." In late 1961, Billy Monk would go the gas chamber under the Lindbergh statute, in this case for kidnapping two women and raping one. Although it was used sparingly, the Chessman and Jensen cases nevertheless illustrated how the Lindbergh Law for a brief period provided the most extreme state reaction to violent, nonreproductive sex crime.[36]

Like the California legislature, several other states issued warnings about the need to control the "sex crime wave" via expanded use of sexual psychopath legislation, if not antikidnapping measures. In a 1950 article for the *Journal of Criminal Law and Criminology*, sociologist Edwin H. Sutherland questioned many of the official assumptions behind such statutes. A careful review of the statistics, Sutherland maintained, demonstrated that, contrary to the claims of Hoover and various articles in the press, no real wave of sex crimes existed. Despite warnings about "tens of thousands" of "sex killers" stalking the nation, the latest statistic showed only six percent of murders of women as fitting the description of a sex crime. Where Hoover supported his claims concerning "degenerates on the loose" by referring to the average of eighteen thousand rapes committed each year, Sutherland pointed out how "at least half of these rapes and perhaps more than three-fourths are statutory rape," meaning "the identification of [all] sex crimes with psychopathy or degeneracy is absurd." Finding the term too vague, and the laws enacted to have no effect on the crime rate, Sutherland flatly rejected the use of psychopath statutes. Finally, Sutherland questioned whether psychiatry should hold a monopoly on discussion of sex crimes, while psychology, social work, and sociology could also make worthy contributions to the debate.[37]

As illustrated by both the California psychopath laws and the Assembly Subcommittee's recommendations, however, the psychiatric perspective indeed dominated all discussion of the problem. Classification, isolation, and segregation were the remedies favored by psychiatrists and public officials. Any efforts to intervene before the commission of the crime would come in the form of psychiatric screening, which advocates saw as a surefire way to detect psychopathy. Attempts to diminish fears of a wave, like the California Assembly report, still found a disturbing prevalence of deviant behaviors in need of increasingly punitive remedies. Experienced more dramatically in California than elsewhere, the postwar crackdown on sex crimes proved to be a reaction against the impact of World War II. Given a more prominent role in diagnosing the mental health of the armed forces, postwar psychiatrists next directed their efforts toward other matters of national mental health, like the "epidemic" of sex crime. In their estimation, sexual psychopaths were a mostly incurable menace, best isolated from the public and segregated from other types of criminals. Politicians and prison officials tended to defer to the psychiatric experts, but the more extreme alternative could still be applied. The most dangerous "mad dogs," in short, could still be eliminated.[38]

Chessman as Psychopath

Toward the end of Caryl Chessman's twelve-year tenure on death row, a *Newsweek* article—titled "Punishment to Fit the Times?"—summed up the latest controversy: "Often, in the affairs of men, great legal issues have turned on odd crimes and obscure people. Thus it was, last week, that great issues of democratic justice and the sovereignty of a state burst upon the world. At the center of the storm stood a 38-year-old habitual criminal, convicted in California twelve years ago. His crime: A sex kidnapping."[39] Even by the end of the case, then, the specific crimes for which Chessman faced the gas chamber were not altogether clear. Though still rather vague, "sex kidnapping" was among the least sensational and most accurate labels attached to Chessman's convictions. The popular press frequently characterized Chessman as a "kidnapper-rapist," a "sex terrorist," a "psychopath" and even a "keen-minded kidnaper sex-pervert"; in true crime accounts, Chessman was a "convicted sadist," a "sex pervert," a "monster," and a "sex fiend." In every instance Chessman was deemed a terrifying, though never clearly defined, sexual menace.[40]

As Paula Fass has recently demonstrated, the crime of kidnapping itself increasingly came to be understood in sexual terms during the 1950s. In particular, the California case of Burton Abbott helped redefine the popular meaning of kidnapping, and it did so in a manner detrimental to Chessman. In May 1955 fourteen-year-old Stephanie Bryan was abducted in Berkeley. Two months later, she was found dead in the Sierra foothills. Her belongings turned up in the basement of the Alameda home of Abbott, who also owned the Sierra cabin where Bryan's body was discovered. Although no concrete evidence of sexual abuse existed, the prosecution offered this charge as its major explanation. Bryan's underpants had been slashed, enabling the Alameda District Attorney to declare, "Those things happen only in murders committed by sex maniacs, by perverts and by psychopathic personalities." Killing the girl, the prosecutor said, gave Abbott "perhaps the greatest sexual satisfaction of his life." To convince the jury to give Abbott the death penalty—under the Lindbergh Statute and, more directly, for murder—the prosecution dramatized kidnapping as a sexually motivated crime. As Fass writes, "It was this vague but sinister gendered sexuality, rather than clear psychological theory, that provided the basis for Abbott's conviction and the public revulsion against him." Executed in 1957, Abbott not only helped redefine the image of the kidnapper as motivated by sex rather than ransom, but his conviction also provided further evidence of the perceived slippery slope from deviant sexual inclination to murder.[41]

In the wake of the notoriety that Chessman gained from *Cell 2455*, his opponents began to portray him in a comparably menacing light. Over the next six years mainstream press accounts would describe Chessman's actual sex crime convictions in cryptic but highly allusive terms. Governor Goodwin Knight, the *Los Angeles Times* reported in 1954, "would not commute Chessman's sentence because the condemned man's crimes were 'atrocious and unprintable.'" Judge Charles W. Fricke, meanwhile, voiced even greater indignation. "After 40 odd years on the bench," Fricke told the press, "I have never had less sympathy for a convicted man. I can't imagine a worse crime than the vicious treatment to which he subjected those two women. It is worse than murder." A 1960 *Los Angeles Times* editorial echoed these sentiments, referring to Chessman's "indescribable crimes whose horrible details are hidden in the decent exclusiveness of court records." The penal code phrased his violations as coercion of his victims to perform "unnatural sex acts;" more revealingly, he was accused in the press of "forcing the women to perform sexual indignities." Although his actual crimes may have been implicit, the absence of clear definition allowed him to be portrayed as a sex criminal of the most frightening variety. Indeed, from 1954 onward, the contours of the argument against Chessman remained intact: the horror of what he did could not be openly discussed, but those crimes surely justified the death penalty.[42]

For his opponents, the plight of Mary Alice Meza most vividly illustrated the lasting impact of Chessman's crimes. Twenty months after the bandit's sexual assault, Meza was diagnosed a schizophrenic and placed in a mental institution, where she would remain for the rest of her life. As Frank J. Parker records, the line against Chessman thus became, "He didn't take a life, he took a mind." Whether directly linked or not, Meza's predicament allowed for the expression of considerable moral outrage against Chessman. An editorial in the *Los Angeles Times* began, "In an institution in Southern California is a young woman whose life was destroyed 12 years ago. She is gently mad, as poor Ophelia was, and mad, they say, beyond the point of return." An even greater tragedy would result, the *Times* went on, if Governor Brown failed to realize the dangers of "turning the creature [Chessman] loose on the community." After Chessman received one of his many stays of execution, a *San Diego Union* editorial cartoon showed Meza alone in desolate cell-like room, her eyes gazing upward toward a beam of light coming from a small window; underneath the caption read, "no reprieve for her." Such indignation was not confined to the California press, however. Writing in *The New Republic*, Gerald W. Johnson viewed Chessman's crime as "so revolting as to raise grave suspicion of [his] sanity," and stated that "one of its effects was to consign a young woman to the living death of a madhouse—a deed by comparison with which murder is almost benevolent."[43]

True-crime accounts of Meza's plight were no less dramatic in their moral condemnation, but they tended to be more openly intrigued by the Bandit's actual assault. *Startling Detective*'s feature story "Why Caryl Chessman Deserves to Die" began, "Eyes that once shone with the joy of youth now stare in a catatonic stupor at the walls in her room." Since the attack, the article continued, Meza had become a "pitiful creature," a "tormented human wreck," and a person "more dead than alive." Nearly comatose, she lay in her hospital room, "occasionally floating back to whimper, 'did they catch him?'" Subsequently, the crimes of the bandit were described in lurid detail. Chessman became "the masked monster [who] yanked his captive into the back seat and told her she would surrender or be left with a corpse. He forced her to submit to perverted abuse." Similarly, *Master Detective*'s "Red Light Terror" paid close attention to the crimes themselves, concluding that the Bandit left Meza a "shivering and sobbing girl." Chessman thus was both a "shrewd, vicious sex criminal" and a "deadly criminal."[44]

Both in the mainstream media and in the tabloids, the narrative of the red light bandit's sexual assault on Mary Alice Meza had all the earmarks of Victorian melodrama: Unsuccessful in his attempt to rob a young woman of her virginity, a predatory monster commits even more heinous crimes, and his victim ends up a "fallen" and institutionalized woman as a result. Although Meza's Latina heritage was seldom mentioned, the plot made for a notable reversal—a woman of color now needed to be protected from a white assailant. Central to Victorian melodrama was the notion of "female purity," which, as Estelle Freedman argues, by the mid-twentieth century had "lost its symbolic power to regulate sexual behavior" in the wake of the sexual liberation associated with both the New Woman lifestyle of the 1920s and the experience of World War II. Despite its anachronistic quality, however, melodrama was perhaps the most convenient way for Chessman's detractors to frame his story. The neo-Victorian moralist J. Edgar Hoover, after all, had warned of the dangers women faced from "predators" on "lovers' lanes." As Freedman observes, it was precisely the motivations of these culprits that seemed most troublesome in the sex crime panics of the postwar period.[45]

In sync with this larger postwar discourse, San Quentin psychiatrists consistently diagnosed Chessman as a psychopath. Though the term was freely used, the connotations of *psychopath* seemed clear—it referred to a sex criminal, who in all likelihood deviated from heterosexual norms. Lindner had described the term as a "pandora's box,"[46] and its use in prison staff evaluations of Chessman demonstrated its utter lack of precision. At the end of their first examination, after detailing Chessman's career of crime, the psychiatrists wrote, "We are all agreed that this man is a Recidivistic, Egocentric, Emotionally Unstable Pathological Psychopathic Personality who wants what he wants when he wants it." Psychiatric social worker J. P. Conrad, however, soon disputed these claims. After noting Chessman's first "heterosexual experiences" at age twelve, Conrad stated "there was some masturbation at the age of 14, but he [Chessman] early arrived at a sufficiently satisfactory heterosexual adjustment to render this practice unnecessary." Chessman, the examiner continued, "denies any homosexual activity." The department's identification of Chessman as a "constitutional psychopath" was therefore "ridiculous." By 1960 San Quentin psychiatrists continued to call Chessman a psychopath, although they were now using the term interchangeably with the more modern (and less sexual) term "sociopath."[47]

Media characterizations of Chessman as a "sexual psychopath" showed how the prosecution's original courtroom contentions continued to provide the basic outline of the anti-Chessman narrative. Prosecutor Leavy, after all, had first dramatized the assault of a "virgin girl" by a "fiend." Both prosecutors and now prison psychiatrists portrayed

Chessman as an incurable monster, guilty of the red light bandit crimes and likely to commit many more. Though rooted in the particularly hostile climate of postwar Los Angeles, the story would be told with equal, if not greater, force by Chessman's opponents throughout the late 1950s. From 1958 on the Southern California press frequently stoked controversy over the case in order to criticize Governor Brown, who appeared to waver in carrying out Chessman's death sentence. Liberal judges and liberal politicians, in this view, were seen to be fostering the enduring climate of sexual permissiveness first brought on by the war. In rejecting the therapeutic approach to criminal justice, which placed emphasis on the ability of professional specialists to alter the lives of the deviant, the right began to implement a radically different view of the criminal. Diseased, unchangeable, forever threatening, and eliciting little sympathy from their fellow citizens, criminals of the sexual variety made good initial public targets. Moreover, the outpouring of anti-Chessman sentiment expressed once the case returned to the headlines in 1954 starkly illustrated the popular potential of the right's emerging criminal justice politics.[48]

The Public Speaks

"Look at the crimes going on today, never heard of before," Mrs. W. J. Spurzem of Long Beach stressed to Governor Knight in the wake of *Cell 2455*'s publication. In fewer numbers than his supporters, concerned citizens like Spurzem wrote to the governors of California explaining their views of Chessman. In these and other statements to Knight, the notion of a lingering sex crime "wave" indeed seemed prominent. "During the last 20 years this country has suffered a mass moral deterioration which must be curbed," said E. J. Lowder, an automobile executive from Los Angeles. Using a common term of gendered derision for death penalty opponents, Charley Jensen of Los Angeles stated that the "sob sisters who want [Chessman's] pardon are only encouraging the terrible crime wave we have in California." To curb the epidemic, said these writers, severe measures needed to be adopted. "Our state has been too lenient with . . . perverts and sex deviates," argued Mr. and Mrs. E. G. Knapp of Huntington Beach. In criticizing the state's hesitance to carry out Chessman's sentence, V. J. Fisher of San Mateo captured the moral outrage of death penalty proponents. "What is the state trying to do," Fisher asked rhetorically, "set him free, so he can carry on with his criminal attacks and ruin the lives of more small children?" Whatever the details of this particular case, nothing short of the death penalty could stop the limitless horrors perpetrated by the state's omnipresent sex criminals.[49]

Not to execute Chessman, several letters stated, would be a failure to protect the sanctity of the postwar family ideal. "When a man has been sentenced with the death penalty for a crime as atrocious as the one Mr. Chessman committed it is surely an affront to the mothers of our nation to allow such a person to live to commit others," insisted four salesmen from Santa Cruz. Writing from what was considered to be the archetypal Southern California suburb, Mrs. D. J. Tuttle warned, "if Caryl Chessman is not put in the electric chair this time, the mothers of Pomona will be completely disgusted with the laws of California." Chessman's opponents regularly identified themselves as mothers in order to bolster the weight of their opinions. Jeanne-Marie Osmond of Arcadia, "a mother of five children," thus wrote, "The laws are not stiff enough for sex crimes." Knight's form letter in response assured Chessman's detractors of his steadfast willingness to defend the seemingly besieged nuclear family: "I have had many comments from mothers to the effect that they are completely disgusted with the laws of California. . . . I am the father of two girls and I am a grandfather, and I can assure you that I sympathize with your viewpoint." [50]

Among Chessman's foes, the avowed concern for postwar family values shared center stage with consideration of the plight of the victims. "There is too much mawkish sentimentality about criminals and too little concern about innocent victims," maintained Henry A. Sammet of Richmond. Not surprisingly, Mary Alice Meza's condition garnered the most attention. Helen Semnacher of Hollywood claimed to be "a personal friend of the young girl who is now in Camarillo and I can remember what a pretty, bright girl she was before she became Chessman's victim." An elderly woman from Angwin, meanwhile, related Meza's experience to her own: "I am nearly 76 and was married over 20 years to a moral pervert and would be now if I hadn't left him in 1928." If not quite accurately, Milla F. Rysberg argued the details of the case with considerable verve: "The one girl who survived his brutal attack, is a completely shattered, mad, never to recover young girl! She is still confined in a madhouse!" The terms were various—"fiend," "menace to society," "sadist and rapist"—but the message was clear: Chessman had ruined Meza's life and should pay the price. Only by doing so would the state's sex crime wave be curtailed, its mothers shielded, and the plight of victims like Meza and Johnson respected.[51]

Purity versus danger, crisis versus cause for study, execution versus

institutional reform—the dichotomies presented by Chessman's opponents seemed superficially clear. The narrative of the sex criminal hound-
ing the nuclear family, distributed nationally by Hoover and via popular media portrayals and reinforced locally by zealous public officials
and a powerful Los Angeles press, was omnipresent in postwar California. By providing resolution to this cautionary tale, the death penalty restored order both legally and psychologically. Purity, as represented by
Mary Alice Meza, was safely protected from the danger symbolized by
Chessman, and the set of social norms governing postwar sexual behavior was temporarily reaffirmed. As they tried to restore an older moral
order, Chessman's detractors roundly rejected the newer, more therapeutically oriented postwar ideas regarding the treatment of criminals.
The debate over Chessman thus revealed a profound division between
postwar liberals and conservatives regarding the malleability of human
nature itself, and it did so precisely as the more optimistic of the two
points of view was clearly ascendant.[52]

The cumulative effect of the story told by Chessman's foes, both
in court and throughout subsequent media discussion, was to keep the
problem of sex crime at the center of popular controversy about the
case. Whether they simply questioned or flatly denied his guilt, Chessman supporters were forced to contend with the prominent fear of sex
crime during the 1950s. Yet, surprisingly, when Chessman's sympathizers did reckon directly with the nature and causes of threatening sexual
behavior, their explanations were virtually identical to those of their opponents. In essence, the two sides parted company only over the matter
of treating sex criminals, as the Chessman supporters held out the possibility that institutional confinement and treatment might eventually pro-
duce beneficial results. Chessman's proponents, in other words, tended
not to dispute what comprised the category of sexual psychopath, just
whether Chessman himself fit the mold.

"The particular crimes of the 'red light bandit' indicate homosexuality," stated Dr. William Graves, former San Quentin physician, on behalf of Chessman in 1960. Upon his resignation from San Quentin in
1954, Graves, in a letter to Governor Knight, gave his disagreement with
the charges against Chessman as a primary reason. Graves would remain at the frontline of Chessman's defense over the next six years, and
his 1960 observations were reprinted in a Justice for Chessman Committee ad in the *New York Times.* "Chessman," Graves explained, "has
none of the psychological makeup that would lead to the kind of crimes
for which he is sentenced to die. The pervert who commits such crimes

tends to be a very weak and dependent individual who cannot satisfy himself by normal means or a man filled with bitterness toward women." In defending Chessman, Graves explained sex crime in reference to homosexuality and what he considered to be other forms of illicit behavior, an argument reinforcing pernicious postwar psychiatric stereotypes. A pervasive cultural fear of same-sex and other nonreproductive sexual behaviors underlay the sex crime panic of the late 1940s, and Graves's comments underscored the lingering resonance of these specious scientific analyses.[53]

In promoting a 1960 rally, the Justice for Chessman Committee (chaired by Elaine de Kooning) answered to its own question—"Why Worry About Chessman?"—thusly: "Popular opinion convicts him of murder and rape, charges which have never even been leveled against him in court." Only the most technical interpretation, based solely on the actual wording of the initial charges, could support the notion that rape did not figure prominently in the prosecution's case against Chessman. In stressing this position, the committee failed to recognize the strength of the narrative popularly told against Chessman. Sexual deviance during the era was construed as a slippery slope, and convictions for crimes like those of the red light bandit placed the culprit on a full-speed course to further sexual assault, murder, and virtually every form of brutal crime. Chessman's leading proponents, however, actually tended to endorse the powerful, seemingly irrefutable consensus among psychiatrists and public officials about the irredeemable makeup of sex criminals. For the majority who spoke out on his behalf, Chessman was a promising writer, not a menacing sexual threat. To the consternation of Chessman's foes, the man they had deemed a "sex terrorist" steadily became a household name in the struggle against the death penalty. Indeed, the emergence of a figure whom the *Los Angeles Times* derisively called a "celebrated rapist" would have profound implications for partisans on both sides of the Chessman divide.[54]

The Rehabilitation of a Criminal "Genius"

(1954–1960)

This young man is completely worthless!
> *Los Angeles Deputy District Attorney*
> *J. Miller Leavy to jury (1948)*

His attitude has always been casual, self-serving and he has always felt that he was not a criminal and never considered it terribly wrong to do any and all of the things that he had done in the past.
> *San Quentin psychiatric evaluation*
> *of Chessman (1948)*

[Chessman's] nothingness, his nonexistence, makes his remarkable articulation, his tireless creation of himself as a fact . . . one of those startling efforts of personal rehabilitation, [and] salvation of the self.
> *Elizabeth Hardwick, "The Life and Death*
> *of Caryl Chessman" (1961)*

Shortly before the 1954 publication of *Cell 2455 Death Row*, Caryl Chessman met with San Quentin psychiatrists for his regular neuropsychiatric exam. "Smiling and affable" because of "fairly good" advance press reports, Chessman discussed his goals in writing the book. "In addition to proving he can write," the exam report stated, "he wanted to tell his side of the story to . . . [show] that rebels always have a cause; and capital punishment is not the answer." At the end of their meeting, the psychiatrists evaluated Chessman: "We are all agreed [that] he has a Psychopathic or Sociopathic Personality and has been a chronic juvenile and adult offender." In referencing Robert Lindner's *Rebel Without a*

Cause: The Hypnoanalysis of a Criminal Psychopath, Chessman's description of himself thus corresponded with the psychiatrists' diagnosis, albeit with a significant twist: he claimed to be a reformed psychopath, one who now had a noble purpose. Between 1954 and 1960, Chessman would write three nonfiction books and one novel attempting to solidify his presentation of himself as a "rebel with a cause."[1]

Precisely what comprised Chessman's cause was open to a variety of interpretations, however. Although he freely confessed to his criminal past, Chessman vehemently denied he was the red light bandit; yet the death penalty, he stressed, was always an unjust punishment no matter who received it. Capital punishment, moreover, was the most dramatic symbol of what Chessman saw as the flawed notion of "retributive justice," which he had encountered throughout his career as a "juvenile and adult offender." As a former criminal psychopath now confronting the most severe punishment of all, Chessman hoped his rehabilitation could provide an instructive example for American society in dealing with its "pressing problems" of crime and juvenile delinquency. While his denial of guilt and his proposal to abolish capital punishment were not uncommon for a prisoner on a death row, it was the question of Chessman's individual character which generated the most debate. The main proof of his reform, according to both the author and his sympathetic readers, was his very ability to write books.[2]

Crucial to Chessman's invention of himself as a rehabilitated man was the support he received from an array of influential criminologists, literary critics, and liberal intellectuals. Because he successfully articulated his criminal past and now offered his own theories on the crime problem, prominent criminologists welcomed him into their ranks. They did so, perhaps, because Chessman's efforts as a writer typified the goals of the "new penology"—reading and writing, the reformers said, were the keys to a prisoner's rehabilitation. A number of literary critics also endorsed Chessman's efforts, seeing in him an author who was no "ordinary criminal" but instead one with a "brilliant mind." To execute him, the specialists said, would not only deprive American society of a perfect "social guinea pig" for the study of crime, but would mean extinguishing a man who had shown obvious signs of "regeneration." Throughout his books Chessman maintained his innocence of the crimes of the red light bandit—meaning his rehabilitation was from his previous life of petty crime, not from the kidnapping charges for which he was sentenced. As Chessman himself knew, and the intellectuals who supported him implicitly realized, confession to the red light bandit's sex crimes would have placed him squarely in the category of sexual psychopath, and thus outside the scope of rehabilitation.[3]

After attempting to prove his reform by writing his autobiography, Chessman wrote, "Guilt or innocence aside, Death Row is doubtless the best thing that ever could have happened to me." The gas chamber, he said, provided the "psychological shock therapy" that now enabled him to "demonstrate . . . that [even] the most 'hopeless' criminal in existence can be salvaged." In *Cell 2455 Death Row*, Chessman appealed to reform-minded social scientists, offering himself as an example of the once-hopeless outcast now ready to contribute to society. The overall effect was that Chessman ended up sounding like a visionary prison warden, an innovative psychiatrist, or a sympathetic guidance counselor. Time and again, he wrote more from the perspective of aspiring criminal expert than incarcerated prisoner. During the late 1950s his strategy attained visible critical success, making him what Elizabeth Hardwick called "one of those startling efforts of personal rehabilitation." A generation of prison writers after Chessman would try to emulate his literary fame and stature, but in the process these writers would steadily begin to reject the rehabilitative ideal. This departure suggested the degree to which Chessman's failure in writing himself off death row nevertheless proved to be instructive for the legions of prison authors who would follow his notable, if ultimately unsuccessful, lead.[4]

Reading, Writing, and Reform

In a preview of *Cell 2455*, *Newsweek* outlined Chessman's apparent goal in writing the book: "To follow in the footsteps of David Lamson, who wrote *We Who Are About to Die* while a resident of San Quentin's death row, but then won a new trial, freedom, and a respectable place in American letters." Published in 1935, *We Who Are About to Die* had been penned after Lamson left San Quentin, while he awaited a new trial for the murder of his wife. A campaign led by Stanford faculty members publicized the case, which eventually went through three trials before being tossed out by a judge in 1936. Rather than allowing him to write his way off death row, Lamson's book instead confirmed his reputation as a man too "respectable" to have killed his wife. In popular memory, however, Lamson had been the most recent (and successful) death row author to precede Chessman. Although both his narrative strategy and his public reputation differed greatly from Lamson's, Chessman would

make frequent use of his predecessor's title phrase in conveying the reality of prison life.[5]

If his status as a death row author was relatively unique, Chessman's
attempt to tell "A Condemned Man's Own Story" (as the subtitle of *Cell
2455* read) followed many of the longstanding conventions of prison literature. In fact, the work is a hybrid of the forms H. Bruce Franklin de-
fines as characteristic of prison literature in general.[6] Initially, *Cell 2455*
reads like a picaresque narrative, as Chessman embarks on a dizzying
ride through wartime Los Angeles; the reader accompanies him on a
endless string of car chases, shootouts, prison escapes, and other sordid
adventures. Though *Cell 2455* also dabbles in the sociology of prison
life, Chessman would develop this approach more fully in his second
work, *Trial by Ordeal* (1955). Rather than write as a sociologist, Chessman more frequently adopted the perspective of a criminologist. Also
prevalent throughout *Cell 2455* is the confessional mode, the meaning
of which was decidedly contemporary. It was the very ability to tell his
story, to offer himself as a "social guinea pig," that comprised Chessman's confession. In other words, there is no single moment in the work
when Chessman "sees the light" and begins to reform;[7] instead, his
transformation is evident on every page, inherent in his ability to recognize and articulate his criminal past. As adherents of the new penology,
most reviewers considered the very act of writing *Cell 2455* to be concrete proof that Chessman's character had indeed changed.

The connection between reading, writing, and rehabilitation was first
made by prison reformers of the early twentieth century. Prior to the
Progressive Era, the holdings of prison libraries generally consisted only
of religious books. In the first decades of the twentieth century, however,
prison reformers increasingly began to view educational instruction as a
necessary part of integrating the prisoner into the outside community.
Yet only a handful of prisons allowed their libraries to include books on
secular subjects. One prison administration which had briefly implemented Progressive educational programs soon took these privileges
away, illustrating in the process the tenuous official linkage between
reading, writing, and reform. Angered by the publication of prisoners'
work (in outlets like H. L. Mencken's *The American Mercury*), San
Quentin officials clamped down on prisoners' ability to write in 1928.
In her *Nation* essay "Shall Convicts Write Books?" Miriam Allen De
Ford criticized such measures. "If prisons really existed for the sake of
reforming criminals, any new interest or talent or means of honest sup-

port that might lead to rehabilitation [should] be hailed with joy by the officials," De Ford observed.[8]

As seen in chapter one, postwar reformers began to establish the Progressive model of rehabilitative imprisonment on a widespread basis. Appropriately, in *New Horizons in Criminology* (1951), Harry Elmer Barnes and Negley K. Teeters devoted a whole chapter to the "New Day in Prison Education." The authors envisioned a modern education program to include classes in academic subjects, as well as in "mental hygiene" and "cultural development." Prison libraries, they said, needed to be enlarged, and prison librarians should be given the power of selecting books. San Quentin, said Barnes and Teeters, offered one of the "most progressive" education programs in the country. In *The San Quentin Story* (1950), Warden Clinton T. Duffy paid special attention to the "three R's," linking the expansion of the education department to the increase in psychiatric treatment each prisoner received. During Duffy's reign, San Quentin's librarian, Herman K. Spector, developed his innovative methods of "bibliotherapy," which encouraged inmates to study classic works. As promoted in a 1949 California Department of Corrections report, the San Quentin library served as model for the rest of the state's prisons, as it helped each inmate become "capable of accepting new ideas and situations in everyday life." Postwar officials, in turn, viewed proficiency in literacy skills as a telltale sign of a prisoner's reformation. Thus included in the dossier that prisoners presented to the parole board were the letters he had written while in prison, as well as his library record.[9]

As Chessman would frequently remind his audience, despite his manifest literary talent state prosecutors had nevertheless declared him, like all of the condemned, to be "beyond the possibility of rehabilitation." Though generally isolated from the therapeutic innovations aimed at the majority of prisoners, Chessman for his part attempted to bring the new penology to death row. Indeed, in order to rejoin the mainstream prison population and then free society, Chessman first needed to appropriate the terms of reentry. Although they disagreed on the specific content, both prison officials and the prisoner himself viewed writing as an initial, mutually beneficial step toward Chessman's therapeutic recovery. Quoting San Quentin psychiatric reports, *Newsweek* said Chessman had been a "difficult prisoner" during his first six years on death row, leading sitdown strikes and fighting with other condemned men. "Because he was tractable when writing," the article continued, "prison authorities urged him to go ahead and write." Those same officials, however, were none too pleased with the result.[10]

Cell 2455 Death Row

Cell 2455 Death Row provides an autobiographical account of Chessman's life, starting from his troubled childhood and eventually leading to death row. From his opening quote of Homer to his Latin section headings, it is clear throughout the work that Chessman wants to establish himself as no ordinary criminal. Instead, he adopts the posture of a lifelong thief with extraordinary intelligence who now wants to invest his unusual abilities in more constructive pursuits; it is this keen observer whom the reader will accompany on a perilous path to the shadow of the gas chamber. Along the way, Chessman makes frequent use of the term *psychopath* as he carefully investigates his rebellious motives. Yet, while he glamorizes his criminal past, Chessman strongly denies he was the red light bandit. To underscore the point, he emphasizes his own steadfastly heterosexual preference, illustrated both by his romantic exploits and his insider analyses of homosexuality in prison. Chessman, in short, seemed well aware that his claim to rehabilitation required him to establish his own sexual "normality."

Fittingly, Chessman's opening description of everyday life on death row demonstrates his identification with men condemned for sex-related crimes. He tells the story of a pair of men, Big Red and Henry, who await their execution. Big Red, "a normally jolly Arkansan in his late thirties," had become convinced that his wife was "cheating on him," and beat another man to death in a drunken rage. Even more sensational was Henry, who had been "convicted of the sex murder of a ten-year-old girl, and doomed." Chessman attempts to humanize these men, mentioning their daily conversation about politics and music. In cinematic fashion, Chessman describes Big Red's final walk toward the gas chamber; as he says goodbye to his fellow prisoners, Red "reminds you of your own plight, and your cell grows smaller in front of your eyes." In *Cell 2455* Chessman frequently uses the second-person voice to describe himself, an obvious attempt to implicate audiences in his plight. In his opening chapter, the reader is thus placed among the men condemned to death for crimes either "caused" by, or committed against, the opposite sex.[11]

After a tour of San Quentin, the author next introduces the man in Cell 2455, to whom he gives the name Whit (short for Chessman's middle name Whittier). For the first third of the book, Chessman tells his own life story in the third person, another strategy aimed at generalizing his experience. Whit, he writes, was born in Michigan in 1921, to loving parents named Hallie and Serl. Because of Hallie's ill health, the family soon moved to Southern California. Initially a promising pianist, Whit's talents diminished after he fell victim to a bronchial condition, encephalitis, and later diphtheria. Such illness caused him to become "a mother's boy, shy, obedient and, on the surface, altogether lacking the normal, healthy aggressions of lads his age." After his mother was left paralyzed by a car accident, Whit began to question God's existence. His father, meanwhile, could not support the family, and during the Depression he twice attempted suicide, both times unsuccessfully. Because he objected to his family being "on relief," Whit began his life of crime. Superficially, Chessman's account of his early entrance into a life of crime seems a conventional Depression-era melodramatic tale.[12]

Yet by analyzing his childhood in terms of his mother's dominance and his father's weakness, Chessman framed his story in popular psychiatric terms. "Momism," first identified by Phillip Wylie in *Generation of Vipers* (1942), linked overbearing mothers to the dangers of Communism. Lindner's *Rebel Without a Cause* (1944) suggested that a weak father figure would make a boy vulnerable to fascism. The weak father/ strong mother dichotomy would also become an increasingly popular stereotype of the roots of male homosexuality. The prominent role that Chessman accords his mother in his criminal past suggested his awareness of these popular debates. After highlighting his success in robbing bordellos, for example, Chessman claims to have used the money to hire a private detective to help Hallie find her parents. Beneath the veneer of nobility, such a claim had the effect of implicating his mother in his life of crime. In general, though, reviewers readily accepted Chessman's account of his youth, describing him as a "sickly, precocious child," or as "victim of an overprotective mother and a weakling father." Chessman, it seems, successfully referenced popular psychological notions of familial danger.[13]

Cell 2455's depictions of Chessman's family life may have been embellished, but prison psychiatric reports confirmed their overall accuracy. "It would seem that both parents were indulgent to the subject," surmised Senior Psychiatric Social Worker J. P. Conrad upon Chessman's readmittance to San Quentin in 1948. Conrad observed that while Hallie "assume[d] a basically uncritical attitude toward him," Serl seemed unusually supportive of his son's activities. Not only had Serl Chessman made Caryl feel "smart to elude officers," but he also "provide[d] as complete a rationalization and a projection of the subject's earlier offenses as the subject himself could have made." Both father and son thus gave the social worker the same family-based explanations of crime that Caryl submitted in *Cell 2455*. An earlier spree of armed robbery and auto theft, the younger Chessman told Conrad in 1948, stemmed from the "need for money to pay for an operation for his mother." Upon his initial arrest for these offenses, though, the *Los Angeles Times* had asked why he and the rest of his "Boy Bandit Gang" chose to rob. "Lucrative," Chessman responded succinctly, mentioning no family hardship. Regardless of his actual motivations, Chessman's accounts of his family background seemed roughly consistent, and were not contrived simply for his *Cell 2455* readership.[14]

Chessman's institutional evaluation as a psychopath carried strong popular connotations of homosexuality. Throughout his autobiography, Chessman sought to counter this diagnosis by presenting himself as resolutely heterosexual. Accordingly, his sexual preference is established early in the work. At age seven, Chessman writes, "Whit loved Annabelle," a neighborhood girl whom he compares to a "goddess." Later, when he became a successful gangster, women seemed to find him irresistible. He took a "wild ride in a hot car" with "two gay young things who squealed with fear and delight." Throughout his adventures as a gangster, Chessman utilizes the second person in order to entice the reader. Thus, "You met gay, sophisticated young things who bestowed their favors liberally, who, for a moment, shared their physical selves with you." In his descriptions of these and other adventures, Chessman frequently referred to himself as a "public enemy." In *Public Enemy* (1931), James Cagney had memorably portrayed a heterosexual playboy and small-time gangster, and Chessman clearly saw himself as cut from the same mold.[15]

In the early sections of *Cell 2455*, Chessman consciously portrays himself as a steadfast defender of both women's honor and heterosexual propriety. When he was about ten, Whit fired his BB gun at a couple "engaging in a sex act" in a car parked in the hills. He was angered because the couple ignored the "tiny, crying girl [who] stood on the front seat and called pitifully for mama." As a teenager, he was engaged in constant struggle with the parents of his girlfriends, who did not want their daughters hanging around him. Chessman, in turn, wanted to save his girlfriends from their parents' "cruel" ways. His "noble" posture was most severely tested by Virginia, the hypersexual moll who hung out with his gang. Virginia smoked, drank, and taunted him as "the little boy." After she asked if Whit had "got" his girlfriend's "cherry," Whit yelled, "Shut your dirty, filthy mouth!" and threatened to kill her. She then challenged him to have sex, and by calling him "either scared or a pansy" provoked his compliance. Afterwards, she told him how "she had been cuffed, cursed, and then compelled to submit" to men. "Whit sobbed," Chessman writes, but then resolved "to fight for her and himself too." The challenge posed by Virginia was profound: she questioned Whit's manhood, he proved himself, and now he would defend her. Beneath his veneer of nobility, in other words, there lurked considerable sexual unease.[16]

Chessman further tried to dispel any questions about his heterosexuality by providing insider accounts of the same-sex activity he encountered in reform school and prisons. At one Sunday service teenage Whit attended, just "as a thundering condemnation of sin was being delivered from the pulpit, a homosexual in the back row seat slid down and committed an act of sex perversion on four boys, one after the other." Such incidents, he wrote, "made it temptingly easy to sneer. Or to vomit." On another occasion in reform school he fought with a "mincing homosexual, big enough to fight grizzly bears." While at San Quentin, he was able to place the issue in perspective. "Prison officials don't have much to say about the very real problem of homosexuality in prison," he wrote. The "prison wolves or 'jockers,'" Chessman continued, were "kept from preying on the young, frightened and physically or morally weak inmate"; meanwhile, the "aggressively active 'queen' is segregated and, when possible, helped medically and psychiatrically." Despite the best efforts of prison officials, nevertheless "the practice of homosexuality still flourishes." This fact, he says, is "inevitable" because the prison inmate has been "locked away from women but he has retained his instincts, his hungers, his needs, and his manhood." As opposed to his initial revulsion, Chessman now adopted an approach based on understanding. Both stances, though, confirmed his main intention: to distance himself from homosexuality.[17]

Chessman's sexual identity was indeed critical to the gangster image he projected in Cell 2455. He had a special fondness for robbing pimps, and for stealing his rivals' girlfriends.[18] He defended friends from the assaults of "mincing homosexuals," and threatened to enact revenge on the "vile animal" who attacked his girlfriend. In short, Chessman saw himself as a defender of heterosexual propriety, not as its assailant. Yet, despite his self-styled credentials as a noble outlaw, Chessman had been labeled a psychopath, thus forcing him to reckon with the popular meaning of the term.

A Former Psychopath

When his story shifts to San Quentin, Chessman no longer tells the story of Whit, the adventurous rebel; instead he speaks as Chessman, the prisoner and criminologist. From the latter's perspective, Whit had been "a grinning, brooding young criminal psychopath in defiantly willing bondage to his psychopathy." In his 1948 report, Conrad noted how Chessman "states that this department's diagnosis of him as a constitutional psychopath is patently ridiculous." Six years later, though, Chessman saw the term as accurate in describing his former self. Yet Chessman's use of the term *psychopath* in *Cell 2455* was no more precise than the experts', and throughout the book he mentions his "psychopathic battles" and his "psychopathic armor." In *Trial by Ordeal* Chessman explains, "I use this term . . . descriptively, not diagnostically, to identify those individuals . . . who keep clashing with the law, defying Authority. I question the validity of the term as a diagnostic label." Conspicuously, Chessman's definition removes all sexual connotations, which, after all, was the reason the term came into popular usage. He denies committing the red light bandit's crimes, yet still calls himself a psychopath. What he did not recognize, perhaps, was the implication of the "diagnostic label." According to the popular discourse of sex crime, the sexual psychopath could not so easily rehabilitate himself, at least not without years of psychiatric correction—and certainly not simply by claiming to be reformed.[19]

Chessman's psychopath more likely corresponded with the modern *sociopath*, a figure whose hatred is directed against society rather than against himself. Whit and the pre–death row Chessman, he said, indeed directed their anger outward. The problem they faced, according to Chessman, was a never-ending series of hostile institutions—places of punishment ruling by force, rather than moral suasion. For the pre–death row Chessman, "crime was an adventure, kicks, glamour; crime was rebellion, a psychopathic crusade, an inviting, deadly pilgrimage." Yet every time he was caught, he encountered harsh cops, mean judges, boorish reform school officials, and bullying prison guards and parole officers, all of whom only threatened him with more punishment. He was warned repeatedly that his recklessness would lead to the gas chamber, but he kept running anyway. Chessman treated his life of crime as inevitable process, the story of a reckless youth combating an enemy he called "Authority," which was always capitalized, and always mean. However broad, this conflict was the basis of Chessman's explanation of his rebellion. He presented himself not as a "constitutionally inferior" psychopath but as a rebel whose war against society could have been redirected if he only had better guidance.[20]

Chessman's exaggerations notwithstanding, large portions of *Cell 2455*'s account of his youthful criminal exploits indeed squared with the historical record. As mentioned above, Chessman first achieved local notoriety as a member of the "Boy Bandit Gang" that wreaked havoc in the Los Angeles area in 1941. According to the *Los Angeles Times,* the gang was captured after "an astounding trail of holdups, running gun duels with police, and automobile thieving." Chessman and the four others in the group—all between the ages of eighteen and twenty-two— had met in juvenile correction camp, where they plotted their course of mayhem. Chessman, "assertedly the leader of the gang," explained their efforts to the press. "I was the car maneuver man. I am practically an expert on cars," he declared. Newspaper headlines equated the Boy Bandit Gang with the Dead End Kids, Hollywood's mischievous band of adolescents. The opening article of a seven-part series on juvenile delinquency in the *Los Angeles Daily News,* moreover, placed a picture of the gang below two photographs of John Dillinger. Of the Dillinger photos, one was captioned "delinquent" and the other "killer." For his crimes, Caryl Chessman, the leader of the Boy Bandit Gang and "self-styled auto expert," received his first sentence to San Quentin.[21]

More than a decade after Chessman's Boy Bandit escapades, the threat of the state's ultimate form of punishment provided him with the catalyst for his own effort at reform. Chessman stated that his rehabilitation began the day he embraced the "new penology." Commending the "humane" basis of the indeterminate sentencing law, he specifically praised Warden Duffy for believing that "those men who genuinely wanted another chance should have that chance." According to psychiatric reports, during his first visit to San Quentin Chessman had been inspired by the prison's Education Supervisor, at one point mentioning his career ambition to become a "Socio-Psychiatrist." In the earlier stay Chessman also taught illiterate prisoners to read and write, and while on death row he authored legal briefs for fellow condemned men. These efforts gave him "great satisfaction," the latter solidifying his reputation as a jailhouse lawyer. By the mid-1950s Chessman's work as author, lawyer, teacher, and criminologist indeed seemed to manifest the goals of postwar penology.[22]

One giant inconsistency hampered Chessman's claim of rehabilitation: he maintained his innocence for the crimes that sent him to death row. Chessman spent a sizable part of each of his three books explaining how the Los Angeles Police, District Attorney Leavy, Judge Fricke, and the local news media teamed up against him. He said his confession had been beaten out of him, and that the Bandit's victims had misidentified him in court. A condemned prisoner protesting innocence, of course, is a phenomenon as old as executions themselves; sex offenses, moreover, historically have been the crimes most frequently denied. More important than its accuracy, though, is the implication of Chessman's claim. To confess guilt would have placed him in the category of sexual deviant, a group deemed inferior by nature and thus outside the scope of rehabilitation. Yet to maintain innocence meant that he refused to accept the fundamental premise of rehabilitation—namely, the admission of guilt and the eagerness to reform. Chessman had indeed admitted he was guilty, but not of the crimes sending him to death row.[23]

More consistent than Chessman's claim to be both innocent and reformed was the role of his own "genius" in linking the two. As Chessman recounted his original argument to the jury in *Cell 2455,* "the red light crimes were committed by a bungling amateur with a sexually twisted mind, not by a coldly calculating professional criminal." He was too rational, professional, and normal, in other words, to have committed the Bandit's sex crimes. Although nothing in his account showed him to be an especially skillful criminal, particularly since he kept getting caught, Chessman nevertheless considered himself to be one; likewise, he now thought of himself as a rehabilitated prisoner, a category much harder to define. The improbable motivations he gave for some of his crimes—to pay for a private detective to find his mother's parents, to escape from prison in order to kill Hitler—in retrospect do not make him completely credible. As he summarized one of his interviews with San Quentin psychiatrists, "No, I was not guilty of the crimes for which I had been sentenced to death. . . . Yes, I would say I was not the red light bandit even if I were." Chessman, it seems, ultimately wanted to be judged by questions other than of his guilt or innocence.[24]

Inside prison walls, Chessman again seemed reasonably consistent regarding what he told *Cell 2455* readers about his innocence. Meeting with San Quentin psychiatric staff shortly after the Red Light convictions, Chessman refused to discuss the details of the case. "He does not want to commit himself with any statements that might be used against him if our records were subpoenaed in court," noted chief psychiatrist David Schmidt. Similarly, Chessman told J. P. Conrad that "when he is clearer about his legal position he may be willing to discuss the charges" against him. Over the next twelve years, Chessman's initial caution gave way to frank discussion with psychiatrists about the detrimental impact of his "not guilty" plea on Governor Brown's clemency decision-making process. Never once did he suggest to these officials that he was reconsidering his stance, however. The antagonism toward sex criminals he evinced in *Cell 2455* also seemed to be an enduring characteristic. As his legal adviser, Al Matthews, wrote to Governor Knight in 1954, Chessman six years earlier "showed extreme repugnance toward anyone involved in sexual crimes. He was proud of being a robber and felt that a person who had also committed the crime with which he was charged had degraded the profession, so to speak." More problematically, Matthews said Chessman knew the identity of the real red light bandit but was "unable under the criminal code" to name him. "I am afraid that man is dead, perhaps at the hand of Chessman," Matthews said in asking Knight to grant clemency (!). Sordid details aside, throughout all of his books, as well as his recorded statements inside San Quentin, Chessman never wavered in his denial of the red light sex crimes.[25]

The Chessman interviewed by San Quentin psychiatrists in 1948 seemed unwilling to see himself as a "criminal," or to find any of his actions to be "terribly wrong." By 1954, though, Chessman adopted the stance of a criminal expert now able to openly assess his former "psychopathy." Prior to *Cell 2455*'s publication, literary agent Joseph Longstreth sought more explanation from Chessman regarding this shift in character. Specifically, Longstreth wondered about the flurry of robberies Chessman admits to in his book that occurred at the same time as the January 1948 Red Light crimes. Noting that Chessman had been released from Folsom in December of 1947, Longstreth asked, why "go out to do a job after a week or two of tranquil living at home?" Echoing his explanation in *Cell 2455*, Chessman responded, "Only one who had been through a 'reformation factory' and then returned to poverty and the sight of a slowly dying, bedridden mother could fully appreciate or grasp" his motivations. "Not stealing, not rebelling, not fighting back," he further stressed, "seemed to imply weakness—and there is the key to psychopathy, the trigger of delinquent conduct." Chessman thus attributed his actions to family necessity and an ensuing, persistent need to challenge authority. Yet as Longstreth pointed out, since the crimes he acknowledged came only a month after his release from Folsom, Chessman seemed to be portraying himself as a career thief. Why, his literary agent thus suggested, should *Cell 2455* readers accept Chessman's claim to be genuinely reformed?[26]

Toward the end of the book Chessman analyzed the transformation he had undergone in the previous six years. "The long years in this crucible called Death Row have carried me beyond bitterness, beyond hate, beyond savage animal violence," he wrote. Chessman further hoped his book was "a beginning contribution" to understanding the "problem of crime." "I would like to believe that it [his book] also signals the beginning for me of a journey back from outer darkness," he added. In *Trial by Ordeal,* he recalled the initial spark, saying that after "four defiant, rebellious years on Death Row . . . [v]irtually overnight I changed radically." An unexpected stay of execution had helped him wake up, as had the warden's criticism of him as an "angry, hating, fighting failure." Chessman responded, feeling he "could tell the story of my life, without pulling punches." *Cell 2455* told the story of a figure who was a noble bandit, a nonsexual psychopath, a "professional" criminal, an aspiring criminologist, and, above all, a rehabilitated prisoner. "Long after I should have been dead," Chessman wrote, "I wrote myself back to sanity." He did so, however, with a little help from his critics.[27]

No Ordinary Criminal

Reviewers generally seemed amazed by both the "authenticity" and "intelligence" of Chessman's first work. Calling it "the most literate and authentic thriller in autobiographical crime literature" he had seen in many years, criminologist Harry Elmer Barnes said "thoughtful students of the crime problem will value the book," which was destined to make a "salutary dent on the criminological horizon." In the *New York Times Book Review,* Frank O'Leary (described in a byline as an "ex-convict") praised the book for its "authentic underworld lingo, gems from the philosophy of penal dusk and sparkling contributions in the field of criminology." For O'Leary, the book clarified the degree to which "Caryl Chessman shows promise, ironically, of the ability to mature into a useful citizen." Chessman's "literate insight" and "brilliant mind" indeed figured prominently in the analysis of many reviewers. As *Saturday Review* staff writer John Barkham wrote, "No condemned criminal . . . has ever produced so literate and lucid and penetrating a piece of self-analysis." "Only Chessman's brain separates him from the criminally commonplace," *Los Angeles Daily News* columnist Tom Gwynne wrote suggestively. The authentic nature of his account, and Chessman's intelligent reflection, made him appear to many as the perfect test case, or "social guinea pig," for criminology. By writing a uniquely intelligent autobiography, the former psychopath had convinced the experts of his readiness to become useful as both citizen and laboratory specimen.[28]

Not all critics viewed Chessman in a favorable light, however. One reviewer, with whom Chessman testily took exception in his next book, wondered if "the book could be the final extension of [a] master plan to fool the rehabilitators again." California Governor Goodwin Knight, meanwhile, voiced his disagreement with the entire connection between reading, writing, and rehabilitation: "There is nothing in the statutes to excuse a man of the consequences of his crimes by writing a book," he declared. Not surprisingly, the California Department of Corrections agreed with the governor. In mid-August 1954, Director of Corrections Richard A. McGee ordered the seizure of all manuscripts written by condemned prisoners. Encouraged to write by prison officials, Chessman was now silenced. Invoking a law which declared prisoners to be "civilly dead" and their work to be public property, state officials sought to counteract the negative publicity generated by the case. To the dismay of prison administrators, Chessman would not remain quiet for very long, though. Despite the ban, over the next six years Chessman—helped by fellow inmates and sympathetic prison officials—managed to smuggle two manuscripts out to his publisher. Chessman's fight for his life, in short, seemed inseparable from his fight for the right to speak.[29]

Trial by Ordeal (1955) thus came into public view as the work of a prolific, now censored death row author. Having written his life story, Chessman here offered an account of life on death row. The insider stance he adopted was not a new approach in prison literature, yet Chessman had few predecessors in terms of his perspective. He now wrote as an embattled public figure, a man literally writing to save his life. "'Fiend' and 'monster' are two of the nicer things you have been called," he wrote in his introduction. "Until death intervenes," he concluded, "I will continue to write." "Writing," he said elsewhere in the text, was "an answer to psychopathy." But if Chessman was on death row, he was not of it. Instead, he wrote from the perspective of a radical criminologist assigned to do fieldwork among condemned men. Since he had proven himself as rehabilitated, he now felt it his task to show how his fellow death row inmates were equally capable of reform.[30]

As he analyzed the character of "the Doomed," the connection between Chessman's own makeup and the perspective he offered came into
sharper focus. Chessman's identity not only as a fledgling expert but as
a white, literate, and heterosexual male lay at the heart of his every explanation. Even when he empathized with condemned African Americans or homosexual men, he showed his distance. His fellow black inmates had nicknames like "the Praying Pimp" or "the Shifter." "Doil,"
meanwhile, "was a small Negro, about thirty years of age, and friendly
as a puppy." After telling how "Danny" had confronted a court preju-
diced against him for his homosexuality, Chessman wondered, "What,
at bottom, is the psychological reason for homosexuality? . . . Is it a
crime or an unfortunate affliction?" This combination of empathy and
analysis did not place the author in the same position as these and other
men; rather, he was writing to show how different he was, or how death
row had rehabilitated him. Men who could not write, though, certainly
could not follow his path. Prisoners like Doil and Danny, meanwhile,
faced an even more severe obstacle: deemed deviant by nature, they
could not so easily lay claim to being rehabilitated.[31]

Throughout *Trial by Ordeal,* Chessman also reassured readers of his
desire to build a stable family life. While at San Quentin, Chessman had
begun a romantic relationship with Frances Couturier, his father's former housekeeper. During his "psychopathic days," he said, he had
"ruined" his first marriage, and now he was determined to do better.
"Death Row," Chessman wrote, "has taught me that a man can live
without the love and companionship of a woman, but if the choice is his,
that he is a fool to do so." Chessman not only wanted to earn Frances's
love and eventually help raise a family, but he wanted to protect her.
"Some vile s.o.b.," he stated, had written Frances "vicious, threatening
letters," yet Chessman "knew how much guts his kind had when fleshed
out in the open." In addition to his professional contributions to criminology, Chessman fashioned himself as ready to become a strong father
figure. Except for his residence, the author of *Trial by Ordeal* seemed to
fit—or at least aspired to fulfill—the image of the postwar breadwin-
ning male.[32]

Critics by and large endorsed Chessman's second effort, seeing in it
further signs of his "maturation." A reviewer for the *New York Herald
Tribune* believed *Trial by Ordeal* showed how "Caryl Chessman has
matured as a writer and a human being." In the *New York Times Book
Review,* Frank O'Leary called it not only a "blistering sequel" to *Cell
2455,* but "a far more disciplined example of objective writing." The

"maturation" and "objectivity" critics found in Chessman's second work, however, gave way to the "arrogant" and "almost screamingly hysterical" voice Chessman adopted in his third book. Published in 1957, again after being smuggled out of San Quentin, *The Face of Justice* offered a blow-by-blow account of the case's legal machinations. According to O'Leary, of the many "faces" Chessman contrived in the book ("legal strategist," "crusading foe of capital punishment," etc.) the most problematic seemed the "boasting and threatening" Chessman, the one who "hurl[ed] invective and innuendo at the officials who have closed in on him." One particular point seemed especially "puzzling" to O'Leary. Chessman claimed to have put together a secret "package" which "indisputably" proved he was not the red light bandit. The exact whereabouts of the package, however, remained undisclosed.[33]

The publication of three books clearly bolstered Chessman's ego. In protest of the seizure by prison officials of the manuscript for his fictional work, Chessman told the court, "One's eyes cannot be shut to the fact that some of the world's greatest literature was written behind prison walls." Whether Chessman's *The Kid Was a Killer* (1960) qualifies as "great literature," though, remains open to debate. The storyline follows Charley Evans, a sportswriter, as he attempts to find out why "the Kid," a boxer, is prone to "savage animal" violence. The hero of the book is Tom Layton, one of the "city's younger psychiatrists" who had recently authored a work on "Psychopathy." Layton soon discovers the Kid's frightening background. The latter had been victim of a tyrannical father, who beat his family and forced the children to watch while he raped his mother; one day the Kid finally rose up and killed his father. Although the Kid dies in the ring at the end, his life illustrates how one can "always find the Authority figure who had precipitated the crisis from which the psychopathic personality was formed." In *The Kid Was a Killer,* Chessman once again cast his lot with the "psychiatric experts" on crime.[34]

The real-life criminal experts in turn lent professional sanction to Chessman's endeavors. Since his account of his own rehabilitation, and his prescriptions for further penological reform, seemed to leap from the pages of *New Horizons in Criminology,* the book's authors, Harry Elmer Barnes and Negley K. Teeters, quite naturally rushed to Chessman's defense. After writing numerous book reviews as well as letters to the governors of California on behalf of Chessman, Barnes presented his overall summation in a post-mortem review of the case. The state of California, Barnes argued, "needlessly executed" a "person who showed signs of future regeneration, and who . . . might have contributed to literature and criminology." Earlier, in a published letter to Governor Knight, Teeters observed, Chessman is "no ordinary criminal; he has a brilliant mind. . . . [S]ociety knows so little about the criminal psychopath that he should be used for scientific purposes to find out how and why a man becomes such a menace to society." "Science, if not humanity," would benefit from the study of criminals like Chessman, the two authors stated in concluding their chapter on the death penalty in the 1959 edition of *New Horizons in Penology*. Influential criminologists like Barnes and Teeters, in short, eagerly invited Chessman into their ranks.[35]

Whether their background was in literary criticism or criminology, Chessman's sympathizers generally steered clear of the author's Red Light convictions; when directly considering the issue, though, they tended to view him as someone who did not fit the category of sexual deviant. Chairing a group of crime writers who formed a committee in Chessman's defense, Wenzell Brown declared: "We are not concerned with his guilt or innocence. . . . [Instead] we are trying to preserve a fund of irreplaceable knowledge which is of great value to psychiatrists, criminologists, penologists, and writers." By contrast, a handful of influential onlookers straightforwardly endorsed the claims to innocence put forth in *Cell 2455*. Max Lerner, for example, said "nothing about Chessman's life seems to fit into this description [of sex offender]." "He was a rebel," Lerner maintained, "not out of sexual sickness, nor did his revenge on society require a sexual form." Similarly, Benjamin Karpman—author of *The Sexual Offender and His Offenses*, a standard work in its field— wrote to Governor Knight, "on the basis of reading his book between the lines and around the margins, I have come to the conclusion that the man did not commit the crime with which he is charged." Remarkably, based solely on reading an autobiographical work, these prominent critics explicitly proclaimed Chessman's innocence. Like such outright denials, the more common evasions of the question of whether Chessman was indeed guilty also underscored the power of the Red Light convictions. For liberal intellectuals, as well as criminological and psychiatric experts, Chessman's value as a model of institutional rehabilitation seemed to rest heavily on his apparent sexual normality.[36]

The Insider Response

According to his closest confidantes, Caryl Chessman died an innocent, rehabilitated man—the latter characteristic depending heavily on the former. In the early 1960s, Bill Sands, a cellmate of Chessman at San Quentin during one of the latter's earlier stints there in the early 1940s, went on speaking tours discussing his own rehabilitation from a life of crime, during which he also highlighted Chessman's reform. The "Caryl Chessman I knew so well," he said, "was a man physically, mentally and emotionally incapable of committing the sex crimes for which he was tried and executed." Rapists, he said, were "weak, frightened individuals," whereas "Chessman was the exact opposite in every way. He had a strong personality and a brilliant mind." Sands agreed with his wife, the journalist Eleanor Garner Black, who had witnessed Chessman's execution. "He was incapable of sex crimes. He was a good person—totally rehabilitated," Black said. According to such logic, to be capable of sex crimes was to be a bad person, and therefore incapable of rehabilitation. *San Francisco Chronicle* journalist Bernice Freeman Davis, in turn, recalled how by 1960 "so many thought" that Chessman had indeed been "rehabilitated" during his twelve years on death row. Although Davis herself was "not so sure," her comment revealed how Chessman had convinced substantial numbers of onlookers to see him as fundamentally changed.[37]

For the former warden Clinton T. Duffy, however, there was no question: Chessman had not lived up to the ideals of rehabilitation. In his death penalty memoir *88 Men and 2 Women* (1962), Duffy—whom Chessman once praised as a "kindly, far-seeing man"—said Chessman combined the "brains of a savant with the morals of a degenerate." Citing prison psychiatrists, the former warden saw Chessman as "incurably psychopathic criminal mind [who] most likely could have never adjusted to the society he hated so intensely." "Once released," he hypothesized, Chessman "would almost surely commit another crime that would land him back in prison." Duffy had no doubts concerning Chessman's guilt as the red light bandit, although he did not support executions for these (or any other) offenses. In general, the former warden characterized Chessman as a man angry at society and authority, and not someone driven by sexual impulses per se. Yet despite diagnosing Chessman more as a sociopath than a psychopath, Duffy would soon write a book which argued that unalterable sexual "deviation" was the root cause of virtually all crime, thus indicating that the former spokesman for rehabilitation had begun to sour on that system's premise.[38]

In his 1959 essay "The Moral Career of the Mental Patient," sociologist Erving Goffman reached a set of conclusions relevant to the conflict between Chessman and his keepers. In assessing the impact of "total institutions" on the lives of their subjects, Goffman saw the "inpatient" stage of his theory as potentially applicable to "jails, concentration camps, monasteries, work camps" and other isolated places operating with their own rules and according to their own regimentation. As the patient proceeds through stages of treatment, he typically follows a definable path: denial, adjustment, manipulation. A "rebirth" in the mental patient might eventually result, Goffman wrote, "taking the form of a strong belief in the psychiatric perspective, or, briefly at least, a devotion to the social cause of better treatment for mental patients." If indeed applied to prison, Chessman's career superficially seemed to follow a similar trajectory. After his initial defiant years, Chessman assumed the persona of a reborn prisoner, in this case voicing the slogans of rehabilitative penology. Yet, unlike academic or popular critics, insiders like Duffy saw Chessman as threatening rather than affirming the principles of postwar penology. In the minds of prison officials, Chessman espoused all the ideals of the institution but actually believed none of them, remaining instead an "incurably psychopathic" criminal throughout his twelve years on death row.[39]

The Art of Reform

To the insiders' dismay, the critical endorsement of Chessman's writings would greatly shape popular opinion, presenting Chessman as the very embodiment of the postwar rehabilitative ideal. Like the supportive critics, Chessman expressed himself via the written word, a shared characteristic that seemed to foster intellectual identification with his cause. As Elizabeth Hardwick wrote about Chessman's books, "The fact that he, from whom nothing could have been expected, was able to write them at all is a circumstance of compelling interest. It seems to suggest that only through 'art,' through some difficult and utterly personal expression is reclamation and prevention possible." To be certain, these grounds would allow only a handful of prisoners ever to achieve "personal reclamation." According to Andrew Ross, postwar liberal intellectuals repeatedly evinced profound antipathy toward the products and influence of mass culture. To be "ordinary," Ross maintains, as in the case of the Rosenbergs, was to be guilty. Given this tendency, it seems only natural that critics like Max Lerner, Hardwick, and many others would rally to Chessman's defense, for surely he was no average criminal.[40]

　　Postwar intellectuals would react similarly to the work of other prison authors, most notably Nathan Leopold and Paul Crump. By the mid-1950s Leopold had spent more than thirty years in prison, and in *Life Plus 99 Years* (1958) he vividly described this experience. As reviewer Robert Hatch wrote in *The Nation*, Leopold's major contention was that "today he is an entirely different person from the youth whom Darrow saved from the gallows." In the book Leopold gladly detailed his many accomplishments, like assembling a prison library, acquiring expertise on parole behavior, becoming a registered lab technician, and working as a prison accountant. "Leopold's mind and will are out of the ordinary," Hatch observed. Once an unremorseful killer, he had become the "most valuable inmate ever known to the history of Illinois," thereby proving that even the most cold-blooded criminal should not "die by the hand of the law." Similarly, in an editorial on "The Rehabilitation of Nathan Leopold," *The Christian Century* saw Leopold's work while on parole—as a medical technician in a Puerto Rican hospital—as evidence of his "atonement" and "redemption." No small part of Leopold's decision to go to Puerto Rico, the articles stressed, was the heterosexual romance he had begun with a pen pal while in prison. According to liberal intellectuals, Leopold's unique intelligence, manifest contributions, and apparently newfound sexual normality coalesced in making him a vivid example of the reformative potential of incarceration.[41]

In the early 1960s Paul Crump, an African American on death row in Illinois, also achieved fame as a writer whose character seemed fundamentally altered by prison. "Once animalistic and belligerent," Warden Jack Johnson told *Life*, Crump—convicted of murder in a payroll robbery—after seven years living under a death sentence had become "completely rehabilitated." According to both Crump and Johnson, the former's transformation began the day he stopped fighting the warden and began to accept the latter's program of reform. Under Johnson's regime prisoners were encouraged to write, and Crump eventually authored the autobiographical novel *Burn, Killer, Burn!* (1962). The book's jacket copy quoted James Baldwin as saying, "I have what can only be called an uncompromising respect" for Crump, whom he saw as "a real writer." In *The People vs. Paul Crump* (1962), an experimental documentary made for public television, director William Friedkin interspersed interviews with dramatic re-enactment of the crime and scenes from black community life in Chicago. Thoughtful and religious, Crump at the end of the documentary faces the electric chair, which the narrator warns "will end his efforts toward redemption."[42]

Endorsed by critics and, more important, by vocal prison officials, Crump's rehabilitation was sanctioned by Illinois Governor Otto Kerner in August 1962. "The embittered, distorted man who committed a vicious murder no longer exists," Kerner stated in commuting Crump's sentence to 199 years in prison. Because Crump's plea was based solely on the claim of rehabilitation, not innocence or any general argument against capital punishment, some death penalty opponents saw Kerner's action as potentially groundbreaking. During his time in prison, *The Christian Century* noted, Crump "gained an education, wrote a novel, reportedly saved a life, earned the respect of both prisoners and jail officials and achieved a wide reputation as a rehabilitated criminal." Such work ultimately showed how "capital punishment, which makes rehabilitation impossible, has no place in modern penology." Unlike Chessman, Paul Crump indeed succeeded in writing himself off death row.[43]

Chessman's specter inevitably influenced contemporary critical reaction to the popular story of another creative prison talent, Robert F. Stroud, better known as the Birdman of Alcatraz. Though promotional ads for John Frankenheimer's 1962 film promised a tale of the "most defiant man alive," the film actually presents Stroud as a shining example of reform. As memorably played by Burt Lancaster, Stroud, after forty-three years of solitary confinement, sheds all traces of his violent youthful behavior, which included two murder convictions, the second for stabbing a prison guard to death for not telling Stroud that his mother had tried to visit him. While at Leavenworth prison in Kansas, Stroud takes interest in a solitary sparrow, and before long he becomes a respected ornithologist. After an unexpected transfer to Alcatraz in late 1942, prison officials deny Stroud the right to continue keeping birds (making the story's title slightly misleading), so he begins to write. Hostile Alcatraz administrators, however, soon confiscate the two-hundred-thousand-word treatise Stroud has produced on the subject of whether prisons "truly rehabilitate." The film ends as Stroud tries valiantly, if unsuccessfully, to stop his fellow prisoners from rioting, thus proving to the warden that he has finally changed.

For the conservative Catholic journal *America*, the older, clearly different Stroud represented "a rare instance of a man who underwent a kind of rehabilitation in prison by finding a creative purpose in life." In the *Saturday Review*, meanwhile, Arthur Knight endorsed the film's statement "that when rehabilitation has taken place the new man ceases to be a criminal and should be returned to the world outside." The positive commentary about Stroud could have been lifted straight from earlier analyses of Chessman. Under the headline "Solitary Rebel," *Time* viewed Stroud's transformation a bit more cynically, however: "Like

Caryl Chessman . . . [the Birdman] had just enough brilliance and flair for publicity to amass widespread public sympathy for his cause." [44]

Yet even as *The Birdman of Alcatraz* garnered further notoriety for Stroud, the prisoner himself languished in a prison hospital at age seventy-three, the reasons for his continued confinement stemming precisely from official hostility toward the notion of his reform. "Off-screen," *Time* said, the real-life Stroud was a "stiff-necked, arrogant, impenitent man and at least initially a homicidal threat to society." Attorney General Robert Kennedy likewise felt that he "could not in good conscience recommend to the President that it would be in the public interest or to Mr. Stroud's benefit that his sentence be commuted at this time." In the pages of *The New Republic*, film critic Stanley Kauffmann sparred with one of Kennedy's predecessors, Francis Biddle, attorney general under Franklin Roosevelt, over whether the Birdman was indeed ready to go free. "Stroud still keeps his defiant attitude," Biddle intoned. More dramatically, Biddle declared that "Stroud remains an aggressive and dangerous homosexual, with homicidal tendencies." In rough outline, then, Stroud's reception matched Chessman's: while vocal critics and other popular opinion makers proclaimed Stroud's rehabilitation, those officials invested with the power to make final judgment saw him as a fundamentally unchanged criminal, one who matched the lingering diagnosis of a psychopath. [45]

In examining the Floyd Patterson–Sonny Liston boxing match (1962), Gerald Early's essay "The Unquiet Kingdom of Providence" explores the ways in which individual reform came to be an official postwar American ideal. Patterson, a "successful product" of reform schools, convinced President Kennedy, Adam Clayton Powell, Jr., and other officials to give Liston (an ex-con) a shot at the heavyweight title. Amid the surrounding rhetoric of "every man deserves a second chance," Liston—an unrepentant mafia thug—demolished Patterson. A year later, Early further observes, Kennedy pardoned the jazz pianist Hampton Hawes, seeing him as fully "rehabilitated" from his drug-related robbery convictions. In the late 1960s prison writers and activists would argue against such subjective, arbitrary practice of the postwar rehabilitative ideal; but Leopold, Crump, Patterson, and Hawes had garnered significant fame, making it seem as though personal reform would indeed be recognized (at least for those successful in popular fields). With the exception of Hawes, however, who was as surprised as anyone by his release, these men went to great lengths to prove both their individual behavioral normality as well as their undeniable institutional utility. From the official perspective, each of the "reformed" figures had manifestly learned the rules of the game. Despite their tireless efforts, neither Chessman nor Stroud managed to join this crowd. Instead, doubts about the genuine nature of Chessman's transformation would always linger, especially among the prison insiders most responsible for assessing whether a change in his character had indeed occurred.[46]

Chessman's Literary Legacy

Caryl Chessman attempted to become one of the experts, trying to beat the system on its own terms; if nothing else, his ultimate lack of success proved instructive to a future generation of prisoners. Many of the classic works of prison literature written in the 1960s offer important contrasts to Chessman's, particularly in their rejection of the rehabilitative ideal. Though not prison literature per se, *The Autobiography of Malcolm X* described what is perhaps the most famous prison transformation in American history. From 1948 to 1951 Malcolm attended the Norfolk (Massachusetts) Prison Colony, which he said specialized in "experimental rehabilitation" programs like discussion groups, debate teams, and courses taught by Harvard education professors. There he had seemingly unlimited access to the vast library the prison possessed (courtesy of a philanthropist) and acquired what he termed a "homemade education." Yet during the course of his studies Malcolm came to embrace the Muslim teachings of Elijah Muhammad, not the "new penology" espoused by the warden; Malcolm's efforts to proselytize, he said, caused him to be transferred to another prison. By contrast, in *Soul on Ice* (1968) Eldridge Cleaver took the exact opposite approach from Chessman—he confessed to rape, and problematically struggled to find the political implications of his acts. For "Soledad Brother" George Jackson, rehabilitative treatment was more accurately described as the "licking process," in which the inmates most compliant with prison officials were considered to be the most reformed.[47]

Indeed, few, if any, prisoners in the 1960s would sing the praises of the "new penology," or claim themselves to be rehabilitated. For African American prisoners, the reasons were many—those who saw sociopolitical injustice as the cause of their crimes, or who preached Black Muslim teachings, or held radical beliefs of any sort, were considered outside the rehabilitation process. Yet neither would many white prisoners or critics in the 1960s echo Chessman's claim that "death row was the best thing that ever could have happened to me," or that prison had in any way been a reformative experience. In his introduction to the prison letters of George Jackson, Jean Genet pointedly declared, "Prison serves no purpose." Paul Goodman, meanwhile, articulated the anarchist point of view in his introduction to a reprinted edition of Alexander Berkman's *The Prison Memoirs of an Anarchist.* "The concept of punishment," he said, "is worthless and the jails must simply be abolished. . . . [T]hey always hinder rehabilitation." Ultimately, it was the work of radical African American and gay prisoners and critics during the 1960s that provided the most vocal rejections of the liberal rhetoric Chessman had made pivotal to his plight.[48]

When "prisoners began to speak," Michel Foucault told Gilles Deleuze, "they possessed an individual theory of prisons, the penal system, and justice. It is this form of discourse which ultimately matters, a discourse against power, the counter-discourse of prisoners and those we call delinquents." Since he espoused the same rehabilitative views as criminologists and prison officials, Chessman's writings superficially possessed little of the "counter-discursive" impact to which Foucault referred. Yet, by making the prisoner himself the judge of his own reform, Chessman (with help from his critics) for a brief moment usurped the prerogative prison officials held to be sacrosanct. Indeed, the unceasing hostility of San Quentin administrators and other state officials clearly illustrated the threats, both discursive and disciplinary, that Chessman's notoriety as a writer had posed. Even more troubling for those same officials, perhaps, would be the prisoner's legacy inside San Quentin and elsewhere. Because the literary fame Chessman gained had helped call attention to his case, and the profits from his books helped sustain his legal campaign, a generation of prisoners would try to emulate Chessman's example.[49]

In *Education of a Felon,* a recent memoir, the prison novelist and screenwriter Edward Bunker recalls his personal interactions with Chessman. While at Los Angeles County Jail in 1948 awaiting sentencing for stabbing a guard at another prison, Bunker, then only fifteen, became acquainted with Chessman and Lloyd Sampsell (the Yacht Bandit), both of whom were en route to death row at San Quentin. Bunker initially did not believe Chessman to be guilty; after all, most prisoners' "moral code didn't allow fraternization with rapists." In retrospect, however, Bunker believes that Chessman indeed committed the red light crimes. Six years after their first meeting, Bunker ended up at San Quentin, where he was temporarily sent to the isolation unit located next to the prison's death row. There a fellow inmate secretly passed Bunker a gift from Chessman, an excerpt from *Cell 2455* that had just been featured in the latest *Argosy*. Rather than the writing itself, it was simply Chessman's achievement in becoming a published author that most excited Bunker. "With the force of revelation," Bunker remembers, "I said aloud, Why *not* me?" As both a well-known writer and the definitive "jailhouse lawyer," Chessman similarly inspired untold numbers of convicts to try to write their way out of prison.[50]

Thus, like few prisoners before or after him, Chessman had clearly "spoken," and he had done so in voluminous detail. "Chessman had shouted from his cell and the world was listening," fellow San Quentin prison writer Malcolm Braly recalled. What the world heard was the voice of a man on death row desperately trying to save his own life. "My chances for commutation," Chessman wrote to Longstreth, his agent, in late 1953, would "improve considerably with publication" of *Cell 2455*. And for a brief moment, Chessman was right. His pragmatic deployment of all available arguments—that he was innocent but still rehabilitated, and now an expert—found a uniquely responsive audience among criminologists and liberal intellectuals of the period. An energetic national debate over Chessman's cause would be the result, causing ordinary middle class citizens to make their voices heard too.[51]

CHAPTER FOUR

A Tale of Two Protests

(1950–1960)

Prior to Caryl Chessman's case, the most notable protests against executions during the twentieth century had been led by working class organizations and their affiliated political parties. The controversies over Tom Mooney, Sacco and Vanzetti, the Scottsboro Boys, Willie McGee, and the Rosenbergs, in other words, originated with the efforts of left unions and—in many of these cases—the Communist Party. In California, radical labor's twenty-year fight resulted in Mooney's pardon by Culbert Olson, the state's only New Deal governor, in 1939. A more recent left success had been scored in the case of Wesley Robert Wells, who, as a result of the campaign led by the Civil Rights Congress, was spared the gas chamber in late March of 1954. Despite the overlap between the Wells and Chessman cases, the protests against their executions stemmed from different sources. Whereas organized labor and African American organizations like the CRC steered the Wells defense, the Chessman opposition sprang from the work of criminologists, mental health experts, liberal intellectuals, religious anti–death penalty activists, and, in no small measure, sympathetic ordinary citizens.[1]

Chessman's case kick-started a renewed middle class campaign against the death penalty in the postwar era, and such protests would once again wed abolition to the larger principle of institutional reform. In identifying the beginnings of a revived national movement in 1956, *The Nation* seemed surprised that "even in California" the controversies over Chessman and executed murderess Barbara Graham had "aroused widespread sentiment in favor of abolishing capital punishment." Though never mustering anything like majority public opinion, the abolitionist position indeed received sanction from a number of top state officials. Viewing the death penalty as inconsistent with California's reputation as a leading "laboratory" of the new penology, state officials like former San Quentin warden Clinton T. Duffy and Department of Corrections director Richard McGee spoke in favor of abolition. In varying degrees, so too would Governors Warren, Knight, and Brown. All of these officials professed reluctance to carry out the death penalty while it remained state law, and each of the governors utilized their power to commute sentences with relative frequency. These same officials, however, were also unanimous in their dislike for Chessman, seeing him as a "troublemaker" and, more important, as a prisoner who was anything but "rehabilitated." [2]

The apparent sympathy for the abolitionist position expressed by Knight and especially Brown inspired thousands of self-styled ordinary citizens to write to the governors about Chessman's case. Rather than simply sign their name on a petition, these correspondents explained exactly why they thought Chessman should not be executed. Chessman's detractors likewise penned letters encouraging the governors to uphold both this particular sentence and the death penalty in general. Unmediated by newspaper editors or direct organizational ties, such direct communication illustrated how and why the case struck a nerve, both pro and con, among the postwar middle class. While the views expressed by Chessman's sympathizers often ratified those put forth by the professional experts, the letters at the same time contained revealing statements about who was writing and why. "I am an ordinary citizen, housewife and mother, writing on behalf of no organization or group," Mrs. Bernard Meer of Stockton told Governor Brown. To view oneself as an "ordinary citizen" indeed sanctioned one's right to speak out politically during the period. Beatrice Petrella of Brooklyn, New York, thus declared, "I know mine is one small voice in this great land. But this is a land where small voices count." As they articulated their opinions about the Chessman case to Governors Knight and Brown, correspondents like Meer and Petrella juxtaposed key frames of reference—group vs. individual, organization vs. ordinary citizen—that illustrated the shifting terrain of postwar debate over the death penalty. Indeed, the voices raised in opposition to Chessman's execution now came less from the left than from those who saw themselves as firmly part of the mainstream of American political life. [3]

Across the nation, but in postwar California particularly, the rise of managerial optimism regarding criminal justice was accompanied by an expansive, inclusive middle class ideology. In the wake of World War II, the state grew by leaps and bounds, as returning servicemen relocated and wartime migrants stayed to work in a now buoyant industrial sector. Whether symbolized by the affordable single-family suburban home or the state's virtually guaranteed access to higher education, California rhetorically promised a middle class lifestyle to both blue collar worker and white collar professional alike. Although home ownership and a college education became realities for millions of Americans, this proliferating stratum of voters—which the political scientist Samuel Lubbell (borrowing from C. Wright Mills) termed the "new middle class"— transformed the political landscape in a different way in California than elsewhere. Firm political loyalties, whether ethnic or party, never took root in California; instead of a strong New Deal coalition, midcentury California instead operated under what one historian has called the "Progressive legacy." Managerial, bipartisan, and nonideological politics held sway, allowing liberal Republicans like Earl Warren and Goodwin Knight to campaign with the support of organized labor. First established by reformist administrators, the rehabilitative ethos of the new penology comprised only one part of a larger technocratic approach to state governance. In considering the merits of issues like the death penalty, California's new middle class thus reckoned with a set of questions posed by state officials and professional experts, rather than by distinct political parties.[4]

To be part of California's expanding middle class hardly translated into fixed political sympathies, however; a vocal fraction of this stratum would reject ideas of therapeutic criminal justice, and their views can in no way be considered less middle class. As outlined in the preceding chapters, a range of behavioral specialists, particularly psychiatrists and criminologists, placed themselves at the forefront of the campaign to save Chessman. In endorsing such expert opinion, a significant component of California's new middle class illustrated an overall shift in its class perspective. In *Working with Class,* the historian Daniel Walkowitz rejects the standard notion of middle class as a universal, rather than relational, category in postwar American history. Instead, Walkowitz locates a fundamental shift during the McCarthy era, in which the notion of a white collar "professional worker" gave way to the "modern professional." Because it suggests an identity increasingly forged in opposition to nonprofessionals, or those without advanced training and college degrees, this transition helps clarify the shifting perspective of death penalty opponents during the late 1950s. While the Wells defense saw the left eventually mobilize professional workers around issues of class and race, the Chessman campaign told a different story. The modern professionals leading the abolitionist movement of the late 1950s believed that their unprecedented access to state policymaking would spell the end of capital punishment in California, and a sizable sector of the public vocally concurred.[5]

A comparison of the Wells and Chessman defense campaigns thus clarifies the broader shift in opposition to the death penalty in the mid-1950s. Like Chessman, Wells, an African American, faced execution for a crime other than murder, namely throwing an ashtray at a prison guard ("assault of a guard by a long-term prisoner" was a capital offense). From death row, Wells helped direct the campaign to save his life through frequent correspondence with Civil Rights Congress leaders, his attorneys, the press, and labor unions. In turn, union and civil rights activists launched an extensive publicity drive to save the life of a prisoner victimized by racism and "segregation within prison walls." Like Wells, Chessman would help steer the protests on his behalf, but he ratified the arguments made by the criminologists, psychiatrists, lawyers, and religious organizations steering the renewed anti–death penalty movement. As a result, the broader audience engaged by Chessman's case now considered abolitionist criticisms cast in the rhetoric of rehabilitation and professional expertise. In their letters to the governors about the Chessman case, members of California's new middle class actively reckoned with the implications of the rehabilitative ideal, at once clarifying their views of the specific issue and showing how it pertained to their larger self-identity as a class. By 1958, with the ascent of avowed capital punishment foe Pat Brown to the governor's chair, it seemed as though liberal abolitionism was on the verge of success. The public opinion mobilized against Chessman, however, ultimately marked the beginning of a larger popular backlash by the New Right against an essentially technocratic campaign to eliminate capital punishment in California.[6]

Against Prison Jim Crow

Nineteen-year-old Wesley Robert Wells arrived at San Quentin in 1928 from Los Angeles, charged with possession of stolen property and sentenced to one to five years. Wells accrued a number of disciplinary in-

fractions, causing him to be transferred to Folsom Prison; there he was
charged with manslaughter after killing another prisoner in a gang fight,
forcing him to remain at Folsom until 1941. Since his stretch preceded
the reform years of World War II, Wells left prison with no work skills
and a criminal record. After a few unemployed months spent living with
his sister in Los Angeles, Wells was arrested for trying to steal a car battery and sentenced to Folsom again. A 1944 confrontation with another
prisoner brought Wells back to San Quentin, this time for five years to
life. Reportedly subjected to persistent physical abuse and racial epithets
from guards and other prisoners, Wells again proved to be a combative
prisoner. In the aftermath of a 1947 disciplinary hearing, Wells threw an
ashtray at a prison guard who taunted him. The officer was not seriously
injured. In August 1947, Wells nevertheless was sent to death row for violation of Section 4500 of the California Penal Code, which specified
that a life-termer guilty of assault could be executed.[7]

At the suggestion of African American lawyer Cecil Poole of San
Francisco, who eventually served as Governor Brown's clemency secretary, white radical attorney Charles Garry took up Wells's case in late
1948. Garry, the future chief counsel of the Black Panthers, was affiliated at the time with both the left-leaning National Lawyers Guild and
the Communist-affiliated Civil Rights Congress (CRC). With strong support from the CRC, Garry developed an initially successful legal strategy
in defense of Wells. In essence, Garry disputed whether Wells's sentence actually qualified as life, which was key to the Section 4500 definition. As a result of his personal contact with Wells, Garry further filed a
1950 suit charging Governor Warren and the California Department of
Corrections with discrimination against black prisoners at Folsom and
San Quentin. With prisoners forced to "eat separately," among other
things, the suit argued that segregation inhibited "proper rehabilitation." Garry's twin legal strategies thus formed an important antecedent
to the arguments later made by radical activists in the late 1960s. The
indeterminate sentence, the Wells lawsuit suggested, was unduly manipulated by prison officials to punish a prisoner they did not like; racism,
moreover, made rehabilitation a system flawed in practice. Effective
only in gaining stays of execution, the legal campaign to save Wells thus
mounted a quite different challenge to the new penology than did Chessman in his writings: rather than present himself as a model of reform,
Wells saw segregation as thwarting "proper rehabilitation." In his 1978
memoir *Streetfighter in the Courtroom*, Garry thus called Wells the "first
Black Panther."[8]

Although the Supreme Court refused Wells's appeal in late 1952 (rendering the legal campaign ultimately unsuccessful), the CRC had already launched an extensive publicity effort on his behalf, making Wells another in a series of death penalty cases taken up by the organization. Throughout its ten-year existence (1946–55), the CRC fought against Red Scare witch hunts and for black prisoners, causing McCarthyite critics to deride the CRC as a "Communist front." According to Gerald Horne, the CRC was a grassroots organization with close ties to the Communist Party. The CRC clearly shared the Party's objectives regarding the race question in America, a fact best illustrated by the career of CRC leader William Patterson, the black Communist attorney who had earlier directed the International Labor Defense during the Scottsboro case. Whether protesting the death penalty for rape in cases like those of McGee and the Martinsville Seven, or contesting the disproportionate severity of Wells's sentence, the CRC tried to stir an international outcry, hoping to simultaneously bring justice to the particular prisoner and call attention to the wider issue of racist inequality in the United States. With strong support from California organized labor, the CRC orchestrated a publicity campaign that by March of 1954 had produced fifty thousand signatures on petitions for Wells. If less notable than some other CRC struggles, the Wells case proved to be one of the group's most visible successes when his sentence was commuted by Governor Knight. Most important to this discussion, though, is the manner in which the CRC, left labor, and the prisoner himself waged the Wells defense.[9]

After the CRC campaign had begun, Wells recalled the details of the CRC's entry into his case in a letter he wrote to the organization's executive secretary, Ida Rothstein. "Friendless" and "penniless" upon his arrival to death row in 1947, Wells hoped only to reach his fortieth birthday (in 1949), a milestone no one in his family had yet accomplished. "Then, on January 2, 1950, when I had less than thirty days to live, I received a letter from the Civil Rights Congress, pledging its assistance in the fight to save my life." In its first press releases on the case, the CRC submitted a number of reasons why Wells should not be executed, most of which centered on his being "a Negro." Other key points made by the CRC included the noncapital nature of Wells's offense, the technical dispute over whether his was a life sentence, and the question of his "mental health." "Wells is not a hardened, vicious criminal as Governor Warren implies," declared CRC West Coast Director Aubrey Grossman in late January 1950; instead, "he is a mentally sick man . . . [and] everyone knows that if Wells were a white man, with some friends in high places, things would be quite different." Initially prominent in the CRC critique, the emphasis on Wells's mental state would fade over the next few years, while the critique of racial discrimination moved squarely to the foreground.[10]

After obtaining a stay of execution for Wells, the CRC proclaimed its success in slowing the pace of "legal lynchings," such as "those of the Martinsville Seven in Virginia, Willie McGee in Mississippi, and Wesley Wells here in California." In granting the stay, moreover, federal judge Louis Goodman supported Garry's contentions regarding the arbitrary use of the indeterminate sentence against Wells. "By deliberate and designed inactivity," Goodman observed, "the Adult Authority [parole board] of California kept the prisoner in an indefinite and indeterminate status for the purpose of making it possible to impose the death penalty on him in the event he committed an offense under Section 4500." Designed to "destroy" someone regarded as an "undesirable citizen," such "overzealousness" violated Wells's right to due process under the Fourteenth Amendment, stated Goodman. The CRC considered this treatment as representative of a larger pattern of "prison Jim Crow" endured by Wells during his more than twenty years of confinement. In September 1950, though, the California State Supreme Court overturned the stay, causing Garry to appeal to the U.S. Supreme Court. In the meantime, the CRC stepped up its publicity campaign. "Like the Scottsboro Boys and Willie McGee," a CRC Fact Sheet maintained, "Wesley Wells is a victim of a government policy that enforces second class citizenship on the Negro people. . . . We must not allow a California version of Mississippi injustice." [11]

A CRC delegation brought Wells's case before California Governor Earl Warren in October 1950. San Francisco CRC Director Ida Rothstein chaired a group of forty-five supporters representing a cross-section of organizations, from both Southern and Northern California; included among the ten with whom Warren met were members of the San Francisco Interdenominational Ministerial Alliance, the International Longshoremen's and Warehousemen's Union (ILWU), and the CRC's Rothstein, Marguerite Robinson, and Decca Truehaft. According to a CRC report, Rothstein led off by telling Warren the two reasons for the meeting: to save Wells's life while obtaining his release from prison, and to demand the end of segregation at Folsom and San Quentin. In the CRC's account, Warren wanted to focus only on the former, and he repeatedly stressed his view of Wells as "a dangerous, bad man" and "a menace [who] cannot be out." Deriding the CRC as a "Communist Organization," Warren said it did not "care about Wells or Negroes" but instead used cases like this one "in order to sabotage our institutions and government." Warren's red-baiting continued after the meeting, as he told a news conference that "this Civil Rights Congress is Communist inspired and made its parade to Sacramento solely for a political purpose, to involve me in the racial discrimination question." As for prison Jim Crow, though, Warren mostly sidestepped the issue, saying only that segregation was not official policy and that attempts to end de facto racial separation had resulted in "bloodshed." Though he had become increasingly liberal on civil rights during his second term as governor, Warren was up for reelection in November 1950, and he now made rejection of clemency for Wells part of a larger anti-Communist campaign.[12]

A Grassroots Campaign

"Quentin Guards Break Up Killers' Sit-Down Strike," blared a *San Francisco Chronicle* lead headline on November 1, 1950. Calling the strike an "incipient riot," the paper described how thirteen of the sixteen death row inmates had refused to return to their cell block after the exercise period. The protest lasted less than an hour, and the strikers' demands were nothing more than new fountain pens, window screens (to keep birds out of their cells), lights on all night, longer exercise periods, and better food. Nonetheless, the *Chronicle* said the "main instigator of the revolt was Wesley Robert Wells, 41-year-old Los Angeles convict sentenced to death for assaulting an official at Folsom Prison." Citing Warden Clinton T. Duffy, the report suggested that Wells "intimidated the other men and has them under his control." There were the three other "ringleaders," though, one of whom was Chessman. Wells, Chessman, and the two others were sent to solitary confinement for twenty-nine days. In the wake of the incident, CRC fliers focused on the treatment of Wells, describing how he had been beaten while in solitary and had been deprived of an attorney at the disciplinary hearing. For a brief moment, then, the two cases overlapped, and Wells urged Garry to attend Chessman's December hearing for a writ of habeas corpus stemming from the response of prison officials to the "riot."[13]

Whether as legal adviser or public relations strategist, Wells was indeed an active participant in all phases of the campaign against his execution. Initially, he sought to define himself as a product of a racist prison system. In a letter to the CRC's Ida Rothstein on the eve of the group's meeting with Warren, Wells took issue with the governor's views of him. "I really do not believe that I am the incorrigible, the anti-social, the mad killer that Governor Warren" portrayed him to be; Wells later used the term "mad dog" in characterizing the official line. Still, "I make no pretension to having been a model prisoner during the many years I've spent in prison." What made him "mean," "hard," or "even savage," though, was the "brutal treatment I've received at the hands of both inmates and my prison keepers." Labeling California prisons as a "system that considered the Negro [worth] less than dirt," Wells further documented several examples of racist mistreatment by prison officials. The CRC then explained Wells's story in a pamphlet entitled "My Name Is Wesley Robert Wells," released in February 1951. In his foreword, Buddy Green of the Communist *Daily People's World* called Wells a "strong, militant, unbreakable spirit . . . [whom] prison authorities are now trying to put to death because they could not subdue his great courage and determination to fight against prison jimcrow [sic]." Wells's account proceeded to address in detail all of the past charges against him and concluded by deeming the November "riot" a "designed act by the Warden calculated to embarrass and discredit my friends," by which he meant primarily the CRC.[14]

Wells continued to elucidate the issues raised by his case throughout his correspondence with attorneys, CRC officials, and other supporters, causing the CRC to publish a sampling of his letters in 1953. Titled *Letters from the Death House,* the booklet tracked Wells's intellectual progression from commentator on his own case to analyst of McCarthyite repression of labor, civil rights activists, and others deemed to be Communist sympathizers. In his preface, screenwriter John Howard Lawson, who had experienced the witch hunts firsthand, called Wells "a hero of our time, not because there is anything spectacular or unusual or 'fictional' in his courage, but because it so common, so rooted in the life and trials of his people, the vast and simple courage of those who hold the future in their hands." Wells indeed seemed to acquire a heroic status among many of his supporters. As CRC leader Patterson told Ida Rothstein on the eve of a 1953 trip to California, "I should like nothing more than to have the opportunity of clasping Wells' hand. Please try to make this possible." After meeting Wells, Patterson described the experience in a letter distributed to editors around the country. "I shall never forget" the two hours spent with Wells, said Patterson, as "he symbolizes for me the depthless spiritual strength of the Negro people." Although California public officials were cynical about CRC's motives, Wells clearly inspired enduring passion for his cause.[15]

In order to turn the spark from the Wells campaign into lasting benefit for the CRC, Patterson wanted the organization to take a cue from the "Negro church." The church, Patterson explained in a letter to Rothstein, "involve[s] all of its members. It establishes all kinds of committees." Such active participation could be the CRC's most effective recruiting tool, Patterson thought. Newcomers, he wrote, "will find in this involvement the first opportunity to express themselves as human beings." In a pair of September 1953 letters to Patterson, Rothstein described the many different spheres of organizing on Wells's behalf. Local 6 of the ILWU planned to circulate twenty thousand copies of a leaflet about the case; the Fillmore (San Francisco) branch of the CRC had gathered more than six hundred signatures from local black churches; CRC "brigades" continued distributing new handouts; the local CRC youth program was preparing a skit based on Wells's writings; letter-writing campaigns were underway; and organizational meetings brought together union committees with the various CRC chapters. CRC literature of the period compared the Wells "injustice" to those of Sacco and Vanzetti, Willie McGee, the Martinsville Seven, and the Rosenbergs. As requested by Rothstein, Patterson made arrangements to get the CRC's Rosenberg Committee mailing list in order to recruit likely supporters. In short, Wells's case provided a catalyst for precisely the type of participatory campaign Patterson envisioned.[16]

A grassroots effort was solidly underway throughout late 1953 and 1954, and the roster of participating labor organizations proved quite extensive. As opposed to the anti-Communist leadership of the state's AFL and CIO, left-wing unions like the ILWU, the San Francisco Building and Construction Trades Council, and local branches of the United Auto Workers (including the large GM plant in Los Angeles) gave their support. In promoting a September 1953 CRC conference, the Trade Union Committee for Wesley Robert Wells circulated a letter the prisoner had written to the Oil Workers International Union in Southern California. "Like the late Tom Mooney, whom I had the honor of knowing quite well during my early years in prison," Wells wrote, "I am to be executed, liquidated, for the 'crime' of believing in and fighting" for what he believed in, in this case "racial equality." In early 1954 the Wells Defense Committee distributed an editorial from *Organized Labor,* the newspaper of the Building Trades Council. The piece focused on

Wells's prison experience, offering no special explanation of why labor should be involved; that "those in positions of responsibility within the labor movement" needed to "speak out" seemed a given. At a March 1954 conference, representatives of the Los Angeles Federation of Teachers, the Fur Workers, and other Left unions joined the growing chorus in support of Wells. Whether spreading literature and petitions inside the workplace or reaching out to the public on the outside, the various labor committees and groups established to fight for Wells formed an integral part of the campaign.[17]

The African American press likewise proved to be a constant source of pro-Wells opinion. After responding to Wells's 1949 letter to her paper by helping to recruit his legal team, Charlotta Bass insured that the leftist *California Eagle* gave full coverage throughout the case. More conservative black papers like the *Los Angeles Herald* and the *Los Angeles Tribune*, meanwhile, climbed on board beginning in late 1953, the latter admitting "We Were Wrong" about its initial reluctance to support Wells. Across the country black editors and columnists publicized the case, and a variety of defense committees often reprinted their columns. *Pittsburgh Courier* columnist J. A. Rogers, for example, kept readers posted about the controversy, at one point recording a donation made by Wells and eleven other death row inmates on behalf of the NAACP. Charlotta Bass's efforts extended beyond publishing sympathetic news stories and editorials in her newspaper. In early 1954 the Wesley Wells Defense Committee of Southern California, chaired by Bass, assembled a weekly newsletter called the *Wesley Wells Defender*. Usually four or five pages, the contents included updates, announcements for upcoming events, and stories such as one about the March 1954 formation of a Youth Division of the Defense Committee. An attentive, often active participant, the African American press comprised a cornerstone of the Wells protests.[18]

A wide range of religious organizations also lent support by early 1954. Initial participants like San Francisco's Baptist-led Interdenominational Alliance were now joined by an expanding number of Protestant and Jewish groups. As recorded in a February 1954 booklet published by the northern California–based Religious Committee for the Defense of Wesley Robert Wells, the Wells campaign enlisted the help of Baptist, Methodist, and Presbyterian ministers, as well as several Jewish leaders, from both ends of the state. After a March meeting, an organization of Southern California Presbyterian churches sent Governor Knight a resolution stating "as no capital crime is involved, the sentence of death is not morally justified." Such qualified opposition to the death penalty contrasted with the views of the Quaker American Friends Service Committee, which also voiced support for Wells. A March 1954 edition of the *California Eagle* included two AFSC letters to Governor Knight, who had assumed office upon Warren's elevation to the U.S. Supreme Court in 1953, and who opposed the death penalty. One called Wells's sentence "cruel and unusual," the other noting that "we find it difficult to believe . . . in California where the penal system has made so many advances, that a man can be executed for throwing a cuspidor at a prison guard." While playing a much smaller role than groups like the Interdenominational Alliance in publicizing Wells's case, the AFSC would soon be at the forefront of the Chessman campaign.[19]

As a result of the work by the CRC, Left unions, the black press, and various religious groups, a groundswell of opinion emerged in favor of Wells, and by March 1954 the campaign would claim the support of significant numbers of middle class professionals. Over three hundred physicians, including the president of the California Medical Association, signed a letter sent to Knight in February 1954. In their statement the physicians particularly referred to the views of prison psychiatrists who had expressed sympathy for Wells. As excerpted in a number of CRC pamphlets, Folsom psychiatrist Burt Howard said the Wells he interviewed after the cuspidor incident was "not a 'wild animal' . . . but a real man, more sinned against than sinning." Seeing Wells as a person able to "courageously resist 'Jim Crow'" outside and especially inside prison, Howard stressed to Governor Knight that "racial hatred and legalistic red tape have robbed him of the consideration due a human being." Similarly, Marcel Frym, a USC criminologist and member of Attorney General Brown's Advisory Committee for Crime Prevention, foregrounded the racial discrimination Wells had endured in prison. Wells's "own individual psychopathology," Frym informed Knight, was due to "the not completely unjustified thought of being persecuted because of his race." Such participation by professionals in the case became substantial enough for the *Los Angeles Daily News* to argue, "Certainly such a wide diversity of groups and persons—criminologists, lawyers, church leaders and laymen—would not have been brought together" if "sufficient grounds" did not exist for Wells's clemency. As evidenced by the views of the Democratic *Daily News*, the participation of professional workers granted legitimacy to the campaign, allowing the mainstream press to minimize the efforts of left labor and the CRC.[20]

As the April 1954 execution date approached, the increased pace of protests began to make an impact. Syndicated columnist Walter Win-chell, who had first endorsed clemency for Wells in 1950, encouraged readers to write letters to Knight; the governor, in turn, assured Winchell that he was taking all opinions into account. A delegation of state assem-blymen, led by black representatives Augustus Hawkins and Byron Rum-ford, brought Wells's case before the governor. Meanwhile, the *San Fran-cisco Chronicle,* which earlier had portrayed Wells as the "ringleader" of an "incipient riot," became an important convert. In a March 21 edi-torial, the paper nodded agreement with Judge Goodman's aforemen-tioned interpretation of the misuse of the indeterminate sentence against Wells. Duly calling Wells a "bad man, unentitled to consideration on any sentimental score," and taking a slap at "the Communists, ever ea-ger for a 'martyr' to exploit for their own evil purposes," the *Chronicle* nonetheless opposed the execution on the grounds of "simple justice." Democratic candidate for governor Richard Graves went on record in support of clemency in mid-March, leaving Knight to weigh the politi-cal benefit of executing Wells. Also in March the CRC delivered a petition with forty-five thousand signatures, the executive board of the heavily Communist Electrical Workers (UE) declared its support, and Knight ac-knowledged receiving "thousands and thousands of communications" in a single weekend. On March 31, after the state Supreme Court con-curred with his recommendation, Knight handed down official word: Wells was a "bad criminal," but the judicial questions of "evidence and fact" provided sufficient grounds for commutation of Wells's sentence from death to life in prison without possibility of parole.[21]

Sparked by the CRC, the popular campaign in defense of Wells scored a visible success. In a letter of March 10, 1954, Patterson had predicted to new San Francisco CRC leader Frances Schermerhorn, "We will win . . . not [because of] the entering of Winchell or any other indi-vidual but [due to] the continuation of our activities along the lines which have been so correctly and aggressively pursued." That same month the *California Eagle* described a key component of the protests: "Ministers, doctors, painters, newsmen, longshoremen—thousands of people are writing to Governor Knight for Wesley Wells' life." A diverse set of grass-roots participants had indeed organized against an execution that they believed was disproportionate to the crime and symbolic of the larger racist practice of the prison system. As Dorothy Healey recalled three years later, Communists certainly participated—the CP's Wesley Wells Campaign Committee "initiated the broadest civil-rights movement in our history," she told delegates at a statewide convention. It would be inaccurate, however, to call all those who protested Communists, or even Party sympathizers. In a 1960 memoir Charlotta Bass observed, "Perhaps the greatest concentration of people from all walks of life in the state of California—labor, the Negro people, civil libertarians, churches, women's clubs, youth organizations—joined in a great defense committee." To save Wells from the gas chamber, the CRC, coupled with left labor, submitted a set of arguments that mobilized Communists, mainstream Democrats, and eventually liberal Republicans alike.[22]

In response to Knight's action, Wells celebrated what he called a "temporary victory." Saying he was ready to "take my rightful place in society," Wells told the *San Francisco Chronicle,* "I hope and am assured that my friends will continue to work for my freedom." Wells further wrote an angry letter to Director of Corrections Richard McGee, taking exception to McGee's hostile comments to the press after the clemency decision. Wells challenged McGee and prison officials to give him the chance "to make good, and eventually earn my release," rather than considering him a "problem." Following this cue, the postclemency issue of the *Wesley Wells Defender* carried a sketch of a white woman and a black man holding a banner reading "You Saved His Life, Now Win His Freedom!" While congratulations were in order for the "fine work of bringing together people from all walks of life of every political creed and religious belief," the article averred, "the job is not finished. . . . Wells must be free." On April 9, the day Wells would have been executed, the *Los Angeles Tribune* published an editorial calling for a continued effort to win at least the possibility of parole. Across the country, meanwhile, Mrs. L. King, chair of the West Harlem Wells Defense Committee, wrote an encouraging letter to Wells. "While rejoicing with you and all those who made a victory possible, we fully realize the job is only partly done," she assured him. In a flier about the case, the West Harlem Committee thanked "the *Amsterdam News,* the churches, ministers, labor organizations, as well as doctors, lawyers, and ordinary citizens who contributed to saving Wells' life." The grassroots effort needed to continue, though, and the Committee concluded, "Our slogan must be NO LET-UP UNTIL WELLS IS COMPLETELY FREE!"[23]

CRC leader William Patterson similarly saw "the follow up in the Wells case [as] a matter of extreme political and organizational importance." The fight for "complete freedom," he wrote to Frances Schermerhorn on April 3, required maintenance of a "united front," the marshalling of which was "magnificent" in the Wells campaign. Patterson indeed hoped the activism generated by the case could be transferred to

the broader political struggle against McCarthyism, a point driven home
at a birthday dinner for the CRC held on what would have been execution day. As reported in the *Daily Worker,* those gathered at the New
York event first heard a recorded message from Wells, then listened to a
number of speakers, including Patterson, denounce McCarthyism. Soon
thereafter, the CRC's Muriel Symington penned letters to I. F. Stone's
Weekly and Carey McWilliams's *Nation,* asking each to use his magazine to speak out for Wells's release and against the "racist mistreatment" of all black prisoners. Out west, the black press would continue
to lead a media campaign throughout April, but Patterson's goal of linking the case to larger issues, whether McCarthy or the "struggle of the
Negro people," would not be tangibly realized. Patterson himself would
soon fall victim to the witch hunts, and the CRC no longer existed by
the end of 1955.[24]

In mid-May 1954, a *Nation* editorial assessed the outcome of the case.
"Left-wing elements first called the Governor's attention to the case,"
editor Carey McWilliams wrote, but the bandwagon joined by various
mainstream officials, members of the press, and others ultimately prevented "a cruel and senseless execution." In his view, the "real 'extrem-
ists' in situations of this kind" were those who refused to join for fear of
abetting the Communists. Curiously, McWilliams offered no opinion regarding the sentence of life without parole given to Wells. In early May,
though, a CRC promotional letter announced Wells's upcoming birthday, proposing "parties, meetings, etc. [which] will give the opportunity
to present the case to new friends." It is not known whether such events
actually took place, but Wells would soon drop out of public view. Awaiting prison reassignment during early May 1954, Wells now watched as
one of his former death row neighbors now took center stage.[25]

A Professional Campaign

The May 1954 publication of *Cell 2455 Death Row* had instantly garnered both attention and support for Chessman. Endorsed first by criminologists and other professional experts, the Chessman protests would
remain largely based among middle class liberals. As Dorothy Healey
later recalled, "The Party had no involvement in the case; it would not
have occurred to us to have gotten involved in a case of this sort where
there was no direct question of racial or class oppression." Indeed, although the time frame of the Chessman case overlapped with that of
Wells, neither the CRC nor the CP was active in the Chessman case.

There would be varying degrees of continuity among other participants from the Wells campaign, however. The AFSC would move to the forefront, while organized labor and the black press would contribute sympathetic statements but not be nearly as active at the grassroots. Instead, the left-liberal press—led primarily by *The Nation*—helped the AFSC sustain interest in Chessman's case through 1960. Bay Area college students would bring the Chessman protests to the gates of San Quentin in May 1960, but the groundwork for the defense had already been established a half-decade earlier. In the post–Red Scare years of 1954 through 1960, a modern professional movement against the death penalty grew up around Chessman.[26]

Like Wells, Chessman helped set the terms of debate by appealing to the constituencies with whom he most closely identified. While Wells linked up with the CRC and left labor, Chessman sought to join the ranks of the criminological experts as well as professional writers and intellectuals. These two different pitches produced contrasting results, influencing both the respective outcomes and—more important to this discussion—the popular debate generated by each case. Specifically, rehabilitation, rather than racial or class discrimination, became the central theme of the Chessman protests. In the Wells campaign, the question of individual reform never gained prominence. To be sure, there were smatterings of such arguments: Patterson told supporters about Wells's character transformation ("self-educated he has grown into a man with a world outlook"); a chess "master" with whom Wells corresponded found it "possible to direct this man's unquestioned vitality into worthwhile channels benefitting himself, his race and society"; and, in urging the possibility of parole, a *Los Angeles Tribune* editorial called him a "shining and much needed example" of "the theory that incarceration can rehabilitate." Even when it moved to the forefront, however, the issue of Wells's rehabilitation could not be isolated from the question of racial discrimination. Though his ability to present himself as rehabilitated was never complicated by race issues, Chessman's conviction for sex crimes rendered problematic—at least for his opponents—his claim to reform.[27]

The different arguments at the center of the Chessman defense reflected both the interests of the prisoner himself and the groups who took up his cause. Active late in the Wells campaign, church organizations like the Methodists and Quakers spearheaded the pro-Chessman drive beginning in May 1954. A petition from the Orange Grove Friends, for example, cited the opinions of Dr. William Graves, a San

Quentin physician who resigned in protest of Chessman's sentence, stating quite inaccurately that it would be the first time "our society has
taken a life where none had been taken." As the case steadily assumed
national and international attention, lawyers, professional specialists,
and the AFSC continued to steer Chessman's defense. A 1959 Pacifica
Radio documentary featured attorney Rosalie Asher, Dr. Graves, and a
sympathetic psychiatrist (Isidore Ziferstein) speaking on Chessman's behalf. At a 1959 clemency hearing with Governor Brown, Asher and
Ziferstein were joined by the ACLU's A. L. Wirin and Chessman's lead
attorney George T. Davis. In March 1960, a public forum held in LA
about the case was sponsored by the ACLU, the Humanist Council of
Southern California, the Council of Liberal Churches, and the Friends
Committee on Legislation. By the late 1950s, both left labor and civil
rights groups had been severely weakened by the Red Scare, yet Chessman never had shown much interest in either cause. Crucial here, though,
is the distinction in leadership between the two campaigns: with middle
class professionals setting the terms of debate, the wider public now confronted a set of pro-Chessman arguments cast in the language of managerial expertise.[28]

A pro-Wells petition sent to Governor Knight in March 1954 anticipated the type of self-identification, as well as the key considerations,
common to participants throughout the early Chessman campaign. "We
young citizens wish to join the ranks of the many notable lawyers, clergy-
men, union leaders, doctors, etc., that seek to be humane in what we feel
is a miscarriage of justice," said more than fifty Los Angeles Young
Democrats, college student body representatives, and church and union
youth group leaders. Singling out the endorsements of Winchell, a
prominent judge, and a few leading professionals, the petition continued, "Is the death penalty in this case, where no life has been taken, society's answer to juvenile delinquency?" These "young citizens," in
effect, endorsed the therapeutic approach to criminal behavior first prof-
fered by prison officials, criminologists, and mental health experts. In responding to the Chessman case, both public officials and private citizens
would indeed amplify their views not simply of one death row prisoner
but of a larger approach to criminal justice. The resonance of the issues
raised in the debate, moreover, was inextricably linked to the reasons
why so many thousands of individuals wrote to the governors about
Chessman. In a period of Cold War conflict and rapid economic expansion, the type of punishment they supported formed a constituent part
of how these citizens identified themselves as a class. "Humane" and

compassionate, Chessman's supporters expressed their views directly to Governors Knight and Brown.[29]

Although not every letter written to the governors about Chessman offered clues to the background of the writer, the vast majority arrived from persons who considered themselves to be part of the growing American middle class—as indicated either by their business letterhead, or, more importantly, by their own statements about their backgrounds. Letters came from insurance salesmen, housewives, school teachers, and aeronautical engineers. There was not a marked imbalance in the number of men and women who wrote, nor could the opinion of Chessman be predicted by the sex of the correspondent. The letters were predominantly from California (and these letters are the focus of this inquiry), but personal statements also arrived both from across the country and various parts of the world. Commonly, letters from within the state began with phrases such as "This is first time I have ever written to the governor," or, as in a letter from Ines Jordan of Salinas, "I know I'm just a very small individual in a great state." To be an individual, many letters implied, meant that the writer saw herself as independent of any organization. Introducing themselves as taxpayers, citizens, and voters, many believed personal correspondence was the primary, if not only, political channel available to them. As Betty and Luis Lopez of West Covina began, "Since this [letter-writing] seems to be the only action open to ordinary citizens like ourselves we sincerely urge you to reconsider this case." Knight supporters, however, would often address the governor as both ordinary citizens and fellow Republicans, thus suggesting the presence of alternative means of influencing state politics. If not a collective source of identification like those provided by unions or specific political organizations, to be an ordinary citizen at least implicitly conferred the right to communicate directly to the governor.[30]

In presenting their views about Chessman, several correspondents explained who they were and how they became interested in the case. James Weakley of Culver City would tell Brown: "I am a male citizen, forty-six years old. I am employed in the personnel department of a defense plant. I am married and have three small children. . . . I am a white American and a democrat by birth." Similarly, Paul Brown of Encinitas responded to his own question, "Who am I?" with "Mr. Average Citizen I hope. Father of two teenage children 18 and 15, Missile Systems Engineer at Convair Astronautics, Registered Democrat." White-collar Mr. Average working in a defense plant would make his voice heard, but so would blue-collar mothers and housewives, often adopting similar rhetoric. Mary Jane Walker of San Francisco, for instance, told Knight she was "not a professional person, however I go about the business of being a mother to a fatherless son and daughter in an apt fashion." Mrs. D. M. Chant, meanwhile, wrote, "My husband is a mechanic in Santa Rosa and I am only a housewife with my family to raise, but we read a lot, also talk with friends that have been successful in business, and they feel as we do that Chessman is getting a raw deal." Not necessarily middle class by occupation, these writers nevertheless stressed their "business"-minded point of view. Indeed, Chessman's case inspired a cross-section of Californians to articulate their views to the governor using the new terminology of ordinary citizenship. In so doing, they fashioned themselves as informed individuals performing what they saw as a political right and a civic duty.[31]

The publication of *Cell 2455* spurred an immediate flow of correspondence to Knight, a sampling of which compared the cases of Chessman and Wells. In the process of writing, these onlookers—for the most part not aligned with any identifiable political organizations—often directly engaged the race question. Writers like Ruth McMaster of Los Angeles pleaded Chessman's case impartially, reminding Knight of his statement that Wells "should not be executed because he had not killed anyone." Others sought to insure the equal application of justice: "Please reconsider, Governor Knight, and grant the same degree of mercy to Chessman, white, as you have to Wells, Negro," wrote Minnie Etzweiler of Los Angeles. A few, like San Francisco's Joseph Harvey, saw Chessman's color as a problem, however. According to Harvey, "Wells had the advantage of being colored, thus exciting all the left wing elements of the population. Chessman, being white, is not drawing as much attention—but I believe that the attention he is drawing is much more sincere." At the furthest extreme stood commentators like Edward Burnett, a white resident of San Francisco's increasingly black Western Addition. Criticizing the "well dressed women possibly from foreign groups" and "the local colored neighbors" who "canvassed the neighborhood" on behalf of Wells, Burnett aligned himself with the "doctor" (Graves) working for Chessman. "Wells seems to be a tough and vindictive man probably trained in foreign subversion," Burnett maintained, whereas "Chessman seems to be a bewildered man who in the past has had every avenue to a better life denied him." These charges cannot be treated as voices from the fringe, especially since they were launched by some professionals involved in the case. L.A. Attorney Rosalind Bates, who had defended Chessman's accomplice David Knowles, introduced her letter to Knight "re: CARYL CHESSMAN, a white man who has no minority group to speak for him." Whether simply acknowledging racial distinctions, distinguishing left-wing protest from that of "ordinary citizens," or sketching a dubious portrait of reverse racism, such correspondence to Knight vividly captured the shifting terrain of protest over the two cases.[32]

Neither Wells nor Chessman had killed anyone, causing their cases to generate similar debate over the appropriateness of the death penalty for crimes other than murder. Mrs. R. C. Dunn of San Francisco began a pro-Chessman letter to Knight, "I am 100% for the death penalty for murderers." "He has taken no life and it would be a shame to take his life," observed Anna B. Mason of Los Angeles. A pair of organizational statements, though, illustrated the new set of terms distinguishing the two campaigns. In July 1954, the Los Angeles–based Unitarian Fellowship for Social Justice sent a pro-Chessman petition signed by over a hundred members. "On humanitarian grounds, and in consideration of the dangerous precedent it establishes for extending application of death penalty in California," the Unitarians opposed Chessman's execution. The Pasadena Council of Churches, meanwhile, argued that it was "inconsistent with the interests of an enlightened society to extend the death sentence where it has not heretofore been imposed." Where the Wells campaign connected his death sentence to a larger pattern of prison racism, Chessman's supporters frequently spoke out in the name of higher idealism. In so doing, their letters to the governor further illustrated how the vocabulary of enlightenment and humanitarianism suffused postwar abolitionist debate.[33]

In the wake of *Cell 2455*'s release, a common pro-Chessman argument focused on the contribution he could make to the study of criminal behavior. With the help of criminal experts and critics, Chessman offered himself as a "social guinea pig" for the study of crime. Jane Butler of Glendale agreed: "Since we are still practically in the dark ages regarding the criminal psychopath [I] think that this man should be used for scientific purposes. . . . In that way we can prevent the growing number of sex crimes and attacks on women." "This brilliant young man," Robert Stevens of Van Nuys observed, "has a tremendous amount to offer society in the matter of curbing and curing delinquency and crime at the very beginning." The reason Chessman seemed so valuable lay in his very ability to write books. As Los Angeles's Helen Fleming averred, Chessman "has already made an outstanding contribution to the study of the criminal mind. He could make a further gift to science." From Redding, Adaline Nixon optimistically predicted that "the book he has written will be a reminder for some of the hoodlums and delinquents who read it." These ideals of contribution and social benefit indeed seemed to hinge on Chessman's individual "genius," a somewhat shaky foundation on which to build an anti–death penalty movement.[34]

Yet Chessman's autobiographical account also convinced a number of onlookers to oppose his execution because the author seemed mentally ill. Throughout *Cell 2455*, Chessman—borrowing from official diagnoses—made frequent use of the label psychopath in describing his former self. Acknowledging the popular connotations of the term, Frances Strain of Pasadena hoped Chessman would be confined in "a psychopathic hospital, [where] he would contribute much needed understanding and prevention of sexual perversion." Several writers ignored Chessman's claim of being a reformed psychopath, and instead saw his mental condition as rendering him unaccountable for his actions. Virginia M. Feagans of Yuba City protested Chessman's death sentence because it was her "understanding that psychopaths are not responsible for their actions." From Los Angeles, John Dailey wrote, "I am not an opponent necessarily of capital punishment; however, I as a civilized individual with some degree of humaneness, do heartily object to the 'putting to death' of mentally ill persons—and the psychopath is definitely a mentally ill person." Similarly, Mr. and Mrs. T. N. Ball of Oakland stressed how "the power of the state should be to protect the mentally ill—not to wantonly destroy them." Chessman's attempt to situate his case within these larger psychiatric debates over criminal behavior was thus problematic. Interpreting *Cell 2455* in a manner not intended by the author, Daniel Blanchfield of Seal Beach told Knight how "after reading the autobiography of Caryl Chessman I am convinced that he has been and is now an insane man, and justice would be better served if he were committed to life imprisonment." If readers like Blanchfield had found him to be perfectly sane, it is doubtful whether Chessman would have obtained their support.[35]

By offering himself as a former psychopath now ready to contribute, Chessman indeed helped initiate the most frequent criticism of his execution, namely its direct contradiction of the ideal of prison rehabilitation. Writing from Long Beach, Mary C. Cooper reminded Knight, "The purpose of punishment of a criminal is to attempt to rehabilitate him. . . . I think [San Quentin's] Warden Duffy has brought this fact out with startling and enlightening results." Mable Bernhart of South Gate, meanwhile, looked forward to "the day when brutalizing legal murder is outlawed and society's outcasts with their socially sick and lost souls can be confined in a manner in which they can go to work rehabilitating themselves and helping others." "There is *always* the possibility for reformation," insisted Carlsbad's Gretchen Mitchell. While emphasizing the stated goals of the correctional system, many such arguments linked the principle of reform to Christian belief systems. Walter Carl Subke, a San Francisco Presbyterian pastor, stated, "In this man's case, there seems to be considerable evidence, in the book he has written, that he has reformed which, of course, is the chief purpose of our prison system." More directly, Hank Maiden of Whittier stressed how "there is something of the Divine in every individual [and it is] therefore our responsibility to appeal to the good and assist the deviant in being rehabilitated back into daily life." Chessman's books certainly bolstered his cause, proving to sympathetic readers that the prison system worked and that rehabilitation was indeed possible. As Henry Donald Frank of San Francisco wrote, "If it is true that the ideal of our prison system is rehabilitation and not revenge then it is obvious from his book that the system has done a pretty good job." In the eyes of his supporters, executing Chessman would violate the core values of the postwar justice system.[36]

Although Chessman's proponents repeatedly voiced their belief in the postwar prison as a site of therapeutic regeneration, the question remains why. In *The Decline of the Rehabilitative Ideal,* criminologist Francis Allen theorizes that the "rehabilitative ideal" depends on "the degree of confidence a society can muster in the capacities of its institutions to effect desirable guidance in character development."[37] First outlined during the Progressive era, the rehabilitative ideal—in which a prisoner convinced a variety of prison officials of his readiness to be released—was enacted on a wide scale during the immediate postwar period, nowhere with more fanfare than in California. This belief, as the pro-Chessman letters illustrated, would resonate among a cross-section of middle class citizens both in the state and across the nation. A larger "confidence" in American institutions indeed seemed to be a staple feature of arguments praising the postwar prison system. Identifying herself as Quaker, Elsa F. Rothschild of Los Angeles wrote, "In one of our fine Reformatories I am convinced that this man's mind can be turned to develop that God given good in him." Oakland's Ruby Harden, meanwhile, recommended "proper confinement for a psychopathic person." While the postwar expansion of the American economy certainly buoyed this outlook, only a few writers made this connection clear. "I think our society is strong enough that we can afford to be merciful," felt William B. Newlin of Glendale. Whether Chessman was placed in the prison reorganized by Warden Duffy or in any other of the state's "fine reformatories," his sympathizers expressed a clear optimism regarding the therapeutic capacities all of the state's institutions.[38]

Such confidence in American institutions arose against the backdrop of the Cold War, and a great number of pro-Chessman writers indeed contrasted the values of "enlightened," "humane" America with those of the "barbaric" Soviet Union. From Modesto, Charles and Florence Baker explained, "We have long abhorred capital punishment because we feel it a throwback to barbarism which does not do credit to a nation so enlightened in most respects." "Capital punishment," according to Bonnie Schultz of Tarzana, was "a holdover from the barbaric ancient civilizations and has no place in a modern nation of thinking people." Toward the end of the case, Mrs. Magruder Eckles of Stockton told Governor Brown, "After eleven years on death row he certainly has suffered enough and it would be barbarous to put him to death now. Even the Russians wouldn't be that cruel." Similarly, George E. Munyer of San Jose feared that if Chessman were executed, America would "become as heartless as those nations behind the 'iron curtain.'" "Barbaric," "cruel," and "heartless" were labels applied to the Soviet Union, whereas America was a nation guided by "enlightenment" and compassion. Opposition to Chessman's death sentence, in short, fit with a larger pattern of national identification in the Cold War era.[39]

New Class Abolitionism

In the debate over Chessman, an engaged citizenry seemed to endorse the larger therapeutic approach to criminal justice first presented by reformist prison administrators and a wide range of behavioral experts. Like the respondents to Chessman's case, this professional strata actively sought to influence the direction of state policy. Such an effort seems an early example of a social movement spearheaded by the so-called New Class, a term later used by '70s neoconservatives to deride all middle class proponents of an activist social policy. The New Class of the era consisted of those whom Barbara and John Ehrenreich termed a "professional-managerial class," and reform-minded prison administrators and public officials seeking to abolish the death penalty surely fit the mold. To bolster public support for their reforms, policymakers appealed to a broader section of the public, which C. Wright Mills first called the "new middle class." As seen by the background of many

Chessman's supporters, one did not have to work in the field of prison administration to draw upon official behaviorist rhetoric. For specialists and ordinary citizens alike, the Chessman case initiated debate as well as compelled action over the principles of the new penology.[40]

A 1957 California Assembly report on whether to abolish the death penalty illustrated how the New Class had access to, and received sanction from, the postwar state. Pushed for two years by Trevor Thomas, executive secretary of the Friends Committee on Legislation, the Assembly judiciary committee held ongoing public hearings on a bill calling for a six-year moratorium on capital punishment. As Dorothy Gardner reported in *The Christian Century,* mass public meetings were held throughout the Los Angeles area in support of the legislation. Sponsoring one such event were the ACLU, the Friends, a criminology professor, and "a number of prominent lawyers." While some rejected the death penalty on religious and ethical principles, the speakers at such events, Gardner said, viewed the death penalty as "a violation of equal justice for all," "not a political but a human issue," "a throwback to the 'barbaric days' of two centuries ago," and of "no use in the administration of justice." Thus, at public events endorsing the Friend's moratorium proposal, a mixture of criticisms—leveled against the death penalty's discriminatory application, its contradiction of liberal humanist principles, and its administrative flaws—reached a wide audience. The legislature, however, had already heard different public testimony on behalf of the bill, and in that discussion such abolitionist analyses were prioritized quite differently.

Held in Los Angeles (late 1955) and San Francisco (late 1956), the Assembly's public hearings provided an official forum for an array of professional experts to critique the state's use of the death penalty. It was this discussion, rather than the ideas circulated at the Friends' public meetings or elsewhere, that made its way into the Assembly's final report on the issue, released in 1957. In fact, the document explained how the committee had sought the advice of "persons who, because of their professional interest or official position, were qualified to make contributions of value." As well as judges and lawyers, this category included "psychiatrists, ministers, educators, public officials and others with informed opinions on the subject." With the exception of one James Alverson, whose affiliation was listed simply as "engineer," the Los Angeles testimony thus included only "informed" modern professionals. According to the Assembly report, the major abolitionist argument presented throughout the hearings concerned the degree to which the death penalty contradicted the "worldwide trend toward abolition." Only Warden Duffy stressed the discriminatory application issue at the hearings, where the death penalty was instead criticized as administratively flawed and fundamentally anomalous in "enlightened" postwar America. Moreover, the punishment could be removed, the New Class critics maintained, in the same manner as all social problems: by corrective government action taken regardless of public sentiment. At the San Francisco hearing, there had been one notable entry into the debate. When Attorney General Pat Brown took the microphone to say the "death penalty brought the law into disrepute," the New Class abolitionist campaign now had its de facto political leader.[41]

When Brown moved into the Governor's Mansion in 1958, capital punishment foes thus considered their views to be well-represented. Attorney General since 1950, Brown—a Democrat, but a protégé of Earl Warren—captured the support of both organized labor and liberal Republicans, benefiting from the right's ill-fated attempt (led by William Knowland) to make "open-shop" legislation the defining issue of the 1958 campaign. Brown came to power with the support of labor, minorities, and middle class liberals—in other words, a New Deal coalition in a traditionally liberal Republican state. The left, meanwhile, had long considered Brown a potential ally, particularly on the basis of his earlier membership in the National Lawyer's Guild. But Wells and his supporters had been mistaken when they thought they could count on Attorney General Brown to fight the execution. In a 1951 meeting with CRC leaders, Brown listened to William Patterson speak highly of Wells's potential to "rehabilitate himself." Responding to a suggestion that he meet Wells personally, Brown reportedly said, "I'm afraid he might attack me." Moreover, after a May 1954 stay granted to Chessman, Brown assured Loyola Law students of his readiness to fight court "interference" in the execution. Four years later, though, Brown included support for abolition in his campaign for governor against Knowland, a death penalty advocate. Such a vocal position would generate an even greater volume of correspondence to the governor's office after 1958, making the Chessman case a controversy Brown would never forget.[42]

As a practicing Catholic, Brown added another flank of religious opposition to the postwar debate over the death penalty. Prominent church leaders helped swing Catholic public opinion against the death penalty for a brief period in the mid-1960s. In a 1972 *America* article, Mary Ellen Leary recalled how both Brown and Ohio Governor Mike DiSalle were notably influential in promoting abolitionist sentiment among

Catholics throughout the late 1950s and early 1960s. Yet while the Vatican officially declared its support for the Chessman defense, Brown never concurred. Even among left Catholics, the case was indeed problematic. In its March 1960 edition, *The Catholic Worker* printed an "Open Letter to the California Legislature" on Chessman's behalf written by associate editor Robert Steed, who proceeded to launch a sixty-day hunger strike in protest of the execution. A storm of angry letters greeted Steed's efforts, however, causing him to print a sampling of reader reaction in the April issue. According to Steed's summary, most of the objections singled out Chessman's status as a "sex pervert" and asked the editor to "remember [Chessman's] victims." Like a wide cross-section of the American public, many Catholics struggled to support a convicted sex criminal. To be sure, Governor Brown's primary objections would focus on the prisoner's refusal to acknowledge guilt and show contrition. Nevertheless, Chessman's particular convictions may have explained why his case did not become an identifiable watershed of either left or mainstream Catholic abolitionism.[43]

As the Chessman case reached the height of national attention during late 1959 and early 1960, Brown's office began receiving thousands of letters every day. Some distinct changes, or refinements, surfaced in the arguments made on Chessman's behalf, not the least of which was the direct nature of the appeals to Brown. Given Brown's stated abolitionist sentiment, Chessman's supporters increasingly asked the governor to follow through on his principles. For instance, a group of eight sent a letter from Los Angeles, declaring, "Since you have publicly denounced capital punishment, and this is obviously a case that does not warrant the death penalty, we the undersigned do not understand your inhumane delay in canceling the execution of Caryl Chessman." Also writing from Los Angeles, Anne Peterson explained that "it is the bounden duty of a public official to lead the people toward changing inhumane or archaic laws." Los Angeles's Eloise Enoch, meanwhile, spoke of the common bond she and the governor shared. "Governor Brown," she wrote, " I too am a Democrat. Ours is the party of humanitarianism, the party with a heart." Extending the Cold War rhetoric of barbarism vs. enlightenment, the terms *humane* and *humanitarian* often sanctioned the arguments made by ordinary citizens to Brown. How, the correspondents implied, could Brown reject an appeal aimed at his most noble instincts and signal political responsibility?[44]

By late 1959, though, a range of issues other than those directly linked to rehabilitation appeared in the letters written to Brown. Inspired by Chessman himself, the ACLU and other supporters began to argue that the lengthy time he had spent on death row constituted "cruel and unusual punishment." For Helen C. Arfe of Daly City, "executing Chessman, or any human being, after keeping him in the death house for eleven years" seemed inappropriate. Spurred by organizations like the American League to Abolish Capital Punishment, a professional group comprised of a number of leading criminologists and prison administrators (including Duffy), the issue of deterrence—or, more precisely, the death penalty's lack thereof—stood at the center of the larger debate. In protesting Chessman's specific case, Diana Conway from Sherman Oaks would thus ask, "How long must civilized man go on killing? . . . Is capital punishment effective?" These questions of constitutional and criminological principle now framed the larger discussion of national policy, the direction of which apparently required an overall humanitarian outlook. After offering a sampling of popular opinions about the case, a group of forty female students from Brooklyn College told Brown, "We appeal to you, therefore, as an humanitarian, to commute the death sentence of this man and thereby set an example for other enlightened leaders."[45]

Although correspondents to Brown frequently stressed the greater ramifications of the case, throughout 1959 and 1960 the new governor also received a steady stream of letters arguing a more particular point, namely Chessman's innocence. Chessman had taken this position both in court and in *Cell 2455*, but, like the prisoner himself, his supporters initially placed primary emphasis on his contribution to society and his rehabilitation. In Pacifica Radio's October 1959 broadcast, however, key supporters like Dr. Graves and attorney Rosalie Asher now calmly stressed Chessman's lack of guilt as their number one argument. Similarly, Dona Shaw of San Francisco notified Brown, "I am an American citizen and by no means a 'sob sister' but I want to add my voice to others who protest Chessman's death sentence for a rape he may not have committed." That Shaw further used the term "hysterical woman" to characterize red light bandit victim Mary Alice Meza was not extraordinary, since many of the letters claiming Chessman's innocence had consistently voiced skepticism about the integrity of the witnesses and the gravity of the crimes. As John Gallagher of Beverly Hills asked, "This '17 year old virgin' . . . Just what was she doing on, of all places, Mulholland Drive at 1 o'clock of a January morning?" Calling Chessman's potential execution a "disgrace," Kathleen Rousseau of Belmont averred, "So far I haven't heard you make any laws requiring women on our streets to cover up." Whether based on consideration of the evidence or simple prejudice, such views of Chessman as completely innocent indeed required dismissal of the courtroom testimony of both of the Bandit's female victims, something Chessman's spokespeople and at least some of his supporters proved willing to do.[46]

The additional viewpoints notwithstanding, during the period leading up to Brown's October 1959 clemency hearing the rehabilitative ideal remained at the core of the Chessman defense. As a group of nine petitioned from Los Angeles, "The policy of prison officials is to rehabilitate. Caryl Chessman has rehabilitated himself with death facing him for 11 years." Also writing from Los Angeles, Edward Mann observed that "Chessman should not die, because he illustrates that which is constructive in our penal system, that he is rehabilitable—that therapeutically he is not hopeless." The behaviorist perspective indeed continued to inform the arguments made on Chessman's behalf. As both a model of institutional success and a source of continued contribution, Chessman, his partisans said, was simply too valuable to execute. Imbued with the managerial optimism of postwar liberalism, these correspondents appeared to believe strongly in the state's capacities to implement sound policy and to create institutions according to humane principles. Those writing to the governors undoubtedly represented only a sampling of broader public opinion about the Chessman case, however. And even as these participants came from the ranks of California's expanding middle class, just as surely they would comprise only a vocal, if influential, fraction thereof.[47]

A "Beastly Intelligence"

In substantially smaller numbers than Chessman's supporters, ordinary citizens opposed to the therapeutic principles of postwar criminal justice wrote to the governor calling for Chessman's execution.[48] On the eve of the October 1959 clemency hearing, a strongly anti-Chessman editorial in William Randolph Hearst's *Los Angeles Herald-Express* addressed the disparity in letters to Brown. Seeing the skewed ratio as "entirely misleading" in its impression of pro-Chessman sentiment, the editorial said most correspondents "wrote to the governor realizing that he is also opposed to the death sentence." By contrast, the *Herald-Express* received a "mass" of letters in which "the ratio has been at least 50–1 against clemency for Chessman." Improbably challenging Brown to allow "a vote of the people on the question" of whether Chessman should be executed, the paper urged all those opposed to the "bleeding hearts" to write to Brown. Like the rest of the mainstream Southern California press, the Hearst papers targeted Brown's stance on the death penalty, viewing it as a key vulnerability. Whether arguing for the "rule of law" or against a "fiendish perpetrator of kidnap and rape," Chessman detractors like Hearst submitted a larger critique of the postwar liberal, managerial state. Through softheaded ideas such as the possibility of rehabilitating "desperate and dangerous" criminals like Chessman, the argument went, reform-minded prison officials and politicians left the society weak and vulnerable.[49]

Rather than "heart" and "compassion," the anti-Chessman letters asked the governors to show "courage," to have the "guts" to stand up for what was right. In urging Knight to "'stay by [his] guns' in the Chessman case," Carrie Jensen of Walnut Creek used a common phrase. Frequently these letters characterized those who supported Chessman as "sob sisters," a derisive label implying excess sentimentality. Glenn Newhouse of San Francisco declared that "it is high time that 'sob-sisters' be 'told off,'" and J. Marsh of San Rafael stated, "We trust you will continue firm in your dealings with [the] 'sob sisters.'" Writing to Brown, Riverside's David Shatto further speculated, "Who among the sob sisters would invite him into their church or recreation hall and say to him: 'Here are our daughters, Do it to them.'" The language of the personal appeals against Chessman was thus heavily gendered: heartfelt sympathy was for sob sisters, whereas the governor needed to act like a gunslinging sheriff in defense of the besieged family and community.[50]

In voicing their desire to curb the apparent postwar sex crime "wave," these correspondents further revealed a deep skepticism about the notion of rehabilitation itself. As Mabel Hunsaker of Fresno put it, "Chessman wrote a book, so what? That only proves he is smart enough to commit other crimes." Mrs. Jack Zehnder of Los Angeles, meanwhile, believed that Chessman's "obvious intelligence ma[de] his crimes even more beastly." For his detractors, Chessman's only future contribution would be more crime. The most direct examples of this argument came in the form of the repeated warnings about what would happen if Chessman's sentence were commuted. As Mr. H. H. Brown of Pomona angrily predicted, "Next thing will be commutation to life imprisonment and in 4 or 5 years, a pardon granted him. Next thing he will do it again and I hope, if he does, it will be one of your family he attacks." In less venomous fashion, James Thornton of West Sacramento would likewise tell

Brown to "remember your wife and children and my wife and children are not safe with them kind of people going around killing and beating society." Chessman opponents tended to see the criminal justice system as far too lenient with criminals (especially those of the sexual type), whom they in general considered to be recidivists. For these reasons, the death penalty seemed society's only safeguard.[51]

Letters to Brown favoring Chessman's execution generally viewed the death penalty primarily as a deterrent to crime, and in this specific case as an affirmation of the rule of law. Sue Sally Jones of Los Angeles observed, "I believe that capital punishment acts as a deterrent from crime in many cases. Also, I believe that, by his various maneuvers, Chessman is making a mockery of our court system." Los Angeles's George Robb concurred: "This USA of ours is a Republic, which is supposed to be a nation governed by Laws. . . . The death penalty is on the laws, [and] statutes of the state of California." Joseph A. Hafner of Arcadia similarly said, "We the people . . . vote and pass laws, to be carried out." For such correspondents, the specific arguments made on Chessman's behalf paled before the general principle of the rule of law itself—the courts had spoken, and only by wily legal maneuverings had Chessman avoided his fate. Many of the most vengeful statements against him—such as offers to cast the cyanide, or proposals to form a lynch mob—came from the same sources as the more reasonable pleas for the rule of law. The ability of a career criminal to make his fate symbolic of California criminal justice clearly affronted the law-abiding perspective of a vocal component of the postwar citizenry.[52]

For some correspondents, Chessman's case also became a forum in which to air a wide range of animosities. The degree of paranoia and irrationality found in the anti-Chessman letters was wildly overstated by Chessman's supporters, however. Not all letters mistakenly called Chessman a "Jew," or labeled Governor Brown a "Communist." Yet for the minority who did use such labels, hatred ran deep, and Chessman offered a convenient target. J. Waller of Los Angeles, for example, urged Brown not to "fall for that Jewish propaganda they are spreading for Chessman, they are rotten to the core." Mrs. Florence Thomsen of Ontario, meanwhile, explained that "Jews are the cause of all of our troubles," because "they commit 80% of crime." Mrs. Mary Ann Crabtree of Boyle Heights found a different menace lurking behind the scenes. She thus began her letter to Brown by stating, "You're a communist." When placed into an outcast category such as Jew or Communist, Chess-

man was effectively stripped of any chance to return to the community
—although for those using such labels derisively, rehabilitation was not
even remotely an issue.[53]

For the citizens who asked the governors to stand tough against Chessman, whether Chessman was a good person who went bad, or someone
who had seen the folly of his ways and reformed, never cropped up in
their arguments. Why, these letters asked, should law-abiding citizens
sympathize with a career criminal, especially when one of his victims
still languished in a mental hospital? For its supporters, the death penalty had always symbolized what the society will not tolerate. The
"compassion" called for by death penalty abolitionists, argued conservative philosopher Sidney Hook in 1961, was better seen as "sentimen-
talism" or, better yet, "treacly humanitarianism." By prolonging his own
case for twelve years, moreover, Chessman had merely compounded his
offense, specifically by causing the legal system to appear weak and in-
effective. From the pro–death penalty perspective, the "sob sisterish"
concern for Chessman's legal rights and moral reform thwarted the
American criminal justice system's enduring ideal of "swift" and "certain justice."[54]

Brown Weighs In

Prior to the mid-October 1959 clemency hearing between Chessman's
attorneys and Brown, no comprehensive public opinion polls of the case
had yet been taken, though Brown could consult polls showing substantially stronger public support for the death penalty than opposition
in California (55 to 30 percent). Nevertheless, Brown would base his decision on the information presented to him from a spectrum of sources
other than simply opinion measurements. In one corner, Brown heard
from a hostile press, led by the *Los Angeles Times* and Hearst, which
stressed the weakness of California justice and the plight of Mary Alice
Meza. Numerous letters, written both to Brown and especially to sympathetic newspapers, made similar pleas for the general rule of law.
From the opposite camp came the equally passionate voices of the "ordinary citizens" who rallied to Chessman's defense, urging Brown to act
on his principles as well as those of the California criminal justice system. Around the world, a variety of pro-Chessman committees likewise
made public calls for clemency. From both Sacramento and San Quentin, meanwhile, Brown received extensive input from prison administrators, state officials, and the prisoner himself. Ultimately, Brown's deci-

sion would weave together important components of each of these divergent points of view.[55]

In preparation for the hearing, Brown's clemency secretary, Cecil Poole (a black attorney who had aided Wells), collected the views of several prominent figures regarding Chessman. A single folder contained the opinions of prison officials, politicians, psychiatrists, the prison chaplain, and judges and attorneys involved in the case. In Foucault's terms, these were the people responsible for managing the "technology of the soul"; each felt a responsibility to pronounce judgment on Chessman's character, and to assess the state of his rehabilitation.[56] Nearly every one of the official opinions flatly said Chessman was unreformed. The dossier included the reports of San Quentin psychiatrists, who by 1960 had not veered from their original diagnosis of Chessman as a "psychopathic personality," and of public officials like District Attorney William McKeeson of Los Angeles, who said Chessman "has exhausted every legal remedy and remains a cunning, deceitful, unrepentant criminal." Most prominent, however, were the views of San Quentin wardens, of a distinguished former governor, of Chessman's victims, and of the prisoner himself.[57]

Chessman's guardians at San Quentin plainly rejected any notion of his rehabilitation. Issued soon after Chessman's initial arrival to death row, Clinton Duffy's 1948 statement—"I believe him to be a dangerous individual"—was echoed by his successors as prison warden. As Warden Fred R. Dickson wrote to Governor Brown, Chessman "has never exhibited any signs that if he was released that he could be beneficial to a prison society or to society in general. . . . [H]e has not shown . . . a good prognosis for rehabilitation." Dickson also maintained that Chessman's sentence should not be commuted to life without parole because he "would cause a great deal of trouble to the institution." Louis S. Nelson, then associate warden and later warden during the turbulent 1960s, explained that "since incarceration at San Quentin Chessman has been arrogant, self-centered, and repugnant." Richard McGee, director of corrections, continued to hold a low opinion of Chessman throughout the case. Although he often spoke against capital punishment, McGee first conveyed his view of Chessman to Governor Warren in 1952: "He is another Sampsell," McGee declared, comparing Chessman to the insubordinate Yacht Bandit of the 1940s, who had since been sentenced to death row. Seven years later, in addition to calling him "almost a textbook case of the psychopathic personality," McGee said Chessman, if commuted, would pose a potential "public relations and management problem of unusual magnitude." Because of his success as a writer and his enduring trait as an outspoken prisoner, both Warden Dickson and McGee believed San Quentin would be better off without inmates like Caryl Chessman.[58]

Brown could also refer to the opinion of former governor and then Chief Supreme Court Justice Earl Warren. In May 1952, before the case became prominent, Governor Warren wrote his review by hand, beginning, "I have studied this record and find no grounds for executive clemency." His reasoning focused squarely on the question of Chessman's character. "The defendant," Warren said, "is an habitual criminal (3 priors). His present crimes, committed while on parole[,] show an abandoned heart. He now shows no contrition. . . . He will always be dangerous." For Warren, Chessman's lack of remorse and lifelong record of crime seemed more important than either the violations themselves or the question of whether those assaults merited the death penalty. The terms Warren used—referring to Chessman's "abandoned heart" and his lack of contrition—showed the prominence of the rehabilitative ideal in the governor's evaluation. "I concur with Earl Warren." Governor Goodwin Knight scrawled across the same page in May of 1954.[59]

Along with the views of participating officials, Poole's clemency folder included testimony from the victims of Chessman's assaults. In his own, decidedly anti-Chessman report, Poole provided excerpts from the original trial, most of which focused on the bandit's threats to kill his victims if they did not meet his demands. Chessman "told me he would kill me, strangle me, if I didn't [perform oral sex], so I did," Mary Alice Meza informed the court. Poole then summarized the views held by Chessman's victims nearly twelve years later. Regina Johnson, Poole noted, "still becomes emotionally disturbed when dealing with this matter." Both Johnson and Ruth Shaw, Mary Alice Meza's mother, voiced their support for Chessman's execution; a letter Shaw wrote to District Attorney Leavy in 1952, which described her daughter's continued fear of Chessman, was excerpted elsewhere in the file. A number of psychiatric reports from Camarillo State Hospital, where Meza had been since 1950, accompanied the personal testimony. Calling the Bandit's original assault "a very severe emotional strain," the 1959 documents said Meza's condition had "systematically worsened." In addition to Chessman's evident lack of remorse, Governor Brown could thus weigh the victims' enduring pain and apparent deterioration.[60]

Somewhat surprisingly, an additional voice in the consensus against clemency came from Chessman himself, who angrily rejected the sentencing option of life without possibility of parole in a letter to Brown dated October 6, 1959. Responding to Brown's ultimatum making acceptance of such a sentence a precondition for clemency, Chessman replied to Poole, "Since I do not happen to be guilty of these so-called Red Light Bandit crimes, I angrily reject the conditions under which our good Governor might deign to consider an application from me." Chessman continued the indignant tone: "I think it is a terrible thing when, after I have spent more than 11 years in a death cell . . . [that] this State's Chief Executive would resort to using his clemency powers in such a nakedly coercive way." In Chessman's eyes, acceptance of a life sentence amounted to a "false confession," whereas he sought another chance for vindication. Confidently, Chessman brooked no compromise on the sentencing issue, and, like many of his leading supporters, he now placed the issue of innocence at the center of discussion. "The mob may applaud treating me so arbitrarily and arrogantly," he concluded his letter to Poole, but "history won't. But, then, history can't vote." Humility, perhaps even more than a direct admission of guilt, was a prerequisite for clemency; but such a trait was never part of Chessman's character.[61]

Going into the clemency hearing, Brown was thus placed in a bind: allowing for the possibility of parole would be politically untenable, neither prison officials nor Chessman himself wanted him to stay at San Quentin, and executing Chessman would contradict his avowed position against the death penalty. At the meeting itself, held in the governor's Sacramento office on Thursday, October 15, 1959, Brown listened to Chessman's attorneys as they added, or perhaps restored, a different set of principles to the forefront of the debate. Brown immediately foreclosed discussion of the guilt question, opening the meeting by telling Chessman's representatives that they could discuss "anything they believe will help him reach a decision regarding clemency," but informing them that any arguments regarding Chessman's innocence would not carry weight. "I, myself, am convinced that the man is guilty of all the crimes with which he was charged and convicted and that have now been affirmed by the courts on several occasions," Brown said. Legally, Brown maintained, the dissents of Supreme Court justices in the case had focused on whether Chessman had received a fair right to an appeal (because of the questionable trial transcript), not on the question of guilt or innocence. Poole then gave an extended description of the case, again quoting court testimony and psychiatric reports. Brown and his advisers thus established their certainty of his guilt, their knowledge of Chessman's diagnosis as a "psychopath," and their sympathy with the plight of the victims.[62]

For the defense, lead attorney George T. Davis made the issue of Chessman's rehabilitation his central theme. Even though Davis's fame resulted from the pardon he had won for Tom Mooney two decades earlier, and his ties to radical labor remained strong, his presentation to Brown almost exclusively emphasized the therapeutic perspective made prominent by Chessman's supporters. Davis began, "I have to discuss this case with you on the assumption that he's guilty . . . that at the time of the commission of these offenses he was a depraved character of some sort." Yet Chessman, Davis said, had changed in the past eleven years, and clemency could provide an even greater "catalytic force" for his rehabilitation. Davis continued by appealing to Brown's humanitarian instincts. "You are a progressive and liberal man," Davis assured Brown, "responsible people . . . consider you the greatest humanitarian to sit in that Governor's chair in this generation." The death penalty, Davis further stressed, contradicted the goals of current penological thinking. California, he declared, "is certainly one of the leading states in the Nation, if not in the World," in the field of penology. Thus, like so many of Chessman's supporters, Davis saw the case as representing far more than the fate of one man—instead, the upcoming execution would be an affront to the postwar ideal of rehabilitation itself.[63]

Throughout the two-hour meeting, Brown repeatedly addressed the question of Chessman's reform, his comments closely resembling those of both fellow state officials and prison insiders. Brown's analysis of Chessman's past record, for example, seemed quite similar to Earl Warren's: "After committing these robberies, while he's on parole he goes out and does exactly the same thing. I mean the element of rehabilitation [is absent]." For both Warren and Brown, Chessman's violations of parole seemed especially galling, and along with Chessman's obstinacy they indicated an utter lack of reform. Brown continued, "There should be, it seems to me, some contrition, some desire to live to make amends . . . [but] I have yet to see a single, solitary thing where Mr. Chessman would be anything other than a psychopath in the prison itself." Brown's depiction of Chessman as a psychopath was influenced directly by what he had heard from San Quentin. As the governor put it, "All of the psychiatric reports show this man to be amoral . . . they all say that this man is just one of those psychopathic personalities that can't be rehabilitated." Swayed by Chessman's wardens, by a former governor, and by the diagnoses of prison psychiatrists, Brown evinced clear skepticism toward the notion of Chessman's reform.[64]

"Chessman Mercy Hinted by Brown," a front-page headline in the

Los Angeles Times nevertheless declared the day after the meeting. The article highlighted an exchange late in the meeting between the governor and the original prosecutor, Los Angeles Deputy District Attorney J. Miller Leavy, in which Brown angrily said, "Don't you think that 11½ years on Death Row, plus life imprisonment from here on out, would be satisfactory to the prosecution?" Although partially intended to deflect Leavy's aggressive pursuit of the death sentence, the comment at least suggested Brown's willingness to consider all sides presented to him. After spending the weekend considering Chessman's fate, however, on Monday, October 19, Brown held a press conference to announce his decision:

> The established findings of this case—a deliberate plan of robberies, sexual attacks, and the use of a loaded gun—have weighed heavily in my thinking. So, too, has Chessman's failure to show contrition. His attitude has been one of steadfast arrogance and contempt for society and its laws. I have considered too the matter of prior felony convictions. . . . Because of all these considerations, I have decided that I will not intervene in the case of Caryl Chessman.

No matter what he or his supporters said, Chessman—according to prison officials—had not changed during his eleven years on death row. Like Earl Warren, Brown combined the perspective of prosecutor and judge, referring to Chessman's "prior[s]" and his "steadfast arrogance" and "lack of contrition." Although Chessman claimed his innocence, and his attorneys argued for his rehabilitation, Brown believed neither. The practice of rehabilitative penology required judgment of the individual, and Brown, with the help of nearly all state officials involved in the case, deemed Chessman to be unreformed.[65]

In both his public statements and his private discussions, Governor Brown also expressed considerable ambivalence toward the views expressed by "the people" about the case. As he told Chessman's attorneys during the clemency hearing, "We have received literally thousands of letters, and I will be perfectly frank with you I haven't been able . . . to read all of them. Some of them have come to my attention." When Davis tactfully urged Brown not to let "public agitation and public outcry" guide his decision, Brown replied, "I am interested in what responsible people think about a case such as this." At various times both Brown and his advisers dismissed the letters on Chessman's behalf by characterizing their writers as "emotional" and untrustworthy. In a press conference in February 1960, Brown noted that he had received letters from all over the world, observing, "Some, of course, [were] from emotionally unstable people, but a great many of them from people whose views

I respect." For many ordinary citizens who had pled Chessman's cause, Governor Brown's stance would be doubly disappointing: not only did he reject clemency, but he also seemed to belittle their views. Calling the "emotionally unstable" populace untrustworthy, Brown instead sought and heeded the advice of professional insiders and other "responsible" people.[66]

According to key advisers like Poole and McGee, Brown clearly had more to lose than gain by granting clemency to Chessman. At the end of his fifteen-page review prepared for the October hearing, Clemency Secretary Poole titled his conclusion "Should Chessman, though guilty of kidnapping, be executed." After acknowledging the diversity of pro-Chessman positions—"general abhorrence of capital punishment," "insistence upon innocence," "contentions of rehabilitation," and Chessman's "value to society"—Poole appealed to Brown's "conscience as Governor." Poole urged Brown to consider the specific "individual" involved as well as "nature of the offenses," and to think about the effect of his action on "the administration of justice and the protection of society." "This society includes Caryl Chessman; it also includes the rest of us," Poole concluded. More dramatically, Director of Corrections McGee told Brown that he doubted whether the "Chessman case or Chessman as an individual is important enough to jeopardize even in the smallest way the great confidence that the people of California have in you and the progressive policies you sponsor." The goals of the new administration's agenda, McGee maintained, "far transcend the importance of any one single human being's welfare, to say nothing of one of the character of Caryl Chessman." Such harsh evaluation suggested a cold political calculus: since Brown's liberalism was not deeply rooted in the California electorate, risking popular support so soon into his administration just to save the life of one unsavory individual was not worth the gamble.[67]

Not Dead Yet

After Brown's rejection of clemency, it seemed certain that Chessman would be put to death on October 24, 1959. Yet on October 21, two days after Brown's announcement, Supreme Court Justice William O. Douglas, no friend of Chessman (nor any convicted sex criminals) but an opponent of the death penalty, granted the prisoner his seventh stay of execution in order to request a full Supreme Court review of lower court rulings. In mid-December, however, the full court refused to hear the case, and a month later it affirmed that decision, causing Chessman's execution to be rescheduled for February 19, 1960. On Thursday, February 18, Chessman was thus brought to the holding cell next to San Quentin's "Green Room," as the gas chamber was known. Less than twelve hours before his scheduled Friday morning execution, word came from Sacramento: Governor Brown had granted Chessman a sixty-day reprieve. "I do this because I want to give the people of California an opportunity, through the legislature, to express themselves once more on capital punishment," Brown's official statement read. A hearing in the legislature was scheduled for March 2. In the span of only four months, Brown had thus visibly changed his position, opening a potential escape hatch for Chessman. Such dramatics, not surprisingly, ignited a firestorm of controversy, one that would continue to haunt Brown's political career for many years afterward.

In explaining his apparently sudden decision, Brown cited a telegram that he had received from the State Department expressing "grave concern" over "anticipated hostile demonstrations of student elements and others when our president visits Uruguay March 2." According to *Newsweek*, though, Brown had sent two representatives to Washington that week to push for exactly such an action by the State Department. A hostile press reaction naturally ensued, with original Los Angeles prosecutor J. Miller Leavy and the Southern California press immediately blaming Brown's action on "Communist agitation." Nationally, pundits and politicians questioned such obstruction of "justice within a sovereign state." For the governor, creating the uproar seemed to be a calculated move. As a candidate in the 1960 presidential campaign, Brown now used the controversy to place himself in the national spotlight and, perhaps, to reconcile himself with death penalty foes angry over the Chessman case.[68]

In granting the temporary stay, Brown for the first time acknowledged the positive influence of the pro-Chessman campaign in his decision-making process. Brown now declared that "The people of California are clearly divided on this basic issue." He continued, "The thousands of communications I have received in this case have centered not so much on the person of Caryl Chessman as on whether this State should continue capital punishment." Contrary to his stated position at the October clemency hearing, Brown now lent credence to the expressions of pro-Chessman opinion, to the point where he exaggerated the extent of the division of public opinion on the case. In a 1961 *Dissent* article about anti–death penalty organizing in California, Frank Harper saw

Brown's actions as fundamentally disingenuous. Brown, Harper maintained, brought the abolition bill before the legislature "knowing [it] would be killed in committee." Even with the certain defeat, the governor would thus be able to claim that "he had done everything possible" to thwart Chessman's execution. Whatever his actual motives, the governor surely could have accurately forecast the impact of his latest decision on the prisoner's fate. Effectively, Brown's temporary reprieve now enabled the legislature to take aim at a specific target—namely Chessman—while reasserting a general pro–death penalty stance.[69]

Indeed, on the same day that Brown outlined his position against capital punishment to the full legislature, state Republicans introduced two bills calling for the extension of the death penalty. Even more damaging to Chessman were the efforts of Assembly floor leader Joseph Schell, a far-right Republican (and future primary challenger to Richard Nixon in 1962) from Los Angeles. Angering Democrats, Schell circulated graphic portions of the Chessman trial transcript among fellow legislators. Since "the Chessman case has been substituted for capital punishment here," Shell said in defending his action, his colleagues needed to be reminded of the danger posed by criminal psychopaths. Convened for a special budget session, state legislators showed little desire to take up the death penalty question. Two days after Brown's address, a complete survey of state legislators by United Press International found increased support for the death penalty over the previous year, as well as overwhelming opposition to clemency for Chessman. Faced with such odds, Brown announced he would not appear at the following week's committee hearing on the bill.[70]

With Chessman's fate severely in doubt, the chair of the Senate Judiciary Committee, Democrat Edward Reagan of Weaverville—known to be a staunch defender of capital punishment—called the hearing to order on Wednesday, March 9. First to speak on the pro-abolition side was former San Quentin Warden Clinton T. Duffy, no ally of Chessman but a vocal critic of the death penalty. Duffy was followed by religious leaders, former police chiefs, state prison officials, a law professor, a psychiatrist, and representatives of the activist organization Californians Against Capital Punishment. The last speaker in favor of the bill, however, was Chessman's attorney (and labor radical) George T. Davis, who presented his views of the case allegorically by focusing on death sentences given to the innocent, using his former client Tom Mooney as his chief example. Speaking on behalf of capital punishment, meanwhile, were a range of district attorneys and law enforcement officials, most notably Los Angeles Police Chief William Parker, who had been invited by the committee chair. Anticipating the arguments soon made by Governor Reagan, Parker warned the senators, "We are the migratory mecca of the world. All of the people who come here are not law-abiding." [71]

The committee, though, would not hear the most newsworthy testimony until the end of the day, when original Chessman prosecutor J. Miller Leavy testified that prior to her 1955 execution murderess Barbara Graham had confessed her guilt to the late San Quentin Warden Harley Teets. As seen in chapter one, the film *I Want to Live!* had presented a strong popular case for her innocence, which Graham had steadfastly maintained. Chessman and his supporters were now making similar claims, and in early March 1960 a documentary titled *Justice and Caryl Chessman* was released in theaters, angering prison officials because it likewise suggested a miscarriage of justice. Prodded by the committee chairman, Leavy said that he had learned of Graham's heretofore unknown confession from Marin County District Attorney William Weissich and San Quentin Associate Warden Louis Nelson, both of whom vehemently favored Chessman's execution. Though later revealed to be a hoax, Leavy's revelations created a media splash. In his 1989 memoir, in fact, Brown, attributed the failure of the March abolition bill to the Graham confession, although the evident hostility of the legislature made for certain defeat anyway. Tabled by vote of eight to seven, the death penalty bill never made it to the floor of the legislature, and Chessman's fate again seemed sealed. [72]

After this defeat, Brown would not fully pursue anti–death penalty legislation for another three years. In response to the March failure, though, a number of influential participants in the Chessman campaign urged a different course, namely a fall ballot initiative. Immediately after the meeting, George T. Davis announced that he would help mount a campaign to get an initiative on the November ballot, saying the qualifying drive might also help sway Brown into an "extraordinary action" on Chessman's behalf. In his *Dissent* article, lead organizer Frank Harper—who had been recruited by left AFL leaders from San Francisco—explained how volunteers, "especially students and housewives, came into the campaign by the hundreds and the most heartening thing was that most of them had always shied away from political involvement of any kind." Yet the grassroots effort was not endorsed by state Democratic Party officials, who were convinced that such a campaign would fail. Even more problematically, neither the state Friends Committee on Legislation nor many of the same religious leaders who testified at the committee hearing would lend support. Lacking effective organizational participation, the referendum drive never got off the ground. While convinced of the death penalty's inappropriateness, the state's liberal leadership instead sought to eliminate it administratively — in Brown's words, listening to "the people of California" as their voices were expressed "through the legislature." Berkeley history professor Richard Drinnon, a vocal supporter of both Chessman and the initiative campaign, saw Brown's approach as illustrative of the "widespread liberal distrust of the people." Whether a sustained grassroots effort would have succeeded is not clear, but the initial momentum generated by the ballot measure seemed a hopeful sign to its participants. If nothing else, the spark fed directly into the ensuing protests over Chessman.[73]

Blaming the People

In response to the media outcry triggered by Brown's February 1960 reprieve, a California Poll took the first sustained measure of public opinion regarding Chessman. By a ratio of 54 to 33 percent, Californians favored Chessman's death sentence, numbers almost identical to their support for capital punishment as a whole. Asked to explain their reasoning, about two-thirds of anti-Chessman respondents referred to the "rule of law"; the other third pointed to "his terrible crimes." Given the overlap between these two explanations, the ongoing campaign waged by prosecutor Leavy and the Los Angeles press highlighting Chessman's "fiendish" sex crimes appears to have strongly resonated with the California public. Of those opposed to Chessman's execution, one-third chose the phrase closest to the slogans of the new penology, namely "life imprisonment is effective and a better punishment." Another quarter did not believe in the death penalty on principle, while between 10 and 15 percent cited each of the following: "[Chessman] didn't kill anyone," "he has been punished enough," and "doubt whether [he is] guilty." While national polls showed a marked downward trend in support for the death penalty in the late 1950s, the above sampling found a slight increase in both support and opposition in California. In his press release, the director of the California Poll, Mervin Field, thus called Chessman's case a "focal point for mobilization" of both sides of the issue. The pro-Chessman forces, however, failed to muster anywhere near majority opposition to his execution.[74]

To explain this inability to win public sympathy for Chessman, a number of prominent critics blamed "mass hysteria" and the "ignorance" of "the people." In a postmortem *Partisan Review* essay, Elizabeth Hardwick wrote, "Perhaps by creating his life, Chessman had to lose it. The vigor of his creation aroused fear, bewilderment, suspicion." In a scathing critique of the letters sent to Governor Brown, Richard Meister expressed even deeper hostility toward "the people." Writing in *The Nation*, Meister pointed out how "those usually too uninformed or too disinterested to write on such matters have been stirred into action." The anti-Chessman letters, Meister said, revealed "the appalling misinformation, the blatant prejudices and the tone of violence and vengeance of those who support the death penalty." The pro-Chessman correspondence had illustrated its own "blatant prejudices," either on behalf of white prisoners and against women, but Meister found flaws only one side of the fence. Uncritical of their own assumptions about Chessman or the reasons why the death penalty should be abolished, liberal analysts of the case preferred to rely on the convenient explanation of popular anti-intellectualism.[75]

As in the Wells campaign, though, the arguments made by Chessman's defenders seemed rooted in the ideals and interests of the respective constituencies involved. Wells cast his lot with the Civil Rights Congress and left organized labor, telling the former of his readiness to fight prison racism and the latter of his great respect for Tom Mooney. By contrast, Chessman aimed his plea toward middle class professionals such as psychiatrists and criminologists, seeking inclusion in their ranks; the experts, along with a vocal sector of self-styled ordinary citizens, seemed ready to welcome Chessman as one of their own. George T. Davis, formerly Mooney's attorney, took Chessman's case directly to Governor Brown, where he drew upon the rhetoric of rehabilitation at the center of New Class opposition to the death penalty. Such different bases of organizational support thus laid the groundwork for two distinct campaigns, one straightforwardly political and the other more technocratically oriented. Reliance on the goodwill of Governor Brown, however, proved no substitute for the sustained grassroots defense waged to save Wells. To be sure, neither case involved murder, making both sentences seem extreme by current standards; yet plenty of influential officials—including Earl Warren and Pat Brown—were ready to follow through with both executions. The process by which the state chose its subjects for execution may have been arbitrary, but the arguments submitted by the two campaigns were not. In aligning himself with the ascendant modern professionals, Chessman adhered to an elusive, conditional set of therapeutic principles around which to build an anti-death penalty movement.

Neither left labor nor African American opposition would entirely fade from the Chessman campaign, however. A March 1960 issue of the Building Employees *Service Union Reporter,* for example, featured an article by International Vice President George Hardy objecting to the death penalty in general, an issue he said had been "clouded" by the particular case of Chessman. Prefiguring the key terms of the critique posed by radical prison activists of the late 1960s, Hardy said the death penalty is "arbitrary and discriminatory," given disproportionately to the "poor and minority groups." Meanwhile, beneath a masthead listing the various programs for political and economic integration it endorsed, a 1960 pro-Chessman editorial in the *California Eagle* called capital punishment "a relic of barbarism." These remaining voices from the Wells campaign thus offered a preview of the left critique of the death penalty made in the late 1960s by groups like the Black Panthers and the American Friends Service Committee. As labor and the black press offered a window to the future, Wesley Wells now seemed a ghost from the past, surfacing only in occasional letters asking the *California Eagle* to help him obtain his freedom. Because of the increasingly charged law and order climate, in 1963 Wells cautiously refrained from sending Brown a thirty-seven-page letter asking the governor to consider the possibility of parole.[76]

Conversely, by early 1960 the Chessman controversy splashed across headlines around the world. A new set of actors—namely, college students from Berkeley and other Bay Area schools—would now perform a crucial role. Inheriting the therapeutic confidence of their New Class elders, the students nevertheless protested Chessman's execution via march, vigil, and other popular means. The liberal state, the new generation believed, would not enact good policy without constant public pressure. Anticipating the criticisms soon to come from the campuses, Bobby L. Jones, a high school American Government teacher from Woodland, expressed his frustration over the Chessman case to the governor shortly after Brown's denial of clemency. "I am getting disillusioned," Jones wrote. "I cannot teach students a respect for the law and the democratic process when the legal machinery and the governor of our state seem so blind to testimony from the other side in this case. You have lost me, Governor Brown."[77]

CHAPTER FIVE

Chessman's Ghost

(1960–1974)

I believe there is something terribly wrong . . . with a government which is supposed to be 'by the people for the people'
[but] which does not yield to public opinion as decisive and
positive as that we sought to exert in the Chessman case.

>   *Anita Jansky of San Francisco to*
>   *Governor Brown, May 5, 1960*

You know, there's a basic difference between the
Governor and me.

>   *Gubernatorial candidate*
>   *Ronald Reagan, October 1966*

On May 3, 1960, the lead story in the *New York Times* began, "Caryl
Chessman was executed today." [1] In dramatic fashion, the article provided a blow-by-blow account of last-minute legal appeals as well as the
preparations of the cyanide. The "convict-author," as the *Times* called
him, eventually "kept his ninth scheduled appointment in the gas chamber at San Quentin prison." That same day, the *Los Angeles Times* provided a somewhat different perspective. According to its front-page
story, "Caryl Chessman, 38, the infamous red light bandit who terrorized
Los Angeles lovers' lanes in 1948, was executed this morning." Whether
a convict-author or a sex terrorist, Chessman now occupied a prominent
place in the national—and international—political scene. Crowds in Rio
de Janeiro denounced the United States as a "miserable country," angry
students smashed the windows of the U.S. embassy library in Lisbon,
and expressions of pro-Chessman sentiment rang throughout Western
Europe. Caryl Chessman's execution, in the words of the *London News
Chronicle,* had finally put an end to America's "squalid melodrama." [2]

   Outside the gates of San Quentin, Chessman's supporters held a can-
dlelight vigil the night before his execution. Quakers, students from lo-

cal colleges, and engaged Bay Area residents were met by Marlon Brando and other celebrities. During the week leading up to the execution, Shirley MacLaine and Steve Allen joined Berkeley history professor Richard Drinnon in a well-publicized visit to Brown's office on behalf of Chessman. On execution day, a small group of lesser-known but no less inspired protesters pled for clemency outside the governor's mansion. A week earlier, pro-Chessman committees had taken out full-page ads in both the *New York Times* and the *Los Angeles Times*. In the latter, 127 self-described "newsmen and writers," including Norman Mailer, Aldous Huxley, Christopher Isherwood, and Dorothy Parker, signed a statement titled "Conscience, Chessman, and Capital Punishment." By early May, thousands of similar pro-Chessman petitions, letters, and telegrams written by equally outraged ordinary citizens had reached the governor's office. Immediately after the execution, Brown received a stormy barrage of statements denouncing him as a "murderer" and comparing him to Pontius Pilate. The plight of one prisoner had struck a collective nerve. As *San Francisco Chronicle* columnist Herb Caen observed, "The Man, Caryl Chessman, is no longer the issue; now he is the worldwide symbol of the farce that is capital punishment" in California.[3]

Despite the severe criticisms he faced from death penalty opponents after allowing Chessman's execution, by early 1960 Brown had begun to define the position that would soon animate the NAACP and ACLU legal campaigns against the death penalty, which gained increasing success later in the decade. After granting Chessman his final, tumultuous stay in February of 1960, Brown had spoken to the legislature in support of his newly proposed abolitionist bill. In the address, Brown stressed that "no matter how efficient and fair the death penalty may seem in theory, in actual practice in California as elsewhere it is primarily inflicted upon the weak, the poor, the ignorant, and against racial minorities." This argument, prioritizing criticism of the death penalty's discriminatory practice over its contradiction of the rehabilitative ideal, indeed became commonplace among activists in the later 1960s. Brown's legal "logjam" approach of staying virtually every execution, moreover, would serve as a model for the NAACP/ACLU strategy later in the decade. Nevertheless, the governor's handling of both the Chessman case and the larger issue would open him to attacks by both the New Left and New Right. Even through his 1966 defeat to Reagan, Brown later recalled, the "shadow of Chessman" lingered.[4]

The emotions expressed both for and against Chessman, in other words, hardly subsided after the May execution. Less than a week afterwards, many of the same student activists gathered outside San Francisco's City Hall to demonstrate against the hearings of the House Un-American Activities Committee. "In our protests against an execution and a witchhunt hearing," Michael Rossman observed, "History was to discover the birthcry of the New Left." In the six years following Chessman's execution, the death penalty would serve as a hot-button issue dividing the radical left and the far right from the liberal center. In 1966, a lengthy *Ramparts* article written by Robert Scheer included Chessman's execution as a primary reason the New Left should not support Brown in his reelection campaign against Ronald Reagan. Meanwhile, the death penalty became an instrumental component of the New Right's rise in California during the 1960s. In his unsuccessful 1962 campaign for governor, Richard Nixon made frequent reference to Brown's handling of the Chessman case, and four years later, in reaction to rising crime rates, antiwar demonstrations, and especially the Watts Riot, the death penalty formed a cornerstone of Reagan's successful "law and order" candidacy. After riding the post-Watts "white backlash" into office, Reagan made capital punishment an fundamental component of his antiliberal regime, speaking in thinly veiled racial rhetoric of the need for an "urban renewal project on death row." [5]

Meanwhile, by the late 1960s both the legal strategists of the NAACP's Legal Defense Fund (LDF) and prison activists led by the Black Panther Party were making racial discrimination the focal point of criminal justice debate. After the LDF's campaign resulted in the Supreme Court's 1972 *Furman* decision ruling the death penalty to be unconstitutional, Reagan immediately launched a referendum calling for the restoration of capital punishment in California, an initiative which passed by more than a two-thirds majority. Matching California trends, popular support for the death penalty rose steadily across the nation throughout the late 1960s and early 1970s. Indeed, precisely as prison activists and legal strategists brought racial discrimination to the foreground of criminal justice debate, Reagan and the New Right created a counternarrative of the death penalty as racial control, successfully using it to anchor a larger assault on postwar California liberalism itself. [6]

The New Left Protests

During the early spring of 1960, pro-Chessman protests spread across the greater Bay Area. Among other highlights, a *Time* cover story noted in late March, were a petition sent to Brown by 384 University of Cali-

fornia faculty members asking for clemency, and the efforts of an "unemployed school teacher" named Norbert Nicholas, who waged a hunger strike outside the Capitol in Sacramento. *Justice and Caryl Chessman* was shown at theaters throughout California, and "on jukeboxes
across the land, a folk song called 'The Ballad of Caryl Chessman'
urged, 'Let him live, let him live!'" After the March hearing at the Capitol, moreover, "California beatniks assembled in North Beach for a reading of save-Chessman poems." As *Time*'s thumbnail sketch suggested,
the most vocal supporters of Chessman by the end of the case were the
students, writers, and artists who comprised the disparate voices of the
early New Left.[7]

A shift in leadership was the most telltale distinction between old left
and new. The New Left, unlike its predecessor, was steered by students and other middle class citizens not directly affiliated with a party
or a union. In accepting C. Wright Mills's rejection of the "labor meta-
physic," student radicals assigned themselves a primary role in left organizing. During the late 1950s and early 1960s, the Bay Area witnessed
several early examples of the activism Mills characterized in 1961 as the
New Left. Berkeley student organizers formed the campus political organization SLATE in 1958, protested Chessman's execution in 1960,
were arrested outside San Francisco City Hall for their demonstrations
against HUAC a week later, and soon joined boycotts of local Wool-
worth's stores over racial discrimination. Small but growing ranks of
students waged these actions, and they indeed seemed motivated by a
distinctly different set of concerns than their predecessors. "The revolt is
not, as in the thirties, a product of sympathy with mass union struggles,"
Michael Harrington, a sympathetic firsthand observer of the New Left,
wrote in 1962, but rather "a radical mood in the midst of a semi-affluent
society, and the key terms are the Bomb, the racist, the executioner."
The Chessman protests best captured what "the executioner" meant to
this new generation of activists.[8]

Bay Area student organizers clearly inherited the orientation of the
New Class professionals leading the period's anti–death penalty movement. "Psychotherapy, not cyanide," "Psychopaths should not be put
to death," "Justice, not revenge"—all were common slogans in pro-
Chessman picket signs. Taken together, the statements summarized the
therapeutic, behaviorist perspective students shared with psychiatrists
and criminologists about the case. Such a standpoint hardly diminished
the passion generated by Chessman's cause, however, as on the eve of the
execution over two thousand people gathered outside the gates of San

Quentin. At least a few hundred students had marched to San Quentin that day from six Bay Area college campuses, many walking across the Golden Gate Bridge from San Francisco State. Among the speakers were psychiatrist Isidore Ziferstein and actor Marlon Brando, the latter remaining at the protests through the night. According to San Francisco State's Stephen Bartholomew, who wrote a first-hand account of the vigil for the school newspaper, the most powerful argument made by students concerned the complicity of middle class citizens in murder. In response to what the *San Francisco Chronicle* described as the "40 young hoodlum types" who cheered in favor of Chessman's execution, Bartholomew and his fellow protesters hoped to make them "realize that a man was dying just past the bend in the road." On the day of the execution, Berkeley student Edwina White argued a similar point in a letter to Governor Brown. White said the question of Chessman's innocence had clouded the larger issue of capital punishment, and she hoped future movements would thus ask, "If any man be guilty of such a crime, should we, the people of this state, take his life." The major arguments students made against Chessman's execution thus complemented one another: rather than implicate themselves in murder, student activists advocated life imprisonment as a more acceptable, humane alternative.[9]

Among participants in the Chessman vigil, a profound sense of disillusionment—with both the criminal justice system and liberal politicians like Governor Brown—was the most palpable and enduring reaction to the execution. After spending "Sunday night lying outside San Quentin prison on a dirty old blanket," Mill Valley's Dorothy McMinn "felt Chessman die within [her]self." Such grief seemed compounded because of the intense campaign that McMinn and others had waged on Chessman's behalf. Sherina Friedlander of San Francisco likewise had "hoped that the marchers, the Quakers, the many different people all bound by their concern over the nearing execution, would somehow be able to influence our government." The contradiction between the professed beliefs and actual practice of the American political system indeed frustrated participants in the pro-Chessman protests. As Michael Rossman recalled a decade later, "Our eyes were opening, a mystification was breaking, we were beginning to see the acts of Official America as ugly, wherever we looked." By allowing Chessman's execution, Governor Brown had irrevocably wounded the liberal idealism of early New Left activists.[10]

The political organizers were joined in the protests by the cultural rebels of the Beat Generation, the latter adopting a different but no less influential critique of what Chessman's execution represented. As Paul Jacobs and Saul Landau observed in *The New Radicals* (1966), "Protests over the execution of Caryl Chessman ultimately brought together students and some bohemians—the loose and overlapping segments of what was to become known as the Movement." To be sure, the two wings were not wholly separate in their views, as evidenced by the Beat writer Terry Southern's characterization of Chessman's execution as a "pellet of nihilism." From the dominant Beat perspective, however, Chessman's sentence most clearly symbolized the stifling sexual norms of American society. In "On Chessman's Crime," Gregory Corso began, "Be abnormal sex a crime? / Then be it everybody's crime / . . . / Gas chamber for every being / who ever fucked or never fucked!" Tuli Kupferberg, in a free-form essay titled "Death and Love," referred to Chessman's "sex so called crimes," which, given their lack of public disclosure, were "left to the luridly vapid imaginations of indignant spinsters & ignorant patres familiarum." Where political activists like Rossman expressed doubt about Chessman's guilt, Beat poets like Corso and Kupferberg went in the opposite direction, viewing the sexual assaults for which he was convicted not as crimes at all.[11]

A pair of prominent left intellectuals whose work blurred the distinction between political and cultural radicalism, Paul Goodman and Norman Mailer, also analyzed Chessman's case in terms of its revelations about American sexual mores. In "The Fate of Dr. Reich's Books," Goodman paid tribute to Wilhelm Reich, the psychologist whose theory of sexual "repression" appealed to many on the cultural New Left. Goodman interpreted Chessman's execution as an example of America's harsh sexual norms, and he characterized the "tone" of anti-Chessman sentiment as "violently, sickeningly, sadistic, pornographic, and vindictive." Elsewhere, Goodman called Chessman's execution a "horrible example" of the "frightening sexual attitude in the general culture." What the anti-Chessman opinion meant for Goodman as an individual was that "when I walk down the streets I am not safe, for these are thoughts and feelings that seethe just beneath the surface in the majority of my fellow-citizens." Like the Beat poets, Goodman thus placed the question of sex at the center of discussion, interpreting Chessman as the victim of a larger pattern of societal repression.[12]

The tendency among some analysts to view Chessman as persecuted because of his "sex so-called crimes" bolstered the notion that he was also a martyr, a view most dramatically expressed by Norman Mailer. In his notable essay "The White Negro" (1959) Mailer located two sources of inspiration for the disenchanted white middle class hipster: the urban negro and the "psychopath." Where the former "relinquish[ed] the pleasures of the mind for the more obligatory pleasures of the body," the psychopath "may indeed be the perverted and dangerous front-runner of a new kind of personality which could become the central expression of human nature before the twentieth century is over." Based on his interpretation of Robert Lindner's *Rebel Without a Cause*, Mailer endorsed the hipster's "decision . . . to encourage the psychopath in oneself," and linked "the unstated essence of Hip" to "its psychopathic brilliance." Such enthusiasm caused Mailer to view the "sexual psychopath" Chessman as representative of the vibrant sexual "underground" of American life. In "Superman Comes to the Supermarket" (1960), Mailer connected the "secret" of John F. Kennedy's appeal to "the private madnesses of the nation which had thousands—or was it hundreds of thousands—of people demonstrating in the long night before Chessman was killed, and a movie star, the greatest, Marlon the Brando out in the night with them." Where others looked at the end result with despair, Mailer viewed the manifest passion of the pro-Chessman campaign itself as a positive sign in the collective struggle for sexual liberation.[13]

The views of Beat poets and influential intellectuals support the dominant interpretation of the case's impact, which identifies Chessman as the first sexual outlaw embraced by the New Left. In *America in the Sixties: An Intellectual History* (1968), the conservative historian Ronald Berman emphasized the left's view of America's stifling sexual norms. For New Left thinkers, Berman stated, "Freedom . . . is seen to derive . . . from unlegislatable sexual needs." Any attempts by government to thwart such desires, according to Berman, were seen as "tyrannous," which explained "why Caryl Chessman was a culture hero of the left." In his concluding chapter, Berman elaborated on the left's embrace of Chessman, distinguishing between what Chessman actually argued and how various radical thinkers interpreted him. Unlike the intellectuals, Chessman "was interested in social pathology not because it symbolized an underlying failure of our culture but because something had to be done about rehabilitating criminals." Moreover, Chessman "never intimated that the crime for which he was accused was a morally relative one. Yet this, most of all, magnetized the intellectuals who declared for him." Relying primarily on the views of the Beat poets and left intellectuals analyzed above, Berman saw the Reichian critique of sexual repression as catalyzing New Left support for Chessman's cause.[14]

Susan Brownmiller reached many of the same conclusions in *Against Our Will* (1975), her influential history of rape. "I am certain that part of the mystique attached to Caryl Chessman," Brownmiller wrote, "had to do with his legend as the Red Light Bandit. . . . as a figure around whom a cause was formed, the sex attacks he may or may not have committed added to his image and made him the ideal personification of society's favorite victim: the arrogant, unloved desperado who never had a decent break or a faithful woman." Similarly, the historian Eric Cummins recently emphasized the enduring impact of the "sexual rebel" Chessman on the New Left. The "reverence for the outlaw," Cummins believes, "was to be Caryl Chessman's biggest contribution to the California Left." Cummins, Brownmiller, and Berman, moreover, all see a logical progression from the left's embrace of Chessman to its lionization of Eldridge Cleaver by the end of the decade.[15]

By no means did all participants in the debate view Chessman as an outlaw hero, however. The opinions expressed by a handful of influential commentators did not speak for the majority of pro-Chessman students, activists, or engaged citizens. Nor did this view correspond with the arguments Chessman himself articulated. Unlike Cleaver, Chessman never attempted to justify the sex crimes for which he was convicted; instead, he distanced himself by saying he was too smart and too "normal" to commit such "depraved acts." Chessman maintained his innocence, argued for his rehabilitation, and spoke of his desire to become a criminologist—three qualities that hardly made him a self-conscious outlaw. For the more politically oriented 1960s activists, the memory of Chessman's execution instead served as a vivid example of liberal hypocrisy. Writing in 1966, Michael Harrington analyzed what he saw as the growing "cynicism" of the New Left. At the beginning of the decade, Harrington stated, radicals "seemed to have believed what they were told about freedom, equality, justice, world peace, and the like." In Harrington's view, "They became activists in order to affirm these traditional values." As examples of their efforts, he listed: "defending civil liberties against HUAC, picketing for the life of Caryl Chessman, demanding an end to nuclear testing, fighting for civil rights." By mid-decade, though, the New Left had begun to reveal itself as more radical than liberal. Harrington attributed this shift to "the shock generated by the society's duplicity in this or that single issue [which] then opened their eyes to larger, and even more systematic, injustices." The protests over Chessman had clearly revealed one of the first instances of this larger New Left conflict.[16]

Nothing confirmed Harrington's point better than the position taken
in the 1966 governor's race by the editors of *Ramparts*. Given the land-
mark events of the intervening years—the Free Speech Movement, the
escalation of the Vietnam War, the conflict at Watts—the prominence of
the Chessman case in their scathing critique of Brown seemed surprising. For editor Robert Scheer, though, the 1960 execution vividly exemplified Brown's unwillingness to lead, his enduring habit of sacrificing
principles for the sake of political expediency. Along with the 1960 California Water Plan, the Chessman case marked the beginning of left "dis-
illusion," or the "alienation of both the politically sophisticated and the
great number of innocents who simply expected Pat Brown to do the right
thing." Contrary to his "professed humanitarian liberalism," Brown
chose to "follow the mob rather than lead the people" in the Chessman
case. Notably, Scheer criticized Brown's seeming "mystic reverence" for
the law, which prevented the governor from acting on his principles regarding issues like the death penalty. In defending his call for abstention
from the 1966 election, Scheer said the "liberal center [brought] the
chaos on itself . . . clobbering the students, killing the Chessmans—and
then wondering why an increasingly disillusioned left won't help it to
gain power." Scheer's position was endorsed at a statewide convention
of more than two thousand activists that October. Still, the anti-Brown
campaign was severely criticized by the left-liberal *Nation* as well as
Dorothy Healey and the California Communist Party, both of which
saw it as grossly underestimating the threat posed by Reagan.[17]

Death penalty foes and New Left activists had rallied behind Chessman, seeing his execution as an example of the contradiction between
the rhetoric and practice of American liberalism. For his supporters,
Chessman's apparently transformed character typified the ideal of rehabilitation central to California's postwar criminal justice system; as
Chessman himself wrote in a letter designed for post-mortem publication, "Capital punishment, it is said, is applicable to those who cannot
be rehabilitated. Yet, the Caryl Chessman who came to death row so
long ago and the Caryl Chessman who was poisoned by gas fumes were
quite different persons." As outlined in the preceding chapter, however,
Governor Brown did not see Chessman's essentially defiant character as
reformed. More important to Brown were political considerations: after
the event the governor claimed he would have been "impeached" if he
had granted clemency. A few months earlier, Chessman had written to
Brown expressing hope that his "execution would lead to an objective
reappraisal of the social validity or invalidity of capital punishment." In

the wake of Chessman's death, Brown now said that his "personal opposition to capital punishment remained as profound as ever," and he
"continue[d] to hope that people of California will change the law."
Within the confines of the legislative approach, Brown would continue
to push for death penalty abolition throughout his next six years in
office. As he did so, the emerging California New Right began to attack
Brown's stance on the issue, eventually resulting in an ominous "reappraisal of the social validity" of the death penalty indeed.[18]

Brown vs. the New Right

In early 1961, former vice president Richard Nixon signaled his intention to run for governor of California. Governor Brown, Nixon maintained, had lost the support of the state's "swing voters." Addressing the
state's Republican Assembly in March, Nixon said "Governor Brown
had lost public confidence because of his handling of the Chessman case
and because of his part in the Democratic National Convention last
year." A year and a half later, with the race in full swing, both Chessman and the larger question of capital punishment remained central campaign issues for Nixon. According to *San Francisco Chronicle* columnist
Jackson Doyle, Brown wanted to avoid capital punishment "for two good
political reasons: 1) The prestige he lost during the Chessman fiasco, and
2) The fact that polls show consistently that the public favors retention
of the death penalty." Indeed, Nixon and the ascendant California New
Right would not let Brown off the hook for the Chessman case. Although
Brown had eventually allowed Chessman's execution, according to the
New Right his wavering had failed to demonstrate a strong stance on
"law and order."[19]

Against the backdrop of the biggest population boom in California
history, the Republican gubernatorial candidate sought to capitalize on
increasing popular concern about crime in the state. A *Newsweek* feature story about the 1962 race captured the reasons why Nixon felt
compelled to pursue the issue. "As governor," the article began, "Brown
has achieved the best school system in America, the biggest water-
conservation project in the state's history, [and] 41 percent of the nation's space industry contracts—all with four balanced state budgets."
Beside a photograph of Chessman, though, the article said Brown
nevertheless remained haunted by the "ghost" of "the kidnapper–sex
offender who staved off death in San Quentin's pale green gas-chamber
for almost nine years." Brown seemed vulnerable on few issues *other*

than capital punishment, making continued emphasis on the Chessman case one of the challenger's only viable campaign strategies. Even with Brown's victory (by more than three hundred thousand votes), the 1962 race set a key precedent: because of the Chessman controversy, the death penalty now became a wedge issue in California political campaigns.[20]

To thwart attacks from the right during the election year, Brown allowed frequent application of the death penalty; eleven executions in 1962 caused California to lead the nation, with Florida and Texas trailing close behind. Once re-elected, though, Brown resumed his fight against the death penalty. Mindful of the Judiciary Committee failure of 1960 (a process repeated with much less fanfare in 1961), early in his new term Brown tried a different tactic, calling for a four-year moratorium on most executions. Urging California to join "other states and nations," Brown singled out New York, "a state similar to ours in population, ethnic concentration and socio-economic structure," for having made no use of the death penalty in 1962. The *New York Times,* in turn, would praise Brown for leading "the rebellion of civilized man's conscience against capital punishment." In an interview with *Look,* Brown explained, "It is a fact that we sentence to death members of minority races, the poor, the friendless. . . . We are prone to minimize [sentences] in defendants who are more like ourselves." Despite a slight overall increase in support for capital punishment (56 percent, versus 28 percent opposition), a 1963 Field Poll recorded even public support for the four-year moratorium (44 to 44 percent). After squeaking through the Assembly by one vote, however, the bill again did not make it past the hostile Senate Judiciary Committee, and it died in June 1963. Brown had continued to pursue a highly visible, if strategically doomed, legislative fight for abolition.[21]

Unable to end the death penalty legislatively, in mid-1963 Brown again shifted gears, utilizing his executive powers to grant clemency and temporary stays. After January 1963, in fact, no more executions would take place during Brown's administration. In contrasting California's efforts with those in Oregon, where voters repealed the death penalty in a 1964 referendum, *The Nation* referred to the former's "*de facto* repeal," attributing it "largely [to] the work of Governor Brown, a man of character and humanity." For a brief moment, a decline in public support for the death penalty in California accompanied Brown's creation of a death row logjam, as shown in a Field Poll of late April 1965. Support for the death penalty had dropped in California to 51 percent, while opposition had risen to 39 percent. Nationally, the rising tide of popular abolitionist support, coupled with the declining frequency of executions, made it appear that the death penalty, in the words of a *Nation* headline, was "on the way out."[22]

While impressed by Brown's executive efforts, *The Nation* nonetheless called Oregon's 1964 referendum the "more honest" means of eliminating the death penalty. Hugo Adam Bedau, a participant in the effort, later said the Oregon campaign "allows us to study the abolition movement at the summit of its success." After a similar initiative was narrowly defeated six years earlier, a handful of activists had formed the Oregon Council to Abolish the Death Penalty. The Council directed an intensive publicity campaign, canvassing neighborhoods, sending position statements to newspapers across the state, and bringing prominent spokespersons like Donal E. J. MacNamara and Clinton T. Duffy to symposia in Portland. The campaign, as recalled by Bedau, attempted to "persuade the public to oppose unnecessary executions, unfair death sentences, and cruel and unusual punishments; and to favor safe incarceration, the possibility of rehabilitation, and the right to life." Sixty percent of the voting public responded favorably to the drive, and capital punishment was effectively abolished in Oregon. The Oregon Council thus engineered a successful public campaign, one which promoted the prevailing criminological arguments against the death penalty. Though confident in the soundness of those same principles, neither Brown nor California's main anti–death penalty organizations showed any interest in such an initiative effort. By mid-1965, it appeared that Brown's logjam strategy, together with the growing reluctance of the courts to allow executions, had provided an alternate, increasingly successful route toward abolition.[23]

Few events had greater impact on postwar California politics, however, than the Watts conflict of August 1965. The aftermath divided the Democratic Party, pitting Brown versus segregationist L.A. mayor Sam Yorty in the 1966 primary; and that the riots ever happened in the first place provided fuel for the right's attack on the incumbent governor. Thus, as Gerald Horne maintains, "The uprising was a rebellion against white supremacy but it also may have been a successful recruiting message for the right wing." In deploring "the rule of the jungle" in Watts, moderate Republican Senator Thomas Kuchel demonstrated the racial coding inherent in the right's critique. As Governor Brown later wrote, "Fear was rampant among white citizens after the ghetto riots in Watts in 1965 and later in the Hunter's Point district of San Francisco." The result was that "the people tended to equate Negro unrest with *all* crime."

Several observers, including Governor Brown, accused Reagan of riding the "white backlash" vote into office. Ultimately, the impact of the law and order issue would be reciprocal: not only did it transform California politics, but the ascendant New Right now created an enduringly racialized politics of criminal justice.[24]

Declaring "our city streets have become jungle paths after dark," Ronald Reagan announced his candidacy for governor in January 1966. "Crimes of violence in California cities," he boldly stated, "now total more than New York, Pennsylvania, and Massachusetts combined." Asked by reporters whether he favored the death penalty, the future governor answered yes, "because penologists say it is a deterrent." Reagan devoted most of his initial statement to attacking the cost of government, but nevertheless promised to strengthen the hand of local law enforcement to fight crime. In making these pledges, the New Right tapped into public fears resulting from escalating crime rates. Though considerably skewed because of Watts arrests, crime was indeed rising in California during the mid-1960s. Although FBI "index crimes"—murder, rape, aggravated assault, burglary, larceny and auto theft—doubled by mid-decade, Columbia University sociologist Sophia Robison disputed whether a national trend toward violent crime actually existed: "The chance of being murdered on a given day is approximately one in two million," Robison told *Time*. Yet by mid-1966 California public opinion polls declared the two most pressing problems faced by California to be "crime, drugs, and juvenile delinquency," and "racial problems." The respective gubernatorial candidates proposed starkly different approaches to the problem of crime, but in the post-Watts atmosphere, Brown's slogan "justice-compassion-understanding" proved to be no match for Reagan's "law and order" candidacy.[25]

In connecting law and order to a broader assault on the welfare state, Reagan thus carried the mantle of Goldwaterism into the 1966 campaign. Covering a Reagan campaign stop for the *New York Times*, Tom Wicker said the candidate did not "mention Goldwater in his speech. . . . He only talked about the same things." Race, Wicker recognized, stood at the center of Reagan's message: "He talked about crime in the streets, the burden of California's welfare program, high taxes, swollen bureaucracy, 'planners,' a Great Society program under which 'we cannot remain a free society,' the 'arson and murder' in Watts, and the 'philosophy that only government has the answer' to people's problems." In his pointedly titled "How to Succeed with the Backlash," *The Nation*'s Carey McWilliams said Reagan's statement about Watts—"We must not recognize the rioters"—was a "code phrase which means that demands for reform made by demonstrators must be rejected out of hand." A Field Poll taken in late September correspondingly found both increased support and substantially diminished opposition to capital punishment (54 percent to 30). Throughout the election, the death penalty formed a staple, if not dominant, component of Reagan's campaign.[26]

In the aftermath of Reagan's landslide victory, Brown reckoned with the fate of the sixty-four men who remained on death row at the end of 1966. A range of anti–death penalty voices—including the Friends Committee on Legislation and San Francisco Catholic Archbishop Joseph T. McGucken—encouraged him to commute all death sentences to life in prison. As Wallace Turner wrote in *The New York Times*, Brown now "ponder[ed] for the last time the question that has been a nightmare haunting him for the last eight years in office." With a single stroke, the outgoing governor had the chance to make a final, definitive statement against the death penalty. Yet, according to Turner, Brown again feared placing "himself above the laws of the state that provide for the death penalty." Another option floated was a blanket reprieve of all death sentences in order to allow the legislature to vote again on it.[27]

Faced with two options quite consistent with his executive and legal abolitionist strategies, Brown chose neither. Instead, on December 28, 1966, Brown commuted the sentences of just four condemned murderers. A story adjacent to the *New York Times* account of this final action asked Brown to assess the role of the "white backlash" in his defeat. "Whether we like it or not, the people want separation of the races," he said in analyzing Reagan's victory. As Brown exited office, nearly one-third of the sixty men left waiting on death row were African American, a fact of no small political importance for the new administration.[28]

The Reagan Revolution

In his first days in office Reagan continued to make law and order his overriding theme. Appropriately, crime was the first subject of the new governor's inaugural speech. "Californians should be able to walk our streets safely day and night," he said, assuring how "lawlessness by the mob, as with the individual, will not be tolerated." Seamlessly transitioning into welfare, "another of our major problems," Reagan laid the groundwork for his most famous pledge: "To squeeze and cut and trim until we reduce the size of government." Writing in *The Nation* nine months later, Phil Kerby began, "California, under its thirty-third Governor, Ronald Reagan, is in the throes of a middle-class revolution against the poor." Throughout his first year in office, Reagan slashed the Medi-Cal budget, enacted drastic cuts in the state's mental heath services, and imposed a hiring freeze for state personnel. Despite firing liberal UC president Clark Kerr, Reagan faced greater opposition in his battle to reduce the state university budget and impose tuition; in fact, the political response to cuts affecting middle class voters was strong enough that Reagan ended up pushing through tax increases to pay for a record 1968 state budget. Nevertheless, in his first year in office Reagan began to chip away at the foundations of postwar California liberalism, making all state welfare spending contested political terrain. Not coincidentally, as they sought to implement the Goldwater vision, Reagan and his staff brought the death penalty back into the political spotlight.[29]

No fewer than twelve executions were scheduled to take place at San Quentin during Reagan's first eight months in office. If realized, the number would have exceeded by four the total number of executions carried out in the entire United States over the preceding two years. Four of the twelve were African Americans, and it was their cases that garnered the most attention. In mid-March 1967, Reagan reached his first clemency decision, refusing to commute the sentence of Paul LaVergne, a Black Muslim who had been sent to death row for the murder of a white cab driver. A San Diego prosecutor had called it a "sacrificial killing" of a white man by a Black Muslim, a point surprisingly seconded by LaVergne's attorney during the clemency hearing. "Society has, by its deprivation of the Negro, created minds receptive to the Black Muslim ideology," the defense lawyer told Reagan's staff, adding that LaVergne "really didn't know that he did wrong." Such a far-flung argument promised to carry little weight with Reagan's clemency secretary, former Free Speech Movement prosecutor Edwin V. Meese III. Although spared the gas chamber by a successful appeal to Supreme Court Justice William Douglas, who was an active participant in the legal logjam strategy, LaVergne provided a useful foil for the new administration. For Reagan, capital punishment insured "self-defense for society" against threats like urban violence, a category now increasingly linked in public debate to black militance.[30]

In early April, Reagan confronted the case of Aaron Mitchell, who had been convicted of killing a police officer during a Sacramento robbery in 1963. Like the increasingly active NAACP Legal Defense Fund, Mitchell objected to the death penalty's racist application. After quoting statistics showing racial disparity in death sentencing, Mitchell told *Eb-*

ony, "I know that my being a Negro has been a big factor in everything that has happened to me." Because the crime was a cop-killing, Brown had refused to commute Mitchell's sentence, but Reagan distinguished himself from his predecessor in how he approached clemency matters. Claiming "I am not an attorney," Reagan let Meese handle the clemency hearing while the governor attended the Academy Awards ceremony in Los Angeles. Responding to charges that Reagan's disregard for "just another Negro's life" was callous, Meese explained that politics were "the only thing I can think of that does enter into his decision." Since Mitchell was to be California's first execution in four years, and the only one in the United States during 1967, political considerations unavoidably shaped Reagan's action. As a *Newsweek* headline declared, Aaron Mitchell's execution proved California's new governor to be a "man of conviction." [31]

Ironically, Reagan's cynical political usage of the death penalty was expressed most clearly in his June 1967 commutation of Calvin Thomas's sentence. Thomas, an African American, had been convicted in 1965 by a Los Angeles jury for throwing a bomb into his girlfriend's home, killing her three-year-old son. Psychiatric examinations, however, showed Thomas to suffer from brain damage and chronic mental illness. A June 21 execution date had been stayed indefinitely by Justice Douglas, but late in the month Reagan announced his decision. Timed to coincide with the first day of arguments in a NAACP lawsuit charging racial disparity in California's use of the death penalty, Reagan commuted Thomas's sentence to life without possibility of parole. "I think this is one where you might want to consider clemency," Meese reportedly advised Reagan. In opposition to critics of the death penalty's racial bias or Reagan's cuts in the state's mental health budget, there could not have been a more perfect public gesture. However appropriate, Reagan's grant of clemency for Calvin Thomas sprang from a crass political calculus, but one entirely consistent with the goals of the new antiliberal administration. [32]

According to journalist Bill Boyarsky, Reagan's staff viewed capital punishment as critical to the success of the new regime. An early administration promotional booklet listed Reagan's "refusal to interfere with court decisions on capital punishment" as one of the governor's signal achievements. An administration insider, Boyarsky wrote, explained that Aaron Mitchell's "execution provided evidence of Reagan's insistence on law and order," which at the time was synonymous with "Negro militance and violence." Largely due to the work of the NAACP, no further executions would take place during Reagan's two terms in office. Yet the ongoing legal battle gave Reagan a further political target, namely the liberal courts and their responsiveness to civil rights organizations. Along with Florida, California was the only state to consistently fight for the death penalty in the higher courts between 1967 and 1972. When an NAACP lawsuit successfully halted a string of five executions planned for a twenty-day period (!) in July 1967, Reagan, the *San Francisco Chronicle* reported, "wished there was a way 'to issue a stay of execution to those people in the days ahead who are going to be murdered.'" From 1966 onward California juries gave out the death sentence with increasing frequency, and a 1969 Field Poll found a whopping 65 percent support for capital punishment. Central to the New Right's law and order critique, the racialized politics of crime during the Reagan years served a larger purpose. When the governor called for an "urban renewal project on death row," postwar California liberalism itself had been condemned.[33]

The right's position on criminal justice had thus triumphed by the end of the decade. The Chessman debate had illustrated the widespread belief among reformers, ordinary citizens, and influential state officials in the ideal of prison rehabilitation. Even key detractors like Governor Brown had argued against clemency in the name of individual reform (or Chessman's lack thereof). In the wake of rising crime rates, urban rebellions, and increasingly defiant black protest, criminal behavior was now popularly associated with African Americans, a group not included in the conception of rehabilitation espoused by public officials. Indeed, from the right's perspective, therapeutic reform was not even an issue: in 1967 Reagan labeled inner city upheavals as the "riots of lawbreakers and mad dogs against the people." "Mad dogs" was a term used by California public officials to characterize sex criminals in late 1940s, but by the mid-1960s it was used by the governor to describe black rioters. The main target of right-wing demonization may have changed, but with Reagan in office, the law and order regime first envisioned by postwar Southern California officials had been firmly put in place.[34]

Just as the right animalized the terms of criminal justice, however, the left began to wholly reject the technocratic principles of postwar penology. African American prisoners and political leaders, as well as the increasingly radical New Left, critiqued the systems of parole, indeterminate sentencing, and institutional therapy as racially biased. In both the

NAACP-led campaign against the death penalty and the Black Panther-inspired prison reform movement, the demand for racial justice replaced the rehabilitative ideal at the center of public debate.

The Liberal Courts

The movement against the death penalty changed dramatically in the mid-1960s. In the first half of the decade, abolitionists waged a political struggle aimed at ending the death penalty by either legislative decision or popular referendum. After the successful Oregon initiative, four states (Iowa, West Virginia, Vermont, and New York) either abolished or virtually eliminated the death penalty. Coupled with the increasing reluctance of the higher courts, the expressed opposition of the Johnson Administration allowed abolitionists to look forward to what the eminent criminologist Thorsten Sellin called "the inevitable end of capital punishment." Led by the Legal Defense Fund and the ACLU, however, the movement charted a different course beginning in the middle of the decade: the courts, rather than the ballot box, became the target of abolitionist efforts. As a number of analysts have argued, this shift from a political to a legal struggle had several ramifications. Most important, popular abolitionist support, which reached its height in the middle of the decade, diminished considerably by the early 1970s. While successful in the courts, the arguments of racial and class discrimination made by lawyers were not linked to a broader popular movement to end the death penalty.[35]

Like Pat Brown, a handful of abolitionists had made the discriminatory application of the death penalty central to their critiques in the early 1960s. This shift away from arguments put forth in the name of rehabilitative penology was evident in anti–death penalty feature stories, many of which highlighted the cases of various African American prisoners. Titled "The Man Who May Break Chessman's Death-Cell Record," a 1960 Look story profiled Edgar Labat, a black man on death row in Louisiana since 1950 for armed robbery and "assisting" in a rape. The next year a Commonweal editorial endorsed the efforts of the NAACP on behalf of Preston Cobb, Jr., a fifteen-year-old African American sentenced to die in Georgia. In a 1962 article in The Nation, Sylvan Shane provided a detailed account of the execution of Nathaniel Lipscomb, an African American; "I was a murderer," Shane concluded, "along with all of the other citizens of Maryland, in whose name Nathaniel Lipscomb had been killed." No longer focused on Chessman, this shifting media representation of the typical death row prisoner corresponded with added official attention to the death penalty's unequal application. A 1963 *New Republic* editorial quoted James V. Bennett, director of the U.S. Bureau of Prisons, as saying "with a few isolated exceptions the persons put to death each year are penniless and friendless. . . . More than half are Negroes." As the civil rights movement brought questions of racial justice to the national stage, abolitionists likewise made discriminatory application their central critique of the death penalty.[36]

Concurrent with this change in mainstream recognition, civil rights organizations like the NAACP's Legal Defense Fund (LDF) gained prominence in the abolitionist effort. As Herbert Haines has recently analyzed, in 1963 the LDF began to attack racial disparities in southern death sentences for rape. These efforts, moreover, coincided with an emerging debate among legal scholars about the constitutionality of the death penalty. Focused on the question of whether capital punishment could be considered "cruel and unusual punishment," the debate gained important attention from Supreme Court justice Arthur Goldberg. In a dissenting opinion in a case involving a death-sentenced rapist (*Rudolph v. Alabama*, 1963), Goldberg questioned whether "in view of the worldwide trend against the death penalty as punishment for rape, such an application is a violation of the 'evolving standards of decency' that go along with the moral evolution of society."[37] Following Goldberg's lead, the LDF began to challenge every execution on these terms; by 1966, it adopted nationally Brown's strategy of creating a logjam in the courts to prevent all executions. To carry out this plan, the LDF began to defend every condemned prisoner, regardless of his color or crime, in order to force the Supreme Court ultimately to rule on the constitutionality of the death penalty. In large part because of the LDF's efforts, executions dwindled in the U.S. to one each in 1967 and 1968, the former (that of Aaron Mitchell) taking place in California.[38]

By mid-decade, then, the main stage of abolitionist efforts had shifted from the ballot box to the courts. After the 1964 referendum in Oregon, political organizing against the death penalty dwindled, and, as Haines observes, "For the first time, *lawyers* became the shock troops of the anti-death penalty movement." Joined by the ACLU, the LDF focused exclusively on legal challenges to the death penalty, and in the process paid little attention to public opinion. The LDF, according to Eric Muller, "simply did not consider the difficult task of public education on the death penalty as one of its important responsibilities." As legal organizations, of course, neither the LDF nor the ACLU could have been

expected to direct a public education campaign. By mid-decade the size
and strength of popular anti–death penalty organizations had steadily
declined, however. The infrequency of executions, as well as the increasing prominence of the Vietnam War, helped reduce the importance of
the death penalty as a national political issue. Independent of an organized movement, abolitionism acquired by the late 1960s a new set of
popular associations. It was now led by a civil rights organization, thus
placing it in an entirely new category in the public imagination. Though
by no means the only cause, the "rise of litigators to a dominant position in the movement," Haines maintains, "contributed to the withering
away of whatever was left of citizen-based, political abolitionism." [39]

The decline of organized abolitionist efforts occurred exactly as both
public and official opinion against the death penalty reached national
high-water marks in the postwar period. In mid-1966, a Harris Survey
showed 47 percent support for abolition, versus 38 percent for retention of the death penalty, and a contemporaneous Gallup poll recorded
roughly similar numbers (47 percent to 42). In these and other polls
women and African Americans expressed clear abolitionist views, while
opinion among Protestants and Catholics both increased to slight majorities against capital punishment. Most notable, perhaps, was the strong
anti–death penalty sentiment among blue collar workers, whom a 1966
Gallup poll recorded as 50 percent opposed (to 40 percent in favor). In
analyzing similar results, Harris pollsters found it "surprising that the
less well-educated, more rural and small-town residents—women especially—carry the day against capital punishment." Such grassroots opposition stood in contrast to the basis of death penalty support identified
in the survey. "The more affluent parts of society, especially among men
and suburban dwellers, are more in favor of continuing capital punishment," the Harris survey said. Less than three years later, though, a Gallup poll reported 51 to 40 percent support of the death penalty. Opposition had plummeted among blue collar workers, Democrats, Catholics,
and Protestants, and it dipped considerably among women. First defined
by Reagan in California, the New Right's stance on capital punishment
triumphed precisely as the NAACP gained increasing success in its legal
campaign.[40]

The gains in popular support for abolition had occurred amidst the
Great Society. Speaking on behalf of LBJ's administration, Attorney General Ramsay Clark told Congress in 1966: "We favor the abolition of the
death penalty. Modern penology, with its correctional and rehabilitative
skills, affords greater protection to society than the death penalty, which

is inconsistent with its goals." Simultaneously, nearly all of the major Protestant denominations spoke in favor of abolition, as did the Conference of American Rabbis and influential Catholic leaders like Cardinal Cushing of Boston. The American Correctional Association, as well as a number of prison officials, voiced opposition across the country. Organized labor, though, was notably absent from public discussion of the issue, as it had been since the participation by left unions in the CRC campaign to save Wells. Yet such official abolitionism was not accompanied by a grassroots organizing campaign, and thus during the explosive late 1960s the New Right quickly captured the popular debate over the death penalty. As a result, the California transition from Brown to Reagan was mirrored at the national level: the death penalty contradicted the principles of the Great Society, but it fit comfortably with the law and order vision of the Nixon regime.[41]

The Radical Critique

As capital punishment appeared increasingly extinct in the late 1960s, anti-death penalty activists like the Friends and those linked to the Black Power Movement turned more directly toward prison reform. Inspired by the emerging prisoners' movement, these groups rejected both the theory and especially the practice of rehabilitative penology. Growing out of the work of Black Muslims and with strong links to the Black Panther Party, the prisoners' movement took root in reaction to the simmering racial hostilities at San Quentin under Louis "Big Red" Nelson, whom Reagan appointed as warden in 1967. The movement spelled out many of the criticisms of rehabilitation made by other activists of the period. At the end of the decade, the writings of prisoners like Eldridge Cleaver and especially George Jackson became increasingly popular among both prisoners and sympathetic left organizers. The growing radicalism of the left in the late 1960s, symbolized by its rejection of nonviolence, further conditioned the embrace of militant prisoners like Cleaver and Jackson. As Eric Cummins demonstrates, the left of the San Francisco Bay Area proved especially responsive to the emerging prisoners' movement. Radical organizers there had lent strong support to groups like the Black Panthers, many of whose leaders were themselves imprisoned (and, like Huey Newton and Bobby Seale, wrote while incarcerated). Berkeley student activists demonstrated their support for militant prisoners by inviting Eldridge Cleaver to teach a sociology course in 1968, a move that outraged Governor Reagan. Radical prison theorists like Jackson, meanwhile, rejected the premise, and criticized the racist practice, of the rehabilitative ideal. Their criticisms were soon echoed by prison activists across the country.[42]

In 1971 Angela Davis published *If They Come in the Morning,* a collection of essays written by prisoners who, like Davis, were strongly influenced by George Jackson. In her essay "Political Prisoners, Prisons and Black Liberation," Davis analyzed the racist application of the rehabilitative ideal. She particularly referred to the disparity between blacks and whites in the length of their indeterminate sentences, and to the "manifest racism of parole boards." The practice of parole and the indeterminate sentence operated as "authoritarian mechanisms" which kept not only black but politically active prisoners incarcerated. Concerning political discrimination, Davis cited San Quentin's Warden Nelson, who publicly stated that "if the prisons of California become known as 'schools for violent revolution,' the Adult Authority would be remiss in their duty not to keep the inmates longer." In general, Davis concurred with the Folsom Prisoners, whose Manifesto (printed elsewhere in her volume) objected to the "ridiculous title of rehabilitation" applied to a system whereby "our program administrators respond to our hostilities with their own." For Davis, the Folsom Prisoners, and others involved in the prisoner's movement, the practice of rehabilitation reinforced the racism of the criminal justice system.[43]

Because of the efforts of both the abolitionist and the prisoners' movements, the issue of racism became a central concern for the Friends during the period. The Friends Committee on Legislation outlined its position on the death penalty in a pamphlet published in 1970. Written by Trevor Thomas, *This Life We Take* illustrated how mainstream Quaker arguments had changed since the 1950s. By 1970 virtually all of their critiques relied on social science research concerning the practical application of the death penalty, completing the Friends' shift toward a secular frame of opposition outlined earlier. In *This Life We Take,* the practical issue of whether the death penalty was indeed a deterrent, rather than the question of its morality, received the most extensive investigation. After concluding it was not a deterrent, Thomas said "the death penalty in this country is predominantly and disproportionately imposed upon Negroes, the poor and the less educated, and upon men." Like the LDF, the Friends saw the unequal application of the death penalty as rendering it unconstitutional. In conclusion, Thomas posed the question, "What is the alternative?"—to which he replied, "The answer is epitomized in two words, *rehabilitation* and *prevention.*" Although the practical application of the death penalty received the bulk of the pamphlet's attention, Thomas's conclusion showed how the rehabilitative ideal remained an integral concern of the Friends.[44]

The very next year, however, the Friends' *Struggle for Justice* outlined a radically new approach toward criminal justice. Written by a study group comprised of veteran activists and former prisoners, the book departed from all prior Quaker advocacy. "The horror that is the American prison system," the Friends wrote, "grew out of an eighteenth-century reform by Pennsylvania Quakers and others against the cruelty and futility of capital and corporal punishment. This two-hundred-year-old experiment has failed." The prison riots witnessed across the United States during the early 1970s, they argued, served to "warn the public that prisoners will no longer submit to whatever is done to them in the name of 'treatment' or 'rehabilitation.'" The quotation marks indicated that the rehabilitative ideal was no longer sacrosanct for the Friends. In fact, the book's introduction declared the entire "reformist prescription," meaning "more 'experts'," "improved therapeutic programs," and greater use of the indeterminate sentence, to be "bankrupt."[45]

Throughout *Struggle for Justice,* the Friends questioned what they termed as the "coercive" nature of a prison system based on rehabilitation. In general, the authors frequently stressed, "The justice system functions to maintain a racist relationship between the white majority and the black, brown, red, and yellow minorities in America." At the heart of the justice system lay the "paternalistic" assumption that prison officials knew precisely what constituted a rehabilitated prisoner. Relying on analysis popularized by the radical left in the late 1960s, the authors explained how this paternalism "becomes an intolerable form of colonialism when invoked by middle class whites to run the lives of blacks, Chicanos, Indians and the poor." Like the LDF, the Friends thus singled out racism as the dominant problem with the American criminal justice system. To confront this issue, the authors advocated the elimination of the rehabilitative ideal, the founding principle of the justice system the Quakers had helped create.[46]

The critique outlined in *Struggle for Justice* reflected an emerging consensus among prison activists concerning the discriminatory practice of rehabilitative penology. With the help of left journalists and scholars, the criticisms initiated by incarcerated prisoners reached a broader audience. In *Kind and Unusual Punishment* (1973), the journalist Jessica Mitford presented a sharply critical view of the criminal justice system based on her research inside prisons like San Quentin. In her conclusion, Mitford endorsed the work of the Prisoners Union, a growing organization dedicated to prisoners' workplace, civil, and human rights, as well as to "abolishment of the indeterminate sentence and all its ramifications." Similarly, in *The Politics of Punishment* (1973), the sociologist Erik Olin Wright brought together a collection of criminologists, radical lawyers, prison psychiatrists, and prisoners. Based on his research inside San Quentin, Wright observed that "the hallmark of the 'enlightened' liberal prison is its rehabilitation programs. Nearly all the prisoners interviewed felt that the rehabilitation programs at San Quentin were almost worthless." Like many prisoners, Wright concluded that in practice, rehabilitation clearly reinforced the racial discrimination inherent in the California criminal justice system.[47]

By the early 1970s prisoners, activists, and left social scientists had thus rejected the rehabilitative ideal. In the eyes of these observers, making a prisoner's release conditional on his proof of his own personal reform amounted to "coercion." The judgment of each prisoner, they said, was made by prison officials who were both politically appointed and motivated by the politics of the period. A little more than a decade earlier, the Friends, as well as virtually all other participants in the abolitionist and prison reform efforts, had espoused great faith in the abilities of middle class experts to manage programs premised on individual therapy. Yet by 1971 the Friends compared the work of those experts to a colonial occupation. Along with the legal abolitionist campaign, the prison reform movement made the issue of racist discrimination its primary argument against American criminal justice practice. And where the LDF ignored the role of public opinion in sustaining anti–death penalty protest, reform advocates like the Friends now rejected the ideal which had historically provided the core intellectual framework of middle class abolitionism.

The *Furman* Decision

In the spring of 1972, the Legal Defense Fund argued its case against capital punishment before the Supreme Court. Led by Anthony Amsterdam, a Stanford law professor, the LDF presented its argument in *Furman v. Georgia,* a case involving the death sentence of an African American convicted of killing a white defendant. Amsterdam began by offering statistical evidence showing how the death penalty had overwhelmingly discriminated against minorities and the poor; since 1930 (when official records began to be kept), more than fifty percent of those executed had been African American. As a result, Amsterdam said the death penalty violated "evolving standards of decency," a key clause in the Eighth Amendment provision against cruel and unusual punishment. By a five to four margin, the Supreme Court sided with the LDF, and in June 1972 ruled the death penalty unconstitutional. The discriminatory application of the death penalty, according to the Court, was not consistent with contemporary "standards of decency." [48]

The widespread popular response to the Furman decision, however, quickly made the LDF's "evolving standard of decency" argument difficult to sustain. President Nixon, who had made his support for the death penalty a staple of his law and order campaign in 1968, voiced immediate criticism of the *Furman* decision; citing the Lindbergh Law as an example of the deterrent effect of the death penalty, Nixon hoped the Court's decision did "not go so far as to rule out capital punishment for kidnapping and hijacking." A Gallup Poll taken that year showed 57 percent support for the death penalty, a significant increase from six years earlier. In response to *Furman*, three states introduced bills to restore the death penalty. Once more, though, the popular politics of the death penalty played out most visibly in California. [49]

In November 1972, two-thirds of California voters supported Proposition 17, a ballot initiative calling for restoration of the state's death penalty. Recognizing the U.S. Supreme Court's intention to end capital punishment, the California Supreme Court had pre-emptively outlawed it in early 1972. After *Furman* was announced, Reagan immediately called on California voters to pass Proposition 17. Writing in *The Nation*, Mary Ellen Leary argued that the measure's eventual success "show[ed] what a gloomy gap exists between the public's view of the subject and the decisions of California and U.S. Courts." Proposition 17, moreover, passed despite the objections of some powerful popular and official voices. Former Governor Brown and the actor Bill Cosby signed the anti-17 position on the official state ballot, and both the *Los Angeles Times* and *San Francisco Chronicle* editorialized against the measure, primarily on the grounds that the death penalty was not a deterrent. Richard McGee, the former head of the Department of Corrections, also expressed his opposition: "Taking human life in this deliberate fashion," McGee argued, "is beneath the dignity of a modern democratic government." In favor of 17, though, were the governor, a powerful network of law enforcement officials from throughout the state, and a notable figurehead—Nancy Reagan, now making her first entry into actual policymaking by campaigning in favor of the death penalty in California. Led

by the Reagans, the overwhelming majority of California voters expressed their opposition to the Constitutional rulings made by the "liberal courts."[50]

Four years later, the Supreme Court allowed the reinstatement of the
death penalty. In *Gregg v. Georgia,* the Court held (by a seven to two
margin) that the enactment of coherent sentencing procedures, as well
as the provision for automatic review by state appeals courts, made the
death penalty constitutionally permissible. As Haines states, "The most
likely explanation for the Court's change of direction lies in public opinion." Justices Stewart and White both cited the California initiative (as
well as a similar Massachusetts referendum) and public opinion polls
as contradicting the LDF's claims regarding "evolving standards of decency." "If the people wanted the death penalty back," Haines summarizes, "standards must not have evolved so much as abolitionists had
claimed."[51]

After Chessman

In the twelve years between Caryl Chessman's execution and the passage
of Proposition 17, the terms of criminal justice debate shifted from institutional rehabilitation to racial control. Yet for all of its symbolic importance, Aaron Mitchell's 1967 execution had generated only limited
public protest, receiving no attention from prominent journals like *The
Nation.* Although much smaller in size than the Chessman vigil, the
crowds gathered outside of San Quentin did exude starkly divided pas-
sions. Saying "Life is getting too cheap," former Governor Brown now
endorsed the protest. Conversely, the lone supporter of the execution on
hand, American Nazi Party leader George Lincoln Rockwell, carried a
sign reading "Gas the only cure for black crime and red treason." Such
notable input notwithstanding, Mitchell's execution failed to generate
national controversy.[52]

Like the rest of the national media, *The Nation* focused on the more
dramatic protests occurring the same week as Mitchell's execution. In
contrast to the few hundred who showed up at San Quentin, sixty-five
thousand people marched in San Francisco to commence the Spring Mobilization Against the Vietnam War. For the New Left, the escalation of
the war made the issue of an individual execution seem quite small; yet,
tapping into public fears of urban unrest and the growing militance of
black protest, the California New Right had already begun to capture
the debate over criminal justice. While the LDF and the Black Panther–

led prisoners' movement posed powerful, influential critiques of a racially biased criminal justice system, neither was linked to a broader political coalition. In the early part of the decade, California's liberal leadership had resisted waging a popular campaign against the death penalty. Ronald Reagan's successful "law and order" strategy in 1966 and passage of Proposition 17 six years later, however, exemplified the strength of voter mobilization around the issue. After Jerry Brown assumed the governorship in 1974, the death penalty would remain at the center of political controversy in the state. But as the nation's most prominent New Democrat took office, postwar California liberalism had been effectively dismantled.[53]

Conclusion:
1974 and Beyond

On July 1, 1974, Wesley Robert Wells walked outside the gates of the California Medical Facility at Vacaville. Freed after forty-six years of incarceration, Wells, now sixty-four, was accompanied by cheers from inside the prison as he met journalists and friends. Asked by the press for his immediate reaction, he responded "Man, don't my expression tell you how it feels?" Assuring reporters he was the "same man walking in that I am walking out," Wells nonetheless added, "I'm older and wiser and more self-controlled." Attorneys Charles Garry and Leo Branton led the reception party for Wells, who was then driven back to San Francisco in a silver Rolls-Royce rented by the Delancey Street Foundation, a self-help program for ex-convicts. For the next eighteen months, before suffering a fatal heart attack, the former prisoner made Delancey Street his new home. With assistance from Assemblyman Willie Brown, the Foundation had helped obtain Wells's parole. Outside the gates of Vacaville, though, Wells explained the source of his freedom: "The power of the people got me out, and I am deeply grateful," he said.[1]

The Black Panther Party could not take full credit for winning Wells's release, but the Oakland chapter, along with the Party's chief counsel Charles Garry, had indeed sustained an ongoing publicity campaign on Wells's behalf. Wells had first written to the *Black Panther* in 1969, voicing praise for Garry while simultaneously providing the details of his own case. "Even more cruel and inhuman" than the death penalty, Wells said, was his sentence of life in prison without possibility of parole. In

July 1974, the Panthers held a welcome home reception for Wells at the Son of Man Temple in Oakland, and that summer the *Black Panther* featured a three-part interview in which the formerly condemned inmate recalled nearly half a century of prison experience. Such a lengthy stretch, Garry noted, basically came for stealing a suit and a car battery, followed by Wells's conflicts with other prisoners and guards. "The story of the indeterminate sentence is the story of Bob Wells," Garry observed in 1974. Initiated by prisoners and criminal justice activists in the late 1960s, the critique of indeterminate sentencing as arbitrary and racially discriminatory was increasingly voiced by the courts, public officials, and criminologists during the next decade. To be sure, the Wells case did not create this consensus, which eventually resulted in California's abolition of the indeterminate sentence in 1977. Yet on two separate occasions—in 1954 and 1974—Wells had been the focal point of successful grassroots campaigns against specific injustices, both of which sprang from different sources, and raised separate questions, than the Chessman protests.[2]

Later in 1974, Jerry Brown was elected governor of California, unhindered by his well-defined stance against the death penalty. In many respects, these two separate events—the release of Wells, the election of the younger Brown—represented the logical outcome of the death penalty debate witnessed in California over the preceding two decades. The Wells defense had first been waged by the state's radical left, which by the late 1950s had largely been wiped out by McCarthyism. In its place came a middle class campaign on behalf of Chessman, a struggle predicated on the idea that the death penalty could effectively be eliminated within the confines of liberal state policymaking. For the Brown family, Chessman thus proved to be both a nemesis and a catalyst. Pat Brown was forever haunted by Chessman's ultimate execution, which neither the New Left, the New Right, nor liberal abolitionists would let him forget. While in Jesuit school in 1960, however, Jerry Brown wet his feet politically in the Chessman controversy. According to his biographers, it was the younger Brown's idea to grant the last sixty-day reprieve in order to allow the legislature to debate a bill aimed at abolition. And, a decade and a half later, while the descendants of the Civil Rights Congress scored a visible grassroots success, the younger Brown began to wage a principled but almost exclusively executive campaign against the death penalty.[3]

During Brown's two terms in office, the California right would indeed continue the pro–death penalty politics it had initiated under Reagan. Future governor George Deukmejian authored 1977 legislation reinstating capital punishment, and the following year saw passage of the Briggs referendum, which vastly expanded the number of capital crimes. Brown's opposition to these measures was unequivocal, and throughout his two terms he would appoint a range of like-minded liberal judges, most notably Rose Bird, chief justice of the state Supreme Court. The right, in turn, repeatedly mobilized popular support for capital punishment, particularly in a successful referendum drive that pushed Bird and other liberal justices off the state Supreme Court in 1986. Yet even as he steadfastly opposed the death penalty, Brown presided over the dismantling of rehabilitative criminal justice in California. With his support, the California legislature enacted the Determinate Sentencing Law in 1977, thus eliminating the cornerstone of the rehabilitative ideal. In turn, state spending on therapeutic programs was slashed during Brown's first term. Detached from its postwar moorings, abolitionism by the late 1970s no longer depended on a wider belief in the principles of the new penology. As governor, Reagan had stoked support for the death penalty while at the same time chopping the state mental health budget, but it was his liberal successor who fully completed the right's assault on the state's therapeutic approach to criminal justice.[4]

A broader, more fundamental linkage tied Reagan's vision to that of the first, or at least most notable, New Democrat. "I take a somewhat jaundiced view of the ability of government to perform," candidate Brown declared in 1974, thus marking the rise of a new generation of fiscally conservative, socially liberal Democrats. As Mike Davis points out, Jerry Brown's belt-tightening measures during his first term came amid an inflationary era when the state sported a three-million-dollar budget surplus. Under Pat Brown, the death penalty contradicted the principles of a state broadly committed to social justice in general, and to welfare spending in particular. No comparable tension would exist, though, for Jerry Brown and the state's New Democrats, who undermined the redistributive promise of postwar California liberalism in much more direct fashion than their New Right predecessors.[5]

Among other major actors in the postwar abolitionist debate, Caryl Chessman's case also left an instructive if diverse legacy. No longer would the postwar rehabilitative ideal be endorsed so easily by criminal justice activists and prisoners, especially after the growing prisoners movement of the late 1960s exposed its fundamental flaws. For the nascent New Left in the Bay Area, meanwhile, the contradiction between official rhetoric and practice, and the perils of relying on liberal politicians simply to do the right thing, both first surfaced in May 1960.

Though equally disappointed, mainstream abolitionists like the Friends and influential liberal voices like *The Nation* would continue to support Governor Pat Brown's legislative and executive strategies as the appropriate, most effective means of ending the death penalty in the state. Active throughout Chessman's defense, the ACLU would help lay the groundwork for the NAACP-led legal struggle, which ultimately succeeded in stopping capital punishment for ten years and slowing its usage for many more. Liberal criminologists and behavioral experts temporarily remained at the forefront of criminal justice discussion, a position they first acquired, and in many ways defined, during the Chessman campaign. Moreover, the reciprocal nature of the specialists' embrace would remain intact—a 1969 issue of *Psychology Today*, in fact, carried a feature article by Chessman, the magazine identifying him on its cover as a posthumous "expert" on crime.[6]

The New Right, however, by the early 1970s had fundamentally altered the terms of criminal justice debate, placing politicians rather than experts at the forefront and making liberal judges rhetorical enemies of the "popular will." A product of the white backlash capitalized on by Ronald Reagan, law and order proved to be an enduring, fundamental component of racialized antiliberal politics both in California and across the nation. Beginning with the Chessman case, state Republicans—spotting a gap between public opinion and executive as well as judicial policy—launched a sustained popular campaign in favor of capital punishment. Confident in their principles, yet reluctant to bring these same views directly to the voters, California abolitionists pursued first a legislative then a legal struggle against the death penalty in the 1960s. The very successes scored by abolitionists in the higher courts during the late 1960 and early 1970s, in turn, provided the New Right with a political opening in which to launch its sustained attack on Great Society liberalism.[7]

Indispensable both to the postwar abolitionist movement and to Pat Brown's larger liberal vision was a profound confidence in the managerial capacities of state administrators and various professional specialists to successfully engineer a well-ordered society. In criminal justice, this outlook translated into tremendous support from vocal professional sectors for rehabilitative penology, complete with a vast network of mental health experts and various state-appointed officials. Yet the Chessman debate revealed the tenuous foothold this therapeutic approach maintained among the voting public, and the terms of derision used by death penalty proponents during the 1950s—criminals as "mad dogs" and psychopaths, their supporters as "sob sisters"—laid the groundwork for the assault on rehabilitative penology launched by the New Right a decade later. As illustrated by Pat Brown's stance in the Chessman case, however, even those who firmly believed in the principle of institutional reform disagreed on the qualities that comprised it. What Ronald Reagan inchoately realized was how politically powerful the negative arguments about rehabilitation could become when applied to entire categories of people, whether common criminals, inner-city rioters, black nationalists, or student protesters. In turn, by separating abolitionism from the state's commitment to therapeutic penology, Jerry Brown solidified Reagan's reactionary effort to demonize a variety of groups as permanently outside the scope of "rehabilitation."

In the wake of Brown's efforts, the ideal of therapeutic reform has largely faded from criminal justice discussion since the 1970s. As outlined earlier, this absence hardly can be seen as permanent: belief in the prison as a site of individual regeneration has periodically resurfaced throughout the course of American history. Yet even if the rehabilitative ideal were to return, as Christian Parenti has recently cautioned, it conceivably could co-exist with popular support for the death penalty; "Therapy and the gas chamber are by no means mutually exclusive," Parenti concludes. Although neither Reagan, who rejected reform and advocated the death penalty, nor Jerry Brown, who eliminated rehabilitation but favored abolition, put forth such a view, this does not at all suggest that a revised combination is not possible. Among contemporary anti–death penalty activists, though, the popular argument proposing life in prison without possibility of parole as a viable substitute for executions illustrates a different mix of Parenti's variables. Aimed primarily at removing the complicity of innocent citizens in state-sanctioned murder, as well as at eliminating the possibility of wrongful executions, abolitionism based on such a sentencing alternative rarely carries with it any consideration of the therapeutic well-being of people consigned to spend the rest of their lives in prison.[8]

In 1995, the *Sacramento Bee* published a three-part series about the fortunes of the formerly condemned inmates who, as a result of the California Supreme Court elimination of the state's death penalty in 1972 (a position reaffirmed in 1976), eventually were paroled. In so doing, the *Bee* study yielded unusual insight into life after death row. Forty-seven of 173 previously condemned convicts were released from prison between 1977 and 1991, nearly two-thirds of them prior to George Deukmejian's election as governor in 1983. Able to locate three-quarters of those freed,

Bee reporter Mareva Brown provided both analysis and a series of biographical sketches. Of the thirty-six parolees she (and researcher Rebecca Boyd) found, nineteen were never rearrested, nine were resentenced for nonviolent offenses, and eight went back to prison for violent crimes. One of the eight violent convictions was for murder (during a robbery), another for serial rape, and most of the rest were for armed robbery, one of which included attempted murder. Thus, though the violent criminal acts cannot be treated lightly, the parole of California's "classes of '72 and '76" hardly resulted in a rash of violent assaults by those once slated to be executed. Among the nineteen who had not returned to prison, a handful had become successful as mechanics or small businessmen, while most struggled to stay away from drugs and the temptations of the streets. Even more dramatically than most ex-convicts, those among this death row cohort faced the difficulty of reintegrating themselves into daily life on the outside, where a criminal record generally precludes gainful employment or good standing in the community.[9]

Two specific cases documented in the *Bee* report provide a fitting, if not altogether rosy, conclusion to this analysis of the death penalty in postwar California. In the late 1960s Robert L. Massie achieved notoriety by obstructing the NAACP's efforts to save his life. Massie, a white man who had pleaded guilty to capital murder in 1965, claimed that he wanted to be executed, but that abolitionists stood in his way. His story reached the pages of *Esquire*, first told by Truman Capote and then by the prisoner himself. No friend of either liberals or the left, Massie in 1971 nevertheless echoed Wells's statements to supporters ever since receiving clemency from Governor Knight, as well as those Chessman had made in rejecting Governor Brown's proposed sentencing alternative. Though opposed to capital punishment in principle, Massie explained how "having my sentence reduced to life in prison would be a fate much worse than death." Massie had grown up in the state's foster homes, reform schools, and prisons during the height of the rehabilitative era, but he had no desire to remain in what he saw as a "dehumanized hellhole" for the rest of his life. Paroled in 1978, Massie stayed free for only eight months before killing a storeowner during a robbery and returning to death row. Whether seen as an innately recidivist criminal or a product of his environment, he clearly had not been "rehabilitated" by the institutions that kept him.[10] After spending better than two more decades on death row, Massie turned down his final right to appeal, and was executed at San Quentin in April 2001.

By contrast, consider the plight of Paul LaVergne, whose execution

slated for early 1967 had provided Governor Reagan with his first opportunity to define a pro–death penalty stance in opposition to black militance. Spared due to the NAACP's efforts, LaVergne had received parole in December 1977. Trying to escape his death row past, LaVergne
changed his name; he further benefitted when his records were lost by the
Board of Prison Terms. In 1989, though, LaVergne was arrested for stealing a wallet, and five years later he was picked up again for petty theft.
As of 1995, he was in drug rehabilitation and on probation while trying
to raise a teenage son. LaVergne's plight illustrates the difficulty faced by
any convict who leaves prison with few work skills, drug problems, and
a criminal record. Increasingly they return, severely stigmatized, to an
already alien environment where there is neither a safety net nor job
training, and the dangers are many. Yet, during the late 1990s, New
Democrats continued to polish off the American welfare state, and both
incarceration and usage of the death penalty (which Democratic politicians from Bill Clinton and Al Gore to California Governor Gray Davis
strongly support) are at their highest points in the nation's history. Neither killing nor permanently confining the Massies and LaVergnes, however, will eradicate the conditions both inside and especially outside
prison that created them. In this decidedly reactionary anticrime environment, it is thus incumbent upon the left to build a broader social vision,
in which the state again becomes an instrument of social justice rather
than wholesale elimination. A grassroots campaign against the death
penalty, targeting it as representative of a larger, more systematic pattern
of racial and class injustice, seems as good a place as any to start.[11]

Notes

INTRODUCTION

1. On Jacksonians, see David J. Rothman, *The Discovery of the Asylum: Social Order and Disorder in the New Republic* (Boston: Little, Brown, 1971); Rothman, "Perfecting the Prison: United States, 1789–1865," in Norval Morris and David J. Rothman, eds., *The Oxford History of the Prison: The Practice of Punishment in Western Society* (New York: Oxford University Press, 1996), 111–129; and Michael Meranze, *Laboratories of Virtue: Punishment, Revolution, and Authority in Philadelphia, 1760–1835* (Chapel Hill: University of North Carolina Press, 1996). On Progressive Era roots of postwar penology, see Rothman, *Conscience and Convenience: The Asylum and Its Alternatives in Progressive America* (Boston: Little, Brown, 1980); Edgardo Rotman, "The Failure of Reform: United States, 1865–1965," in Morris and Rothman, *The Oxford History of the Prison,* esp. 169–171; and Jonathan Simon, *Poor Discipline: Parole and the Social Control of the Underclass, 1890–1980* (Chicago: University of Chicago Press, 1993). On the "new penology" of the 1950s, see Harry Elmer Barnes and Negley K. Teeters, *New Horizons in Criminology: The American Crime Problem* (New York: Prentice Hall, 1951), ix–xiii.

2. The titles of two of the many articles written during the case are illustrative: "Chessman's Challenge" and "How Many More Chessmans?" See *The New Republic* (March 7, 1960), 14; and *The Nation* (March 26, 1960), 439–440. On Chessman's representativeness, see Elizabeth Hardwick, "The Life and Death of Caryl Chessman," *The Partisan Review* (Summer 1960): 503–513. Many books written about the larger movement devoted single chapters to Chessman's case; see, for example, James Avery Joyce, *Capital Punishment: A World View* (New York: T. Joyce, 1961), 19–55; and Eugene B. Block, *May God Have Mercy: The Case Against Capital Punishment* (San Francisco: Fearon Publishers, 1962), 1–12, 147–152.

3. William L. O'Neill, *Coming Apart: An Informal History of America in the 1960s* (Chicago: Quadrangle Books, 1971), 276–277. For a discussion of the trial transcript appeals, see Frank J. Parker, *Caryl Chessman: The Red Light Bandit* (Chicago: Nelson-Hall, 1975), 143–198.

4. Maurice Isserman, "Where Have All the Convict Heroes Gone: Long Time Passing?" *Radical History Review* 64 (1996): 113–117. Isserman's point was made in a review of a recent work which connects the Chessman case to the prisoners' movement of the late 1960s, namely Eric Cummins, *The Rise and Fall of California's Radical Prison Movement* (Stanford: Stanford University Press, 1994).

5. William M. Kunstler's *Beyond a Reasonable Doubt? The Original Trial of Caryl Chessman* (New York: Morrow Press, 1961) found him not guilty beyond a reasonable doubt; Milton Machlin and William R. Woodfield's *Ninth Life* (New York: Putnam, 1961) declared Chessman's innocence; Parker's *Caryl Chessman*, meanwhile, concluded that he was guilty.

6. On Chessman's early years, see Machlin and Woodfield, *Ninth Life,* 13–17.

7. Machlin and Woodfield, *Ninth Life,* 17–28.

8. On the "red light crimes," see Kunstler, *Beyond a Reasonable Doubt,* 3–20; Machlin and Woodfield, *Ninth Life,* 41–64; and Parker, *Caryl Chessman,* 7–17. On Chessman's confession, see Parker, 69–77. On Section 209 (adopted 1933), see Parker, 93–117. Even though he found Chessman guilty, Parker believed that the victims' initial identifications (prior to the trial) took place in dubious circumstances. Meza identified Chessman from her bedroom window, while Johnson saw him at the police station just prior to identifying him in a police line-up. See Parker, 61–68.

9. On Chessman's decision to represent himself, see Kunstler, *Beyond a Reasonable Doubt,* 21–35; on the timetable (and the Court Reporters' Association quote), see Kunstler, 292–293. Once convicted, Chessman retained several attorneys, beginning with Rosalie T. Asher in September 1949. See Kunstler, 293.

10. On the legal skirmishing after *Cell 2455*'s publication, see Machlin and Woodfield, *Ninth Life,* 187–202; Brown quoted, 196.

11. On transcript hearings, see Machlin and Woodfield, *Ninth Life,* 202–244. Poole to Brown, October 1959, Edmund G. Brown Collection, Bancroft Library, carton 207.

12. On the events of 1960, see chapter four.

13. On the postwar discourse of sexual psychopathy, see Estelle B. Freedman, "'Uncontrolled Desires': The Response to the Sexual Psychopath, 1920–1960," *Journal of American History* 74, no. 1 (June 1987): 85–111; and Allan Berube, *Coming Out Under Fire: The History of Gay Men and Women During World War II* (New York: Plume, 1990), esp. 1–33.

14. Caryl Chessman, *Cell 2455 Death Row* (Englewood Cliffs, N.J.: Prentice Hall, 1954).

15. Franklin Zimring and Gordon Hawkins, *Capital Punishment and the American Agenda* (New York: Cambridge University Press, 1986), esp. 3–25, 154–156, quotes on 155.

16. "Distrust of the people" is a quote from UC Berkeley history professor Richard Drinnon. See Peter Loewenburg, "An Interview with Richard Drinnon," *Studies on the Left* 2 (1961): 76–81. For recent criticisms of the legal campaign against capital punishment, see Herbert H. Haines, *Against Capital Punishment: The Anti–Death Penalty Movement in America, 1972–1994* (New York: Oxford University Press, 1996); David von Drehle, *Among the Lowest of the Dead: The Culture of Death Row* (New York: Times Books, 1995); Michael Mello, *Dead Wrong* (Madison: University of Wisconsin Press, 1997); and Michael Mello and Paul J. Perkins, "Closing the Circle: The Illusion of Lawyers for the People Litigating Their Lives at the *Fin de Siecle*," in James R. Acker, Robert M. Bohm, and Charles S. Lanier, eds., *America's Experiment with Capital Punishment: Reflections on the Past, Present, and Future of the Ultimate Penal Sanction* (Durham, N.C.: Carolina Academic Press, 1998).

1. THE ANTITHESIS OF REFORM

1. Viewing death penalty opposition as cyclical prioritizes the roles of both an organized movement and corresponding legislative successes. This does not mean that there was no opposition outside of the three periods in question, but suggests that such protest did not constitute a widespread movement. For more on the cycles of death penalty opposition, see Haines, *Against Capital Punishment*, 7–16; Hugo Adam Bedau, ed., *The Death Penalty in America: An Anthology* (Chicago: Aldine Publishing, 1964), 1–32; and Louis Filler, "Movements to Abolish the Death Penalty in the United States," *Annals of the American Academy of Political and Social Science* 284 (1952): 124–136.

The Macnamara quote in the epigraph is from his "Statement Against Capital Punishment," in Bedau, *Death Penalty in America,* 183. This was the first among his ten arguments against the death penalty. James Simmons to Governor Goodwin Knight, July 10, 1954, Brown Collection, carton 205.

2. Examples of such analyses include Haines, *Against Capital Punishment,* and David Brion Davis, "The Movement to Abolish Capital Punishment in America," in *From Homicide to Slavery: Studies in American Culture* (New York: Oxford University Press, 1986), 1–35. In his *Rites of Execution: Capital Punishment and the Transformation of American Culture, 1776–1865* (New York: Oxford University Press, 1989), Louis Masur devotes an entire chapter to the link between death penalty opposition and prison reform made by early proponents of the prison, but does not analyze the abolitionist movement of the 1830s and 1840s in terms of this connection (71–92). In "Movements to Abolish the Death Penalty," however, Louis Filler stressed the historic connection between these two movements (124–136).

3. The foremost historian of prison reform, David J. Rothman, makes only passing reference to the death penalty in his three aforementioned works on the subject: *Discovery of the Asylum, Conscience and Convenience,* and "Perfecting the Prison."

4. In his recent work *Laboratories of Virtue,* Michael Meranze provides a useful summary of the historiography of Jacksonian prison reform (1–9).

5. On Progressive attempts to make prison more like the outside community, see Simon, *Poor Discipline*, 31–38; Rothman, *Conscience and Convenience*, 23–27; and Rotman, "The Failure of Reform," 169–171.

6. Most historians treat reform and rehabilitation as synonymous, although the latter—which, as discussed later in this chapter, indicated the clinical orientation of prison specialists—did not come into popular usage until the early twentieth century. See Simon, *Poor Discipline*, 1–14.

7. W. David Lewis, *From Newgate to Dannemora: The Rise of the Penitentiary in New York, 1796–1848* (Ithaca, N.Y.: Cornell University Press, 1965). On the origins of the Pennsylvania system, see Rothman, *Discovery of the Asylum*, 79–92; Meranze, *Laboratories of Virtue;* and Paul Takagi, "The Walnut Street Jail: A Penal Reform to Centralize the Powers of the State," in Tony Platt and Paul Takagi, eds., *Punishment and Penal Discipline: Essays on the Prison and the Prisoners' Movement* (San Francisco: Crime and Social Justice Advocates, 1980), 40–50.

8. Masur, *Rites of Execution*, 77, 27–30. Also see M. J. Heale, "Humanitarianism in the Early Republic: The Moral Reformers of New York, 1776–1825," *Journal of American Studies* 2, no. 1 (1968): 170–175.

9. On colonial execution narratives, see Karen Halttunen, "Early American Murder Narratives: The Birth of Horror," in Richard Wightman Fox and T. J. Jackson Lears, eds., *The Power of Culture: Critical Essays in American History* (Chicago, 1993), 67–101. On the influence of Lockeian environmentalism and phrenology, see David Brion Davis, *Homicide in American Fiction, 1798–1860* (Ithaca, N.Y.: Cornell University Press, 1957), 23–55; and Davis, "Movement to Abolish Capital Punishment," 18–20.

10. On the prison discipline societies, see Lewis, *From Newgate to Dannemora*, 108–109, 221, 252–254. Foucault described early-nineteenth-century British prison reformer Jeremy Bentham's idea of the "panopticon" (or central prison watchtower) thusly: "It is polyvalent in its applications; it serves to reform prisoners, but also to treat patients, to instruct schoolchildren, to confine the insane, to supervise workers, to put beggars and idlers to work." Michel Foucault, *Discipline and Punish: The Birth of the Prison* (New York: Vintage Books, 1979), 205.

11. On the growth of abolitionism in the 1840s, see Masur, *Rites of Execution*, 117–124; Phillips quoted on 122.

12. For general connections between prison reform and the other movements of the period, see Lewis, *From Newgate to Dannemora*, 200–204. For the impact of the market economy on reform movements of the period, see especially David Brion Davis, *The Problem of Slavery in the Age of Revolution, 1770–1823* (Ithaca, N.Y.: Cornell University Press, 1975); and Paul Johnson, *A Shopkeeper's Millennium* (New York: Hill & Wang, 1978). Davis, "Movement to Abolish Capital Punishment," 27–33.

13. Davis, "Movement to Abolish Capital Punishment," 39–40. In *Rites of Execution*, Masur also emphasizes how the issue of slavery far outweighed both the death penalty and prison reform movements by the 1850s (158–161).

14. On general conditions in the post–Civil War period, see Rothman, *Conscience and Convenience*, 23–27; and Rotman, "Failure of Reform," 169–171.

Of the composition of the prison population, Rothman writes, "Since inmates and patients were typically the immigrant and the poor, incarceration seemed a convenient policy, at least to a society that was acutely apprehensive about alien hordes and dangerous classes." By 1890, 60 percent of the population of Illinois penitentiaries were immigrants; in California, immigrants comprised 45 percent. See Rothman, *Conscience and Convenience*, 23–24. On Southern convict leasing, see Alex Lichtenstein, *"Twice the Work of Free Labor": Convict Leasing and the New South* (New York: Verso, 1996); and David Oshinsky, *"Worse Than Slavery": Mississippi's Parchman Farm and the Ordeal of Jim Crow Justice* (New York: Free Press, 1995).

   15. Rothman, *Conscience and Convenience*, 31–32, 34–35. Also see Rotman, "Failure of Reform," 171–175.

   16. Rothman, *Conscience and Convenience*, 45, 46–50. The difficulties of prison management at the end of the nineteenth century created the initial impetus for prison reform. By the 1890s most states had enacted severe restrictions on prison labor, thus depriving prison administrators of a key disciplinary weapon. Along with poor conditions, overcrowding, and the wide disparity in prisoners' sentences, this fact led many wardens and others to look for alternative means of internal control. Wardens, according to Rothman, thus favored the indeterminate sentence because it "would supply them with a genuinely powerful weapon: the authority to determine inmates' release time." Placing a prisoner's release time in his own hands, in short, insured greater conformity with prison rules and regulations. Prison administrators could also assure the public that just as only prisoners ready to become "productive citizens" would be released, the indeterminate sentence would insure that the most dangerous criminals would remain behind bars. On prison conditions at the end of the nineteenth century, see Rothman, *Conscience and Convenience*, 23–27; and Rotman, "The Failure of Reform," 175–176. On wardens, see Rothman, *Conscience and Convenience*, 73–74.

   17. Rothman, *Conscience and Convenience*, 54–80.

   18. Osborne quoted in Rothman, *Conscience and Convenience*, 121. Simon, *Poor Discipline*, 38.

   19. Rothman, *Conscience and Convenience*, 45–46. Simon, *Poor Discipline*, 49. On Progressive prison innovations, Rothman speculates, "Perhaps the confidence of the reformers was founded upon their secure sense of themselves as humanitarians—and their sense that therefore they could decide who should and should not be released into the community" (72).

   20. Robert H. Dann, "Abolition and Restoration of the Death Penalty in Oregon," in Bedau, *Death Penalty in America*, 344–345. Ellen Elizabeth Guillot, "Abolition and Restoration of the Death Penalty in Missouri," in Bedau, *Death Penalty in America*, 351.

   21. Dann, "Abolition in Oregon," 345. Guillot, "Abolition in Missouri," 354–356.

   22. John F. Galliher, Gregory Ray, and Brent Cook, "Abolition and Reinstatement of the Death Penalty During the Progressive Era and Early 20th Century," *The Journal of Criminal Law and Criminology* 83, no. 3 (1992): 551, 560–565, 573–576.

23. On the severity of Depression-era prisons, see Rotman, "The Failure of Reform," 183–186; and Rotman, *Conscience and Convenience,* 144–158. Gallup Poll cited in Hazel Erskine, "The Polls: Capital Punishment," *Public Opinion Quarterly* (Summer 1970). Where the early 1930s witnessed more than 150 executions per year, the late 1950s saw an average of sixty. See James A. McCafferty, "The Death Sentence, 1960," in Bedau, *Death Penalty in America,* 94–97.

24. *Sacramento Bee* (May 1, 1944). On McGee's career as penal innovator, see Daniel Glaser, *Preparing Convicts for Law-Abiding Lives: The Pioneering Penology of Richard A. McGee* (Albany: State University of New York Press, 1995).

25. *Sacramento Bee* (May 1, 1944). on California's emergence as the national leader in therapeutic penology, see Blake McKelvey, *American Prisons: A History of Good Intentions* (Montclair, N.J.: P. Smith, 1977), 336–338.

26. Clinton T. Duffy, as told to Dean Jennings, *The San Quentin Story* (New York: Doubleday, 1950), 250, 218–219, 6; Clinton T. Duffy, with Al Hirshberg, *88 Men and 2 Women* (New York: Doubleday, 1962), 181. *The San Quentin Story* was excerpted in *The Saturday Evening Post,* March 25–May 13, 1950.

27. On the emergence of criminology as a separate discipline, see Gregory Shank, "J. Thorsten Sellin's Penology," in Platt and Takagi, *Punishment and Penal Discipline,* 28–30. Barnes and Teeters, *New Horizons in Criminology,* 717–730. During the war, Jonathan Simon writes, Barnes had envisioned prisons "designed to maximize the efficiency of production and the rehabilitative potential of industrial work and education" (63). For use of *New Horizons in Criminology* as a training manual in the California correctional system, see letter, Harry Elmer Barnes to Governor Goodwin Knight, December 15, 1958, Brown Collection, carton 204.

28. For general background on the postwar growth of scientific management in California prisons, see Simon, *Poor Discipline,* 68–74.

29. New York Committee to Abolish Capital Punishment, "Abolish the Death Penalty: Murder and Executions in New York State" (1960), Peace Collection, Swarthmore College. For more on the American League to Abolish Capital Punishment, see Haines, *Against Capital Punishment,* 10–11, 40–41.

30. Friends Social Service Committee, "A Statement on Capital Punishment: Why We Should Abolish the Death Penalty" (1960), Philadelphia Yearly Meeting, Joint Committee on Capital Punishment, Peace Collection, Swarthmore College. Elizabeth Walker Mechling and Jay Mechling, "Hot Pacifism and Cold War: The American Friends Service Committee's Witness for Peace in 1950s America," *Quarterly Journal of Speech* 78 (1992): 176.

31. Karl Menninger, "Verdict Guilty—Now What?" *Harper's Magazine* (August 1959), 61–64.

32. Bedau, *Death Penalty in America,* 123.

33. Bedau, *Death Penalty in America,* 167. Charles S. Milligan, "A Protestant's View of the Death Penalty," in Bedau, 179. Sidney Hook, "The Death Sentence," in Bedau, 147, 152.

34. Bedau, *Death Penalty in America,* 23. "Death Penalty Must Go," *Christian Century* (April 3, 1957), 413. Giles Playfair and Derick Sington, *The Of-*

fenders: The Case Against Legal Vengeance (New York: Simon & Schuster, 1957), vii. Edmund G. Brown, "A Matter of Conviction," *Fellowship* (July 1, 1960), 1.

35. Friends Social Service Committee, "Statement on Capital Punishment," 1. "Capital Punishment: The Debate Continues," *The Nation* (March 10, 1956), 190. Fred J. Cook, "Capital Punishment: Does It Prevent Crime?" *The Nation* (March 10, 1956), 194. Jacques Barzun, "In Favor of Capital Punishment," in Bedau, *Death Penalty in America,* 156.

36. William O. Douglas, foreword to Judge Jerome Frank and Barbara Frank, *Not Guilty* (New York: Doubleday, 1957), 12. Bedau concluded that by 1964, there had been twenty-three erroneous executions in the twentieth century (*Death Penalty in America,* 438).

37. On the postwar European effort to eliminate capital punishment, see Zimring and Hawkins, *Capital Punishment and the American Agenda,* 3–21.

38. Bedau, *Death Penalty in America,* 339. Sara R. Ehrmann, "The Human Side of Capital Punishment," in Bedau, 492–519. Cook, "Capital Punishment," 197–198.

39. J. Edgar Hoover, "Statements Against the Death Penalty (1960–61)," in Bedau, *Death Penalty in America,* 130–134. Hoover's views were first published in various law enforcement bulletins during the period.

40. Playfair and Sington, *The Offenders,* vii. Robert Hovda, "The Death Penalty," *Commonweal* (July 17, 1959), 367–368.

41. Albert Camus, "Reflections on the Guillotine," in *Resistance, Rebellion, and Death* (New York: Modern Library, 1961), 176, 211, 230, 233; also published in *The Evergreen Review* (Fall 1957). At the end of the essay, Camus argues that in lieu of abolition, the use of a sleeping pill rather than the gas chamber "would [at least] put a little decency into what is at present but a sordid and obscene exhibition" (233). As Peter Linebaugh has argued, Camus based his argument on the opposition between "obscenity and decency. He wishes to remove something that is offensive to the senses . . . [thus making] . . . an aesthetic critique rather than a moral one." Peter Linebaugh, "Gruesome Gertie at the Buckle of the Bible Belt," *New Left Review* 209 (1995): 22.

42. *Omnibus* (1958), Museum of Broadcasting, New York.

43. *Knock on Any Door* (Nicholas Ray, 1949).

44. *I Want to Live!* (Robert Wise, 1958). See also Tabor Rawson, *I Want to Live! The Analysis of a Murder* (New York: Signet, 1958). Convicted of murdering an elderly Burbank widow in 1953, Graham became one of only four women executed in California between 1940 and 1963. Her case involved many of the same principal figures as Chessman's: the district attorney, judge, and public defender, among others.

45. *Herald Tribune* quoted in John Laurence, *A History of Capital Punishment* (New York, Citadel Press, 1960), xv. Magazine titles from *Saturday Review* (April 23, 1960), 26; *Reporter* (April 14, 1960), 2; *The Nation* (May 21, 1960), 439; *The New Republic* (March 7, 1960), 14. "Must Chessman Die? An Appeal to the National Conscience," *The Nation* (March 26, 1960), 264–265. Norman Cousins, "Of Death and One Man," *Saturday Review* (April 23, 1960), 26. For Friends endorsement, see letter, Arthur Springer to A. J. Muste,

April 19, 1960, in Papers of A. J. Muste, "Correspondence" (18), Peace Collection, Swarthmore College.

46. "Capital Punishment: The Debate Continues," *The Nation* (March 10, 1956), 191. The American Institute of Public Opinion and the Harris Survey, "Public Opinion and the Death Penalty," in Bedau, *Death Penalty in America*, 237. Joyce, *Capital Punishment*, 21. Other examples of Chessman's prominence include Laurence, *History of Capital Punishment*, xxv–xxvi; and Block, *And May God Have Mercy*, 1–2, 6–12. In his introduction to *The Death Penalty in America*, Bedau explained why the book would include no "extensive discussion" of cases like Chessman's or the Rosenbergs'. The intrinsic importance of these cases, Bedau wrote, "has, understandably enough, permitted them to obtrude upon every discussion of capital punishment in America. The powerful emotions aroused and the far-reaching political and social consequences of each case have usually carried the controversy far beyond the question of capital punishment itself. Rarely has this helped put the larger question in a clearer light" (v–vi).

47. *Herald Tribune*, quoted in Laurence, *History of Capital Punishment*, xv. "The Value of Chessman," *The Nation* (May 14, 1960), 414. *Christian Century* (April 27, 1960), 499–500. Friends Committee on Legislation, "Facts to Be Considered in the Chessman Case," Southern California Friends (circulated 1960), Brown Collection, carton 206; emphasis in original.

48. Barnes and Teeters, *New Horizons in Criminology*, 4th ed. (1960), 321. Harry Elmer Barnes, *Saturday Review* (August 5, 1961), 16, 26.

49. *Dallas Morning News* (March 14[?], 1960), editorial page; in Brown Collection, carton 214.

50. Letter, Northern California Regional Office, American Friends Service Committee, to Governor Knight, January 11, 1955, Brown Collection, carton 205.

2. THE SEX CRIMES OF THE RED LIGHT BANDIT (1948–1954)

1. *Time* (May 8, 1960), cover. Gerald W. Johnson, "Chessman's Challenge," *The New Republic* (April 7, 1960), 14. *Time* (February 29, 1960), 21–22.

2. The classic account of the origins of white attitudes toward black sexuality is Winthrop Jordan, *White Over Black: American Attitudes Toward the Negro, 1550–1812* (New York: Norton, 1968), 550–610. W. Fitzhugh Brundage, *Lynching in the New South: Georgia and Virginia, 1880–1930* (Urbana: University of Illinois Press, 1993), 58. For women's response, see Jacquelyn Dowd Hall, *Revolt Against Chivalry: Jessie Daniel Ames and the Women's Campaign Against Lynching* (New York: Columbia University Press, 1979).

3. Nancy MacLean, "The Leo Frank Case Reconsidered: Gender and Sexual Politics in the Making of Reactionary Populism," *The Journal of American History* (December 1991): 917–948.

4. Paula S. Fass, "Making and Remaking an Event: The Leopold and Loeb Case in American Culture," *Journal of American History* (December 1993): 919–

95 1. Fass argues that the initial narrative of the case highlighted concerns over the dangers of childhood and popularized psychiatric standards of normal versus abnormal child-rearing. However, as the case has been reinterpreted—by the press at the time of Loeb's death in 1936 over an apparent lover's quarrel in prison, by Meyer Levin in his 1955 bestselling novel *Compulsion,* and most recently by Tom Kalin in his 1992 film *Swoon*—the homosexuality of the two murderers has become the key issue.

5. James Goodman, *Stories of Scottsboro* (New York: Pantheon, 1994). In the last two decades of the nineteenth century, Ida B. Wells waged a tireless campaign against lynching, although she had to leave the South in order to do so safely. A year before the Scottsboro case began, meanwhile, Jesse Daniel Aames launched the Association of Southern Women for the Prevention of Lynching. See Ida B. Wells, "Southern Horrors: Lynch Law in All of Its Phases," in *Selected Works of Ida B. Wells-Barnett,* ed. Trudier Harris (New York, 1991), 14–45; and Hall, *Revolt Against Chivalry,* 78–80, 159–221.

6. On the McGee defense, see Gerald Horne, *Communist Front? The Civil Rights Congress, 1946–1956* (Rutherford, N.J.: Fairleigh Dickinson University Press, 1988), 74–98. On the Martinsville Seven, see Eric W. Rise, *The Martinsville Seven: Race, Rape, and Capital Punishment* (Charlottesville: University of Virginia Press, 1995).

7. For an overview of the case, see *Time* (June 22, 1959), 21; and *Newsweek*'s ominously titled account, "On the Night of the Prom" (June 22, 1959), 26–27. In Florida, thirty-seven blacks and no whites had received the death penalty for rape in the previous forty years.

8. For the breadwinner vs. homemaker distinction, see Barbara Ehrenreich, *The Hearts of Men: American Dreams and the Flight from Commitment* (New York: Doubleday, 1983), 1–28. For more on the domestic ideology, see Elaine Tyler May, *Homeward Bound: American Families in the Cold War Era* (New York: Basic Books, 1988); and Michael Rogin, "Kiss Me Deadly: Communism, Motherhood, and Cold War Movies," in *Ronald Reagan, The Movie: And Other Episodes in Political Demonology* (Berkeley: University of California Press, 1987), 236–271. John D'Emilio and Estelle B. Freedman, *Intimate Matters: A History of Sexuality in America* (New York: Harper & Row, 1988), 300. In her article on the discourse of the "sexual psychopath" during the period (discussed below), Estelle B. Freedman argues that the unequal application of sex crime laws, as well as divergent rates of institutionalization among blacks and whites, revealed the following difference: "In short, white men who committed sexual crimes had to be mentally ill; black men who committed sexual crimes were believed to be guilty of willful violence." Freedman, "'Uncontrolled Desires,'" 97–98.

9. John D'Emilio, *Sexual Politics, Sexual Communities: The Making of a Homosexual Minority in the United States, 1940–1970* (Chicago: University of Chicago Press, 1983), 16–17.

10. Freedman, "'Uncontrolled Desires,'" 100, 103; emphasis in original.

11. *Literary Digest* (April 10, 1937), 5–7; Sheldon Glueck, "Sex Crimes and the Law," *The Nation* (September 25, 1937), 318–320.

12. Berube, *Coming Out Under Fire,* 1–33. For general wartime atmosphere,

see D'Emilio and Freedman, *Intimate Matters,* 260–261, 288–290. Ellen Herman, *The Romance of American Psychology: Political Culture in the Age of Experts* (Berkeley: University of California Press, 1995), 1–123. Berube records a number of examples of GIs being diagnosed as sexual psychopaths after they were caught committing homosexual acts (148–168). For analysis of psychiatric approach to homosexuality, see D'Emilio, *Sexual Politics, Sexual Communities,* 15–19. In addition to its direct influence in American lives, psychiatry received legitimation from popular culture, especially in films like *Spellbound* (1945) and *The Dark Past* (1947). For a discussion of the transformation of psychiatrists from villains to heroes in Hollywood films during the period, see Peter Biskind, *Seeing Is Believing: How Hollywood Taught Us to Stop Worrying and Love the Fifties* (New York: Pantheon Books, 1983), 21–33.

13. Robert M. Lindner, *Rebel Without a Cause: The Hypnoanalysis of a Criminal Psychopath* (New York: Grune & Stratton, 1944), 13–14.

14. *Newsweek* (July 29, 1946), 5; *Time* (July 29, 1946), 19; *Newsweek* (August 19, 1946), 25. Frank C. Waldrop, "Murder as a Sex Practice," *American Mercury* (February 1948), 144–150. "What Can We Do about Sex Crimes?" *Saturday Evening Post* (December 11, 1948), 30–31, 47, 58, 62–63. The figure of the werewolf cropped up frequently in popular culture accounts of sex crime during the period. For example, the press coverage of the sex-murder of the Black Dahlia in Los Angeles in 1947 focused on the search for the "werewolf"-killer. See Theodore Hamm, "Fragments of Postwar Los Angeles: The Black Dahlia in Fact and Fiction," *Antipode* 28, no. 1 (January 1996): 24–41.

15. J. Edgar Hoover, "How Safe Is Your Daughter?" *The American Magazine* (July 1947), 32–33, 102–104.

16. J. Edgar Hoover, "How *Safe* Is Your Youngster?" *The American Magazine* (March 1955), 19, 99–102.

17. 1950 report quoted in *Time* (March 2, 1953), 42; *Newsweek* (March 9, 1953), 50. Benjamin Karpman, *The Sexual Offender and His Offenses* (New York: Julian Press, 1954), 22–24.

18. Daniel Bell, "The Myth of Crime Waves: The Actual Decline of Crime in the United States," in *The End of Ideology: On the Exhaustion of Political Ideas in the Fifties* (Glencoe, Ill.: Free Press, 1960), 137–158; Hall et al. quoted in Philip Jenkins, *Moral Panic: Changing Concepts of the Child Molester in Modern America* (New Haven, Conn.: Yale University Press, 1998), 6, 8.

19. Hamm, "Fragments of Postwar Los Angeles."

20. For complete list of sex murders linked by local police and press to the Dahlia case, see *Hollywood Citizen News* (June 17, 1949). Simone de Beauvoir, *America Day by Day* (London: G. Duckworth, 1952), 95–96. On trial coverage, see *Los Angeles Daily News* (May 4–May 22, 1948). Aside from Chessman's *Cell 2455* account, Machlin and Woodfield's *Ninth Life* and the 1977 TV movie *Kill Me If You Can* (starring Alan Alda as Chessman) also emphasize media hype, yet the attention initially given to the case did not match that given the Black Dahlia or other notable cases of the period. See "Did the Press Kill Caryl Chessman?" *The Progressive* (December 1960), 12–17.

21. Leavy quoted in Machlin and Woodfield, *Ninth Life,* 81; *Equalizer* article cited in Kunstler, *Beyond a Reasonable Doubt,* 43–44. Chessman, Kunstler

notes, unsuccessfully petitioned for a change of venue on account of the tabloid article (43).

22. Kunstler, *Beyond a Reasonable Doubt*, 43–46. On juror backgrounds, also see Parker, *Caryl Chessman*, 36.

23. On Knowles and other Section 209 cases, see Parker, *Caryl Chessman*, 93–117. Leavy's arguments quoted at length in Kunstler, *Beyond a Reasonable Doubt*, 46–123, and Machlin and Woodfield, *Ninth Life*, 83–106.

24. Trial quotes from Kunstler, *Beyond a Reasonable Doubt*, 124–170, and Machlin and Woodfield, *Ninth Life*, 107–140, 152–154. Leavy further stated in summation, "You heard the doctor testify that her hymen was bruised. It could not have been less than an attempt to commit sexual intercourse on her. . . . She is under the law raped, ladies and gentleman. That is rape. It is only charged as attempted rape. I am willing to leave it that way" (Machlin and Woodfield, 137). This charge would not be the focus of the subsequent legal and press campaign against Chessman, however.

25. See Kunstler, *Beyond a Reasonable Doubt*, 211–245; Machlin and Woodfield, *Ninth Life*, 141–161.

26. On Fricke's background, see Parker, *Caryl Chessman*, 45–59. See Fricke, "Instructions to Jury," *State of California vs. Caryl Chessman* (#117963, 117964), Los Angeles Superior Court Records.

27. See Machlin and Woodfield, *Ninth Life*, 158–161; Kunstler, *Beyond a Reasonable Doubt*, 267–268.

28. *Los Angeles Daily News* (May 22, 1948). On usage of Little Lindbergh Law, see Parker, *Caryl Chessman*, 93–117.

29. Fricke to Judiciary Interim Committee, December 7, 1949, in California State Assembly, *Preliminary Report of Subcommittee on Sex Crimes* (Sacramento: California State Assembly, 1950), 194. On De River's testimony, see Kunstler, *Beyond a Reasonable Doubt*, 23–24, 248–249; on Leavy's use of De River's gallery of graphic photos, see Machlin and Woodfield, *Ninth Life*, 75–76. On Leavy's continued pursuit of Chessman's death sentence, see "State Starts Fight to Get Chessman Executed," *San Francisco Chronicle* (May 17, 1954).

30. "Death Penalty Urged for Child Molesters," *Los Angeles Times* (December 8, 1949). Stroble, a seventy-year-old grandfather, had been convicted in November 1949 for the sex murder of a six-year-old girl. After a jury found him guilty, Fricke sentenced him to die in January 1950. He was executed two and a half years later. For a recap of the case, see *Los Angeles Times* (July 26, 1952).

31. See "Tests Proposed in All Sex Cases," *Los Angeles Times* (December 8, 1949); and "Sex Criminals 'Mad Dogs,' District Attorney Asserts," *Los Angeles Times* (December 9, 1949).

32. State Assembly, *Preliminary Report*, 10–25, 33.

33. State Assembly, *Preliminary Report*, 27–29, 34–35.

34. State Assembly, *Preliminary Report*, 30–33, 45–48, 59–63.

35. State Assembly, *Preliminary Report*, 72–73. On Dugger and the use of Section 209, see Parker, *Caryl Chessman*, 112–117.

36. On subsequent use of Section 209, see Parker, *Caryl Chessman*, 112–

117. On Jensen, see Parker, *Caryl Chessman,* 112, and *Los Angeles Times* (January 12, 1955); Jensen, as the latter highlights, had a previous record of murder. On Brown commutations of Wein and Langdon, see *Los Angeles Times* (June 5, 1959, and October 9, 1959; quotes from former). On Monk, see *Los Angeles Times* (November 20, 1961).

37. Edwin H. Sutherland, "The Sexual Psychopath Laws," *Journal of Criminal Law and Criminology* (January–February 1950): 543–554.

38. On recommendations for segregation and isolation, see State Assembly, *Preliminary Report,* 72–78.

39. *Newsweek* (February 29, 1960), 21–22. In a feature story that same week, a *Time* photo caption called him "Kidnaper Chessman." See *Time* (February 29, 1960), 21.

40. Examples include: "Kidnapper-Rapist," *Los Angeles Examiner* (February 23, 1960); "sex terrorist," *Sacramento Bee* (May 4, 1960); "psychopath," *Los Angeles Times* (October 16, 1959); "keen-minded kidnaper sex-pervert," *Time* (February 29, 1960), 23. Leland Swanson, "Why Caryl Chessman Deserves to Die," *Startling Detective* (April 1960), 36–40. For a summary of these and other labels, see "Did the Press Kill Caryl Chessman," 14.

41. Paula S. Fass, *Kidnapped: Child Abduction in America* (New York: Oxford University Press, 1997), 146–171; quotes on 153, 159.

42. *Los Angeles Times* (May 11, 1954). *Los Angeles Times* (May 13, 1954). 1960 editorial quoted in "Did the Press Kill Caryl Chessman," 12–17. The phrase "worse than murder" had also been frequently applied to the crimes of the Rosenbergs.

43. Parker, *Caryl Chessman,* 113. *Los Angeles Times* (October 16, 1959). *San Diego Union* (February 23, 1960). Gerald W. Johnson, "Chessman's Challenge," *The New Republic* (March 7, 1960). Writing to Governor Brown in 1959, the court psychiatrist who interviewed Meza disagreed with the linkage between the assault and Meza's schizophrenia, arguing that a diseased thyroid condition since age twelve had caused her illness. See Parker, *Caryl Chessman;* and "Did the Press Kill Caryl Chessman," 14.

44. Swanson, "Why Caryl Chessman Deserves to Die," 36–40. "Red Light Terror: The Shocking Truth about Caryl Chessman," *Master Detective* (September 1954), 16–17, 59. *Saga: Adventure Stories for Men* (February 1960), 34–35. *Rogue* (March 1960), 21.

45. Freedman, "'Uncontrolled Desires,'" 86–87. Rather than melodrama, postwar Los Angeles is more commonly represented by film noir, a genre which, as it explores the dark spaces of the city, contains far more moral ambiguity. See Mike Davis, *City of Quartz: Excavating the Future in Los Angeles* (New York: Verso, 1990), chapter one; and Hamm, "Fragments of Postwar Los Angeles." Judith R. Walkowitz, meanwhile, analyzes the relationship between sex crime, melodrama, and Victorian London in *City of Dreadful Delight: Narratives of Sexual Danger in Late-Victorian London* (Chicago: University of Chicago Press, 1992).

46. Lindner, *Rebel Without a Cause,* 1.

47. "Neuropsychiatric Report," August 17, 1948, San Quentin execution file

#66565, California State Archives. "Psychiatric Social Worker's Report," August 21, 1948, San Quentin execution file #66565, California State Archives. The evaluations reveal the slippery transition between these terms—in 1955, he had a "psychopathic or sociopathic personality"; in 1959, simply "a psychopathic personality"; and in his final evaluation "a Sociopathic, Emotional Unstable, Anti-social Personality." "Sociopath" appeared to represent an outward hatred of society rather than a "condition" developed directly from within one's self. Dr. David Schmidt remained the chief psychiatrist from 1948 to 1960. For 1959 reports, also see San Quentin execution file #66565.

48. "Did the Press Kill Caryl Chessman," 13–15.

49. The ratio of pro- to anti-Chessman letters was about five to three. Given the raw numbers (by 1960 "thousands daily"), this still resulted in a significant cross-section of anti-Chessman opinion. Mrs. W. J. Spurzem to Knight, July 24, 1954; E. J. Lowder to Knight, May 12, 1954; Charley Jensen to Knight, July 25, 1954; Mr. and Mrs. E. G. Knapp to Knight, May 13, 1954; V. J. Fisher to Knight, October 26, 1955; all in Brown Collection, carton 205.

50. Four Santa Cruz Chrysler dealers to Knight, October 8, 1954; Mrs. D. J. Tuttle to Knight, August 29, 1957; Mrs. Jeanne-Marie Osmond to Knight, May 18, 1954; Knight to Hazel Paus, July 26, 1954; all in Brown Collection, carton 205.

51. Henry A. Sammet to Knight, May 10, 1954; Helen Semnacher to Knight, May 12, 1954; M. Holbek to Knight, May 12, 1954; Rysberg to Knight, February 18, 1957; all in Brown Collection, carton 205.

52. These terms are from Mary Douglas, *Purity and Danger: An Analysis of the Concepts of Pollution and Taboo* (New York: Routledge, 1995), esp. 130–140. "If pollution dangers were placed strategically along the crucial points in [a culture's] moral code," Douglas writes, "they could theoretically reinforce it. However, such a strategic distribution of pollution rules is impossible, since the moral code by its nature can never be reduced to something so simple, hard and fast" (131).

53. Justice for Chessman Committee Ad, *New York Times* (April 29, 1960). Governor Knight, however, downplayed Graves's disagreement over the charges against Chessman as a reason for his resignation. See *Los Angeles Times* (May 12, 1954).

54. Justice for Chessman Committee Ad, *New York Times* (April 29, 1960); *Los Angeles Times* cited in "Did the Press Kill Caryl Chessman," 14.

3. THE REHABILITATION OF A CRIMINAL "GENIUS" (1954–1960)

1. "Neuropsychiatric Committee Examination," April 23, 1954, San Quentin execution file #66565, California State Archives. Leavy's address to the jury in the epigraph is quoted from *Los Angeles Daily News* (May 18, 1948). *Daily News* headlines also called Chessman a "criminal genius"; for examples, see ibid., and "Crime Genius Sentenced to Death" (May 22, 1948). As local news stories often noted, "Chessman was rated as having the highest I.Q. of any

prison inmate in California"; see *Daily News* (May 17, 1948). "Neuropsychiatric Report," August 17, 1948, San Quentin execution file #66565, California State Archives. Hardwick, "Life and Death of Caryl Chessman," 504.

2. Chessman, *Cell 2455 Death Row*.

3. As outlined in chapter one, the "new penology" refers to the Progressive ideal of modeling prison life on the modern industrial community. See Barnes and Teeters, *New Horizons in Penology*, 644–679.

4. Caryl Chessman, *Trial by Ordeal* (Englewood Cliffs, N.J.: Prentice Hall, 1955), 92.

5. *Newsweek* (February 22, 1954), 28–29. Lamson was accused of murdering his wife in their Palo Alto home in 1933, and his trial took place in the public spotlight—the press sensationalized the case as one of sex murder. At the time of his wife's death, Lamson was the sales manager of the Stanford University Press. Because the evidence of his guilt seemed questionable, and because of Lamson's "respected" place in the community, a number of Stanford faculty members and others formed a Lamson Defense Committee. As Dorothy Van Doren wrote in *The Nation*, Lamson's "relationship with his wife, his own character, and the circumstances surrounding the tragedy made it inconceivable that he could have committed the murder." Lamson went on to write feature stories—not about prison life—for the *Saturday Evening Post* and other magazines. See *The Nation* (November 20, 1935), 602–603; and *The Nation* (September 26, 1934), 341–342. For an overview of the case, see *Time* (April 13, 1936), 18–19.

6. In his seminal work *Prison Literature in America*, Franklin argues that the confessional narrative was the most common form of prison literature until the early nineteenth century, when narratives similar to the picaresque novel emerged. Although normally sprinkled with pious confessions of the author's hope that "young readers would not follow his path of vice," the picaresque narratives sought to titillate readers with accounts of the author's criminal exploits, and frequently offered detailed advice about the arts of horse thievery or counterfeiting. Prison literature became more sociological in the late nineteenth century, as many works turned away from the adventures of a lone criminal toward a focus on the class status of the prisoner. After O. Henry's success as a short-story writer in the early twentieth century, Franklin argues, prisoners "began to think of themselves as potential professional authors rather than just criminals with their own tale to tell." The confessional, picaresque, and sociological modes would survive, often in hybrid form, in both nonfictional and, increasingly, fictional prison literature of the twentieth century. H. Bruce Franklin, *Prison Literature in America: The Victim as Criminal and Artist*, rev. ed. (New York: Oxford University Press, 1989), 124–178.

7. Although Chessman would make the problematic argument that death row helped rehabilitate him, he both denied the red light bandit's assaults and celebrated his prior life of crime. Because he never really saw himself as a sinner, his story did not fit into the form of a traditional confessional narrative. Unlike Malcolm X, whose autobiography fit this mold, Chessman never seemed able to say, "The truth can be quickly received, or received at all, only by the sinner who knows and admits that he is guilty of having sinned much." Malcolm X, with

Alex Haley, *The Autobiography of Malcolm X* (New York: Ballantine Books, 1964), 63.

8. Miriam Allen De Ford, "Shall Convicts Write Books?" *The Nation* (November 5, 1930), 495–497. On the history of prison libraries, see Cummins, *Rise and Fall of California's Radical Prison Movement,* 5–10.

9. Barnes and Teeters, *New Horizons in Criminology,* 719–730. Duffy, *The San Quentin Story,* 250, 218–219. California Department of Corrections, *The Prison Library of San Quentin: Its Programs and Achievements* (Sacramento: State Department of Corrections, 1949), 3. According to the report, the average inmate checked out sixty-nine books a year, from a library of over twenty-three hundred titles (p. 9). On dossier, see Cummins, *Rise and Fall,* 21–32.

10. Chessman, *Cell 2455,* 331; *Newsweek* (February 22, 1954), 28–29.

11. Chessman, *Cell 2455,* 3–11.

12. Chessman, *Cell 2455,* 16–32.

13. On Wylie's Momism, see Rogin, "Kiss Me Deadly." The private-detective rationale is from Chessman, *Cell 2455,* 109; later he claimed to have found out about a special surgeon who could help his mother recover from her paralysis, making him want to join the Canadian Royal Air Force to help pay for the trip (172). For reviews, see Wenzell Brown, "California Villon," *Saturday Review* (May 22, 1954), 36; and *America* (June 19, 1954), 322. Brown's title corresponds with Chessman's stated desire to emulate François Villon, the seventeenth-century imprisoned French poet (See *Cell 2455,* 247).

14. "Psychiatric Social Worker's Report," August 1948, San Quentin execution file #66565, California State Archives; Chessman quoted in "'Boy Bandit Gang' Rounded Up: Pair Shot and Three More Held," *Los Angeles Times* (February 3, 1941).

15. Chessman, *Cell 2455,* 28, 158, 184, 162. For more on Cagney, as well as others who fit the gangster type, see Robert Sklar, *City Boys: Cagney, Bogart, Garfield* (Princeton: Princeton University Press, 1992), esp. parts I and II.

16. Chessman, *Cell 2455,* 37, 74–79. Many of Chessman's conflicts occurred on lovers' lanes or other secluded spots in the hills—an especially peculiar pattern, given his red light bandit convictions. After making love "joyously, gladly" in the hills, Chessman and his female companion got in a fight. Doing the "ungentlemanly thing," he told her that "her only virtues were biological." After she slapped him, he warned that "I've got a notion to kill us both" (163). Even more problematically, Judy, his "true love," was the victim of an attempted rape on lover's lane. Chessman wrote that her assailant "tore off her undergarments and attempted to rape her, possibly succeeding," which sounds almost exactly like one of the red light bandit's assaults. As with Virginia, "He comforted her [Judy], resolved to beat the life out of the vile animal who attacked her, and a few days later they drove to Las Vegas and got married" (169–170).

17. Chessman, *Cell 2455,* 92, 158, 220–221.

18. Here the always tricky second-person voice fails to implicate the reader: "You robbed. You hijacked. You snatched a pimp here; you knocked over a bookie or gambling joint there. You sat at your paralyzed mother's bedside and talked the night away." Ibid., 184.

19. Ibid., 129, 134, 152; "Psychiatric Social Worker's Report," August 1948,

San Quentin execution file #66565, California State Archives; Chessman, *Trial by Ordeal*, 176. Of his diagnosis as a psychopath, Chessman writes, "I knew . . . that the prison's chief psychiatrist had tagged me a 'constitutional psychopathic personality' and predicted that my chances for living within the law after release were slim" (*Cell 2455*, 223). In *Trial by Ordeal*, Chessman argued that "unquestionably today's most baffling, most pressing criminological problem is the young criminally aggressive psychopathic personality, the violent rebel, the tough guy." He went on to quote Robert Lindner's views of psychopathy at length (176–182).

20. Chessman, *Cell 2455*, 157.

21. Chessman was eventually sentenced for auto theft, assaulting a police officer, and robbery. For accounts of the Boy Bandit Gang, see *Los Angeles Times* (February 3, 1941); *Los Angeles Examiner* (February 4, 1941). For comparison to the Dead End Kids (later the Bowery Boys), see *Los Angeles Daily News* (February 7, 1941); for Dillinger references, see *Los Angeles Daily News* (March 3, 1941; delinquency series continues for following week). Thus, one year prior to the local media campaign against Mexican American juvenile delinquency that resulted in the notorious Sleepy Lagoon case, the threat posed by white adolescents commanded local attention. For a contemporary account, see Carey McWilliams, *Southern California Country: An Island on the Land* (New York: Duell, Sloan & Pierce, 1946), 318–320.

22. Chessman, *Cell 2455*, 331, 215–222; "Psychiatric Social Worker's Report," August 1948, San Quentin execution file #66565, California State Archives. In *Cell 2455*, Chessman often praised himself for his efforts as teacher and lawyer: "By far my greatest satisfaction was teaching an earnest group of illiterates to read and write" (222); "I'm the first condemned man ever to defend himself at his trial and then handle all subsequent litigation of the case without being represented by counsel" (320).

23. According to Peter Linebaugh, "In 1721 it was said 'there is a hardly a day of Execution [which] passes without an instance of some condemn'd Criminal, who, by solemn Protestations in the last moments of his life, does not endeavor to persuade the World that he dies Innocent." Peter Linebaugh, *The London Hanged: Crime and Civil Society in the Eighteenth Century* (Cambridge: Cambridge University Press, 1992), 18. One reason sex crimes are frequently denied involves the code of justice inside prisons. Rapists, and especially child molesters, are the target of unceasing hostility from other prisoners. See Bruce Jackson, *In the Life: Versions of the Criminal Experience* (New York: Holt, Rinehart and Winston, 1973), esp. 353–412.

24. Chessman, *Cell 2455*, 293, 351–352. At the outset of *Trial by Ordeal*, Chessman continued, "All along you've vehemently denied being southern California's notorious red-light bandit, a strange, depraved bird who amateurishly committed a string of penny-ante robberies, attempted rape, and, on two occasions, compelled female victims to commit what the newspapers have called 'unnatural sex acts'" (5). Chessman's long record of convictions, however, made his claim to professional criminal status questionable. For a summary, see Parker, *Caryl Chessman*, 207–208.

25. "Neuropsychiatric Report," August 17, 1948, San Quentin execution file

#66565, California State Archives; "Psychiatric Social Worker's Report," August 1948, San Quentin execution file #66565, California State Archives; Matthews to Knight, May 10, 1954, Brown Collection, carton 205.

26. Chessman to Joseph Longstreth, December 8, 1953, Brown Collection, carton 205.

27. Chessman, *Cell 2455*, 359; Chessman, *Trial by Ordeal*, 95.

28. *Chicago Tribune Book Review* (May 9, 1954), 5. *New York Times Book Review* (May 2, 1954), 28. Barkham, syndicated review (May 1954), Brown Collection, carton 205. *Los Angeles Daily News* (May 6, 1954), 8.

29. Chessman, *Trial by Ordeal*, 34; *Newsweek* (August 2, 1954), 20. On Chessman's legal struggle, see Cummins, *Rise and Fall of California's Radical Prison Movement*, 41–51. Chessman wrote his third book, *The Face of Justice* (Englewood Cliffs, N.J.: Prentice Hall, 1957), on carbon paper, and he once wrote a writ of habeas corpus on a roll of toilet paper. The promotional staff at Prentice Hall duly added the following teaser to the cover of *The Face of Justice*: "This is the plea for life that was smuggled out of death row."

30. Chessman, *Trial by Ordeal*, 4, 293, 183–184.

31. Ibid., 150–164, 192–194, 19, 32–33, 69–70, 90–91.

32. Ibid., 32–33, 69–70.

33. *New York Times Book Review* (October 6, 1957), 35; extended in *The Saturday Review* (October 5, 1957), 32–33. One example from *The Face of Justice* illustrates O'Leary's point: "This is not a story for those sanctimonious souls who for so long have danced and gloated around my unfilled grave" (201). Included in the "package," according to Chessman, were "some affidavits and original photostats of police records and reports and other material which establish indubitably that the wrong man now occupies Cell 2455, Death Row." Yet he had placed the package "where it cannot be found, seized and suppressed or destroyed against my wishes." Chessman offered no explanation why he withheld such "vital information" (226–227).

34. *Chessman v. Teets* (354 U.S. 157), 5. Chessman, *The Kid Was a Killer* (Greenwich, Conn.: Fawcett Publications, 1960), 140. In his appendix to *Writers in Prison* (Oxford: Basil Blackwell, 1990), Ioan Davies calls the book a "classic of prison writing" (245). This is in sharp contrast to the appraisal of Anthony Boucher, then the crime editor of the *New York Times Book Review,* who argued in 1961: "David Lamson was an incomparably better writer. . . . *The Kid Was a Killer* quashed forever the myth of his [Chessman's] literary potential." *Contact* 8 (1961), 31.

35. *Saturday Review* (August 5, 1961), 16. *San Francisco Chronicle* (May 11, 1954), 4. Barnes and Teeters, *New Horizons in Penology* (1959 ed.), 320. In the *Saturday Review* piece, Barnes maintained that since Chessman had shown such signs of "regeneration," his execution contradicted the "principles of contemporary correctional philosophy and practice—principles which have, perhaps, been most highly developed and most proudly paraded in the state of California" (16, 26).

36. Brown quoted in *San Francisco Chronicle* (May 11, 1954). Lerner in *New York Post* (May 26, 1954). Karpman to Knight, July 26, 1954, Brown Collection, carton 205.

37. Bill Sands, *My Shadow Ran Fast* (Englewood Cliffs, N.J.: Prentice Hall, 1964), 61–62, 154, 176–181. Black quoted in Bernice Freeman Davis, *The Desperate and the Damned* (New York: Crowell, 1961), 224. Bill Sands dedicated his book to the Warden and Mrs. Duffy, "who gave my life back to me" (vii). Bernice Freeman Davis was a crime reporter for the *San Francisco Chronicle* for many years, and her book is based on her "inside" knowledge of San Quentin. Of Chessman, Davis wrote, "Was he actually rehabilitated, as so many thought? He might have been, but I wouldn't bet on it. I'm sure he wasn't ready for freedom the last time I saw him. Right to the end, he broke rules, flouted authority, got into petty arguments, hated cops, considered himself a con. I remember how pleased he was when he chortled over the embarrassment of prison authorities after one of his books was smuggled out. He was proud, too, that other inmates kept the manuscript a secret. Yes, I believe that Chessman took his greatest satisfaction when so many convicts joined him in defeating the forces of law and order" (224).

38. Chessman, *Cell 2455*, 221. Duffy, *88 Men and 2 Women*, 142–154. In *Cell 2455*, Chessman wrote, "San Quentin had a new warden, a kindly, practical, far-seeing man named Clinton Truman Duffy, and this bespectacled, thoughtful penologist was destined to write penal history in California" (221). Contrasting Sands to Chessman, Duffy, in his introduction to *My Shadow Ran Fast*, recalled how "On his arrival at San Quentin Prison on a gun robbery charge, Bill Sands would pass as a boy you would like to know and one that you would welcome into your home as a friend of your children" (vii–viii). In *Sex and Crime*, Duffy stated his thesis in the opening sentence—"Sex is the cause of nearly all crime"—and proceeded to explain how crimes ranging from forgery to arson were caused by sexual "deviation." In his chapter on "homosexuals," Duffy argued that "the deviation, not the felony, was the basic problem." "Most homosexuals are potential convicts," he wrote, except for those who had been "cured of their deviation" after "lengthy professional treatment." Clinton T. Duffy, with Al Hirshberg, *Sex and Crime* (New York: Doubleday, 1965), 1–9, 28–39.

39. Erving Goffman, "The Moral Career of the Mental Patient," in *Asylums: Essays on the Social Situation of Mental Patients and Other Inmates* (New York: Anchor Books, 1961), 127–169.

40. Hardwick, "Life and Death of Caryl Chessman," 506; Andrew Ross, "Reading the Rosenberg Letters," in *No Respect: Intellectuals and Popular Culture* (New York: Routledge, 1989), 15–41.

41. Nathan Leopold, *Life Plus 99 Years* (Garden City, N.Y.: Doubleday, 1958). *The Nation* (March 29, 1958), 278–280. *The Christian Century* (April 2, 1958), 397.

42. "Facing Death, A New Life Perhaps Too Late," *Life* (July 27, 1962), 28–29 (reprinted as "Rehabilitation on Death Row" in Bedau, *Death Penalty in America*, 556–563). Baldwin quoted on jacket copy to Paul Crump, *Burn, Killer, Burn!* (Chicago, 1962). *The People vs. Paul Crump* (William Friedkin, 1962).

43. Kerner quoted in Bedau, *Death Penalty in America*, 563. *The Christian Century* (August 1, 1962), 929.

44. References are to *The Birdman of Alcatraz* (John Frankenheimer, 1962). The contradiction between the film's ad campaign and its overall message is pointed out in Philip T. Hartung, "That Little Tent of Blue," *Commonweal* (August 10, 1962), 446. *America* (July 26, 1962), 552. Arthur Knight, "Maximum Security," *Saturday Review* (May 19, 1962), 31. "Solitary Rebel," *Time* (July 20, 1962), 79.

45. *Time*, "Solitary Rebel," 79. Kennedy fully quoted in Hartung, "That Little Tent of Blue," 446. Stanley Kauffmann, "Crimes and Punishments," *The New Republic* (August 13, 1962), 28, 30. Francis Biddle, letter to *The New Republic* (September 17, 1962), 30.

46. Gerald Early, "The Unquiet Kingdom of Providence: The Patterson-Liston Fight," in *The Culture of Bruising* (New York: Ecco Press, 1994), 46–65. In his autobiography, Hawes says his unexpected release came shortly after he played in a concert attended by Lady Bird Johnson; later he heard that all his fellow inmates were writing letters to President Kennedy, arguing (unsuccessfully) that they too were "rehabilitated." Hampton Hawes, with Don Asher, *Raise Up Off Me: A Portrait of Hampton Hawes* (New York: Coward, McCann & Geohegan, 1979), 122–128.

47. Malcolm X, *Autobiography*, 157–158, 173–189; Eldridge Cleaver, *Soul on Ice* (New York: Dell, 1968), 25–29, 145–162; George Jackson, *Soledad Brother: The Prison Letters of George Jackson* (New York: Bantam Books, 1970), 26. On Chessman's influence on subsequent San Quentin prison writers, see Cummins, *Rise and Fall*, 63–64.

48. Jean Genet, introduction to Jackson, *Soledad Brother*, 3. Paul Goodman, introduction to Alexander Berkman, *Prison Memoirs of an Anarchist* (New York: Schocken, 1970), ii.

49. Michel Foucault, "Intellectuals and Power—A Conversation with Gilles Deleuze," in *Language, Counter-Memory, Practice: Selected Essays and Interviews,* ed. Donald Bouchard (Ithaca: Cornell University Press, 1977), 209.

50. Edward Bunker, *Education of a Felon: A Memoir* (New York: St. Martin's Press, 2000), 50–53, 124–125. Chessman's main piece of advice to Bunker in 1948 illustrated the former's perspective as a seasoned convict: in prison, Chessman instructed, "If you gotta take somebody out, if you want to avoid the gas chamber or life make sure you stick him from the front—not in the back. In the front you can make a case for self-defense" (50). Another notable, and quite controversial, prison author who identified with Chessman was Jack Abbott, who declared, "I was sent to prison for the same reason Caryl Chessman was executed: arrogance." See Jack Henry Abbott, *In the Belly of the Beast* (New York: Random House, 1981), 93.

51. Malcolm Braly, *False Starts: A Memoir of San Quentin and Other Prisons* (Boston: Little, Brown, 1976), 299; Chessman to Longstreth, December 8, 1953, Brown Collection, carton 205. In *Trial by Ordeal,* Chessman struggled to define his identity as an author: "I began by letting Caryl Chessman, the condemned man, speak. Of course it was not he who would write the book. The writing itself would be done by Caryl Chessman, the author. . . . Both Chessmans threw themselves into the task" (202).

4. A TALE OF TWO PROTESTS (1950–1960)

1. The literature on some of these cases is quite vast, but the most thorough descriptions of the popular campaigns are: Richard H. Frost, *The Mooney Case* (Palo Alto: Stanford University Press, 1968); Louis Joughin and Edmund M. Morgan, *The Legacy of Sacco and Vanzetti* (New York: Harcourt, Brace and Company, 1948); James Goodman, *Stories of Scottsboro* (New York: Pantheon, 1994); Gerald Horne, *Communist Front*, 74–98; and Walter and Miriam Schneir, *Invitation to an Inquest* (Garden City, N.Y.: Doubleday, 1965).

2. "Capital Punishment: The Debate Continues," *The Nation* (March 10, 1956), 191. For a summary of the California governors' positions, see Burton Wolfe, *Pileup on Death Row* (New York: Doubleday, 1973), esp. chapter one.

3. Mrs. Bernard Meer to Governor Edmund G. Brown, August 20, 1959, Brown Collection, carton 205; Beatrice Petrella to Brown, July 20, 1959, Brown Collection, carton 210. All of the letters quoted in this chapter are found in the Edmund G. Brown Collection at the Bancroft Library, cartons 204–215. The collection contains more than four thousand letters written to both Governor Knight and Governor Brown about the case. The letters collected are by no means all of the letters written to the governors, making it difficult to provide an absolute breakdown of the letters by gender, race, region, or any other category. Of the letters in the collection, there is a virtually equal division between men and women writers, and the ratio of pro-Chessman letters to anti-Chessman letters is approximately three to one. For ratio, see *The Economist* (February 20, 1960), 14; and informal tally sheet (1960), Brown Collection, carton 209.

4. On postwar California, see Richard Walker, "California Rages Against the Dying of the Light," *New Left Review* (March–April 1995): 42–74; Jackson K. Putnam, "The Progressive Legacy in California: Fifty Years of Politics, 1917–1967," in William Deverell and Tom Sitton, eds., *California Progressivism Revisited* (Berkeley: University of California Press, 1994), 250–263; Samuel Lubbell, *The Future of American Politics* (New York: Harper and Row, 1951), esp. 69–89; C. Wright Mills, *White Collar* (New York: Oxford University Press, 1951), esp. 289–301. As the outline of this chapter makes clear, by 1960 opposition to the death penalty had become an issue clearly linked to the Democratic Party.

5. Daniel J. Walkowitz, *Working with Class: Social Workers and the Politics of Middle Class Identity* (Chapel Hill: University of North Carolina Press, 1999), esp. 230–235. Among social workers, Walkowitz writes, "McCarthyism made it both dangerous and unprofessional to express an identity of interest with poor or African American or Hispanic clients" (235).

6. For a general outline of the CRC's role in the Wells case, see Gerald Horne, *Communist Front*, 323–330.

7. For chronology, see Horne, *Communist Front*, 323–330; and Charles Garry and Art Goldberg, *Streetfighter in the Courtroom: The People's Advocate*, foreword by Jessica Mitford (New York: Dutton, 1977), 25–36. Between 1930 and 1967, eight prisoners were executed in California for violations of Section 4500, including three for nonlethal assault; see Parker, *Caryl Chessman*, 115.

8. Garry, *Streetfighter in the Courtroom*, 25–36, Black Panther quote on 25.

9. On the link to CRC involvement in other cases, see Horne, *Communist Front*, and promotional booklet *Civil Rights Congress Tells the Story* (Los Angeles, 1951[?]), in Civil Rights Congress Collection—Southern California Library for Social Studies and Research (hereafter CRC-SCSS). On Patterson's career see Horne, *Communist Front*; Goodman, *Stories of Scottsboro*, 103–105; and William L. Patterson, *The Man Who Cried Genocide* (New York: International Publishers, 1971). All of the cases in which the CRC was active—including Wells's—were mentioned in the CRC's 1951 "We Charge Genocide" petition brought before the United Nations by Paul Robeson; see Patterson, *Man Who Cried Genocide*, 169–184, text of petition 225–232, Wells mentioned on 231.

10. Wells to Ida Rothstein, August 10, 1952, in Civil Rights Congress Collection—Schomburg Center for Research in Black Culture (hereafter CRC-SC). CRC press release, January 15, 1950, CRC-SC.

11. CRC circular, August 31, 1950, CRC-SC. Goodman cited in CRC "Fact Sheet—Wesley Robert Wells" (October 1950), CRC-SCSS. Goodman fully quoted, and legal history of the case explained, in Royce Brier, "This World Today: The People vs. Wesley Robert Wells," *San Francisco Chronicle* (March 19, 1954).

12. "Report on Delegation to Governor Warren" (October 16, 1950), CRC-SC. *Sacramento Bee* (October 17, 1950). *San Francisco Chronicle* (October 17, 1950). In the 1950 gubernatorial race, Warren needed to appease the Republican right wing, which, as best evidenced in Nixon's concurrent campaign against Helen Gahagan Douglas, made Communism the defining issue; Warren would easily defeat James Roosevelt (FDR's son) in the November election. See Burton R. Brazil, "The 1950 Elections in California," *Western Political Quarterly* (March 1951): 67–71.

13. "Quentin Guards Break-Up Killers' Sit-Down Strike," *San Francisco Chronicle* (November 1, 1950). Wells to Garry, December 3, 1950, CRC-SC. Two other residents were child killer Fred Stroble and the one-time Yacht Bandit Lloyd Sampsell, now back for murder. In *88 Men and 2 Women* (1962), Warden Clinton T. Duffy refers to a "vicious fight" between Wells and Chessman. Duffy's only indication of Wells's reputation among prison insiders is a mention of him as a "tough, consistent troublemaker" (188).

14. Wells to Ida Rothstein, October 14, 1950, CRC-SC; excerpted in CRC, *My Name Is Wesley Robert Wells* (San Francisco, 1951), 26–27. Green quoted in *My Name Is Wesley Robert Wells*, 5–6. Wells quoted in ibid., 29.

15. John Howard Lawson, preface to Wesley Robert Wells, *Letters from the Death House* (Los Angeles: Civil Rights Congress, 1951), pages not numbered. Patterson to Rothstein, September 10, 1953, CRC-SC. Patterson to Editors, November 12, 1953, CRC-SC.

16. Patterson to Rothstein, February 5, 1951, CRC-SC. Rothstein to Patterson, September 1, 1953, and September 16, 1953; both CRC-SC.

17. For a list of participating unions, see Religious Committee for the Defense of Wesley Robert Wells, "Appeals to the Governor of California to Save the Life of Wesley Robert Wells" (San Leandro, Calif., 1954), 25, 29, CRC-SCSS. Wells to Oil Workers International Union, August 20, 1953, CRC-SC.

Organized Labor excerpted in Religious Committee, "Appeals to the Governor," 23. March conference described in *Daily People's World* (March 9, 1954). For more on the anti-Communist purge by California's AFL-CIO leadership, see Gerald Horne, *Fire This Time: The Watts Uprising and the 1960s* (Charlottesville: University of Virginia Press, 1995), 3–9; for a survey of the Communist affiliations of many of the participating unions—the ILWU, UE, Fur Workers, et al.—see Ellen Schrecker, *Many Are the Crimes: McCarthyism in America* (Boston: Little, Brown, 1998), 26–31. A further example of grassroots participation was the fact sheet put together by Willard Harper, a civics teacher at Jordan High School in South-Central Los Angeles; see "Does Striking a Guard Warrant Death?" CRC-SCSS. Harper also explained the case a letter published in *The Nation* (February 27, 1954), 188.

18. On the politics of the black press, see Horne, *Fire This Time*, 6–7. Views of black press collected in Religious Committee, "Appeals to the Governors," 21. Rogers's *Pittsburgh Courier* articles (e.g., October 3, 1953; November 7, 1953) circulated by the State Defense Committee for Wesley Robert Wells, CRC-SCSS. Wesley Wells Defense Committee of Southern California, *Wesley Wells Defender* (e.g., March 5, 1954; March 12, 1954), CRC-SCSS.

19. Religious Committee, "Appeals to Governor," 9–15, 29. Presbyterian resolution cited in *Daily People's World* (March 12, 1954). AFSC members quoted in *California Eagle* (March [?], 1954), CRC-SCSS.

20. Text and signatures of letter from physicians cited in Religious Committee, "Appeals to the Governor," 16–17. Howard and Frym excerpted in ibid., 8, 24. *Los Angeles Daily News* (ally of Democrats) cited in *Wesley Wells Defender* (March 12, 1954). Another influential official supporter was Superior Court Judge A. A. Scott, who had sentenced Wells to prison for his 1942 theft: "I have been in touch with him on many occasions and noted a great change in his outlook. . . . Some of his letters are real masterpieces," Scott wrote to *California Eagle* editor Robert Ellis. Letter reprinted in Religious Committee, "Appeals to the Governor," 22.

21. Winchell's 1950 support cited in Religious Committee, "Appeals," 24. Knight quoted in Winchell's *New York Daily Mirror* column (March 16, 1954). Meeting of Hawkins (Los Angeles) and Rumford (Berkeley) with Knight cited in *Wesley Wells Defender* (March 12, 1954), CRC-SCSS. "Justice Issue in Wells Case," *San Francisco Chronicle* (March 21, 1954). Graves, Knight, unions, et al., cited in *Wesley Wells Defender* (March 5, 12, and 19, 1954). Full text of Knight's commutation in execution file #24155, California State Archives. In a recent biography, Neal Gabler off-handedly notes, "Thanks largely to Walter's intervention, Wells's sentence was eventually commuted." Neal Gabler, *Winchell: Gossip, Power and the Culture of Celebrity* (New York: Knopf, 1994), 409.

22. Patterson to Schermerhorn, March 10, 1954, CRC-SC. *California Eagle* (March [?], 1954), CRC-SCSS. Dorothy Healey, "Report to Southern California District Convention," HUAC hearings, 86th Congress, IB, 64. Charlotta Bass, *Forty Years: Memoirs from the Pages of a Newspaper* (Los Angeles: Charlotta Bass, 1960), 180; quoted in Horne, *Communist Front,* 325.

23. Wells quote in *San Francisco Chronicle* (March 27, 1954). Wells to McGee (dated March 21, 1954, but includes quotes from the next week's news-

papers), CRC-SC. "Free Wells Move Now in Order," *Los Angeles Tribune* (April 9, 1954), reprinted by CRC, CRC-SCSS. *Wesley Wells Defender* (April 7, 1954). West Harlem Wells Defense Committee, "American Love of Justice Cheats Gas Chamber!" (April 1954), CRC-SC. L. King to Wells, April 8, 1954, CRC-SC. After the clemency decision, Director of Corrections McGee told the press, "We can't have any sympathy for Wells as an individual," and "Some of the inmates have said . . . 'the only way to be sure to live a long time is to get Wells before he gets them first.'" Quoted in Wells to McGee, March 21, 1954, CRC-SC.

24. Patterson to Schermerhorn, April 3, 1954, CRC-SC. *Daily Worker* (April 13, 1954). Symington to Stone and McWilliams, April 11, 1954, CRC-SC. Patterson to Schermerhorn, April 27, 1954, CRC-SC.

25. "The Quality of Mercy," *The Nation* (April 15, 1954), 413–414. Schermerhorn to CRC chapters, April 3, 1954, CRC-SC (in handwriting atop the letter: "Sent to all CRC chapters . . . [and several participants]").

26. Dorothy Healey and Maurice Isserman, *Dorothy Healey Remembers: A Life in the Communist Party* (New York: Oxford University Press, 1990), 184–185.

27. Patterson to editors, November 12, 1953, CRC-SC. Attorney Henry Gross (Chess "Master") to Knight, February 3, 1954, cited in Religious Committee, "Appeals to the Governors," 26. *Los Angeles Tribune* (April 9, 1954).

28. Sampling of church statements included in Brown Collection, carton 205. In protest of Chessman's sentence, Graves resigned on May 10, 1954. See also *San Francisco Chronicle* (May 11, 1954); Orange Grove Friends to Brown, March 19, 1960; transcript of KPFK broadcast, "The Coming Death of Caryl Chessman" (October 18, 1959), Brown Collection, carton 209; transcript of clemency hearing, October 15, 1959, Brown Collection, carton 207; telegram, Martin Hall of Humanist Council to Brown, March 19, 1960, Brown Collection, carton 210.

29. Petition to Knight, March 25, 1954, CRC-SCSS. Among others, signers included student representatives from L.A. City College, USC, and UCLA; Methodist and Jewish youth leaders; and committee leaders from the Urban League and UAW locals.

30. Ines Jordan to Knight, May 5, 1954; Betty and Luis Lopez to Knight, July 27, 1954; both in Brown Collection, carton 205. For a letter from an "ordinary citizen" and Republican, see Ernest Peters to Knight, May 11, 1954, Brown Collection, carton 205. Many nonwhite letter writers used a common form of address. For example, Roger Portis of Spokane, Washington, wrote to Governor Knight, "Dear Sir, I am a colored man," and Helen Strong of Los Angeles began a letter to Brown, "I am a Negro." While it would be a mistake to assume that every letter that did not begin this way came from a white person, most writers made special note when they were not white. Portis to Knight, January 7, 1955, carton 205; Strong to Brown, May 10, 1960, carton 210.

31. Weakley to Brown, October 5, 1959, Brown Collection, carton 210. Paul Brown to Brown, August 11, 1959, carton 210. Walker to Knight, July 28, 1954, carton 205. Mrs. D. M. Chant to Knight, December 7, 1954, carton 205. In his analysis of middle-class opinion during World War II, Robert Westbrook argues, "Just because most citizens are not political philosophers does not mean that they do not on occasion advance significant theoretical arguments or that we

should not subject these arguments to the same scrutiny that we give those of intellectual elites." From 1954 to 1960, Chessman's case provided another occasion when many ordinary citizens advanced "significant theoretical arguments." Robert Westbrook, "Fighting for the American Family: Private Interests and Public Obligations in World War II," in Fox and Lears, *The Power of Culture,* 196.

32. McMaster to Knight, May 5, 1954; Etzweiler to Knight, May 5, 1954; Harvey to Knight, May 12, 1954; Burnett to Knight, May 12, 1954; Bates to Knight, May 7, 1954; all in Brown Collection, carton 205.

33. Mrs. R. C. Dunn to Governor Knight, May 13, 1954; Anna B. Mason to Knight, July 29, 1954; both in Brown Collection, carton 205.

34. Butler to Knight, May 12, 1954; Stevens to Knight, May 6, 1954; Fleming to Knight, December 10, 1954; Nixon to Knight, May 10, 1954; all in Brown Collection, carton 205. This view was also expressed by Walter Wanger, the Hollywood film producer later responsible for the anti–death penalty film *I Want to Live!* (1958). Wanger's home had been the target of one of Chessman's red light bandit robberies, causing him to testify at Chessman's trial (see Kunstler, *Beyond a Reasonable Doubt,* esp. 211–213). In a telegram to Knight, Wanger argued, "I trust you will consider the advantages that would be gained by keeping Chessman alive in order to allow the criminologists and psychiatrists who are seeking to solve the problems of the prisons to avail themselves the chance to study this individual as well as allowing him to make further contributions to the subject of dealing with crime." Wanger to Knight, May 4, 1954, Brown Collection, carton 205.

35. Strain to Knight, May 13, 1954; Virginia M. Feagans to Knight, May 11, 1954; John Dailey to Knight, May 13, 1954; Ball to Knight, May 10, 1954; Blanchfield to Knight, July 27, 1954; all in Brown Collection, carton 205.

36. Bernhart to Knight, September 27, 1955; Mitchell to Knight, January 12, 1955; Subke to Knight, July 28, 1954; Maiden to Knight, January 10, 1955; Frank to Knight, May 11, 1954; all in Brown Collection, carton 205.

37. See Francis Allen, *The Decline of the Rehabilitative Ideal: Penal Policy and Social Purpose* (New Haven: Yale University Press, 1981), 11. As Allen outlines, the larger retreat from the "rehabilitative ideal" began in the early 1970s, after the political and cultural protest of the 1960s (1–31).

38. Ella Rothschild to Knight, July 28, 1954; Ruby Harden to Knight, May 6, 1954; William Newlin to Knight, July 28, 1954; all in Brown Collection, carton 205.

39. Charles and Florence Baker to Knight, July 27, 1954, Brown Collection, carton 205; Mrs. Magruder Eckles to Brown, August 30, 1959, carton 210; George Munyer to Knight, May 13, 1954, carton 205.

40. For a review of the New Class literature, see Barbara Ehrenreich, *Fear of Falling: The Inner Life of the Middle Class* (New York: Doubleday, 1987), 144–195. Barbara and John Ehrenreich, "The Professional Managerial Class," *Radical America* (March–April 1977). In *White Collar,* Mills observed, "The probability that people will have a similar mentality and ideology, and that they will join together for action, is increased the more homogenous they are with respect to class, occupation and prestige" (295).

41. Dorothy L. Gardner, "May Ban Death Penalty," *Christian Century* (May 1, 1957), 575; California State Assembly, *Hearings of the Assembly Interim Committee on Judiciary to Study Capital Punishment* (Sacramento: California State Assembly, 1957), committee view on 31, Alverson on 37, Brown on 45–46. In his pro–death penalty testimony, Judge Fricke discussed judicial "interference" with Chessman's execution (32). As the report noted, the major argument against capital punishment during the hearings was the "worldwide trend toward abolition" (23), a view stressed by Richard McGee in his testimony (45). The discriminatory bias by class and race—a point the report attributed to Warden Duffy—was fifth among the reasons for abolition (25–26).

42. Brown's career outlined in an interview, "The Campaign Against Death," *Look* (May 7, 1963), 29. Totton Anderson, "The 1958 Election in California," *Western Political Quarterly* 12, no. 1 (part II) (March 1959): 276–300. "Brown Says He Won't Aid Wells," *People's World* (September 19, 1951). "Brown to Push for Execution of Chessman," *San Francisco Chronicle* (May 19, 1954).

43. For a review of Catholic opposition in California and elsewhere during the period, see Mary Ellen Leary, "California Views the Death Penalty," *America* (August 5, 1972), 55–59. Robert Steed, "Open Letter to the California Legislature," *The Catholic Worker* (March 1960), 1. Robert Steed, "Reactions to the Chessman Case," *The Catholic Worker* (April 1960), 1, 2, 8.

44. Petition to Brown, October 5, 1959; Anne Petersen to Brown, September 1, 1959; Mrs. Eloise Enoch to Brown, October 5, 1959; all in Brown Collection, carton 210.

45. Helen Arfe to Brown, October 4, 1959; Diana Conway to Brown, October 17, 1959; Petition, Brooklyn College students to Brown, July 25, 1959; all in Brown Collection, carton 210.

46. Dona Shaw to Brown, September 11, 1959, Brown Collection, carton 210; John Gallagher to Knight, July 26, 1954, carton 205; Kathleen Rousseau to Knight, May 13, 1954, carton 205.

47. Petition to Brown, September 17, 1959; Edward Mann to Brown, October 5, 1959; both in Brown Collection, carton 210.

48. Although not all the letters written to the governors are contained in the Brown Collection, it is clear that the overwhelming majority of letters came from supporters of Chessman. Toward the end of the case, *The Economist* reported that letters on behalf of Chessman outweighed letters supporting his execution by three to one; an informal tally sheet by one of Brown's secretaries made the ratio appear much higher (Brown Collection, carton 209). However, in his memoirs about the case, Brown wrote, "the thousands of letters that poured into my office were almost evenly split." Given the hostility toward Chessman in the popular press of California, many of those who supported his execution may not have felt the need to voice their opinion directly. See Edmund G. Brown, with Dick Adler, *Public Justice, Private Mercy: A Governor's Education on Death Row* (New York: Weidenfeld & Nicholson, 1989), 37.

49. "Chessman's Last Chance?" *Los Angeles Herald-Express* (October 14, 1959).

50. Carrie Jensen to Governor Knight, May 12, 1954; Glenn Newhouse to

Knight, May 11, 1954; J. Marsh to Knight, May 13, 1954; Shatto to Brown, October 16, 1959; all in Brown Collection, carton 205. Chessman's supporters often made use of the phrase "sob sisters," declaring themselves immune from this label. For example, Benjamin Petrie of Monterey began a telegram to Knight, "[I] am not one who sides with sob sisters." Petrie to Knight, May 13, 1954, Brown Collection, carton 205.

51. Mabel Hunsaker to Knight, July 27, 1954; Mrs. Jack Zehnder to Knight, May 13, 1954; H. H. Brown to Knight, May 15, 1954; all in Brown Collection, carton 205.

52. Sue Sally Jones to Governor Brown, March 26, 1960, Brown Collection, carton 210; George Robb to Brown, March 27, 1960, carton 210; Hafner to Brown, February 16, 1960, carton 208; Thornton to Brown, March 24, 1960, carton 210.

53. J. Waller to Governor Brown, April 27, 1960, Brown Collection, carton 210; Mrs. Florence Thomsen to Governor Knight, October 28, 1957, carton 205; Mrs. Mary Ann Crabtree to Brown, May 6, 1960, carton 210. The best example of a critic taking these opinions as representative of all Chessman opponents is Richard Meister, "Who Hates Chessman: A Study of the Governor's Mail," *The Nation* (March 26, 1960), 275–277.

54. Sidney Hook, *The New Leader* (April 3, 1961), 18–20; reprinted along with other pro–death penalty arguments (by J. Edgar Hoover, Jacques Barzun, et al.), in Bedau, *Death Penalty in America* (1964 ed.), 120–165.

55. For a summary of the three opinion polls it had taken since 1956, see *The California Poll* (March 3, 1960). Unlike in other states—especially those in the Northeast—support for capital punishment stayed strong (averaging around 55 percent, compared to around 35 percent for opposition) in postwar California.

56. Foucault, *Discipline and Punish*, 30.

57. Clemency folder; McKeeson to Brown, October 8, 1959; both in Brown Collection, carton 207.

58. F. R. Dickson to Brown, October 14, 1959; Nelson and McGee in Brown Clemency Folder (October 1959); Duffy memorandum, August 19, 1948; all in Brown Collection, carton 207. In *88 Men and 2 Women* (1962), Duffy still strongly held this view of Chessman, even though he did not favor the latter's (or any other's) execution. See Duffy, *88 Men and 2 Women,* 126–139.

59. Earl Warren to McGee, Inter-Office Memorandum, October 9, 1952 (Knight annotation, May 1, 1954), Brown Collection, carton 207.

60. Report for Clemency Hearing, Cecil Poole to Brown, October 14, 1959, Brown Collection, carton 207, 1–11.

61. Chessman to Poole, October 6, 1959, Brown Collection, carton 207.

62. Transcript, Governor's Executive Clemency Hearing, October 15, 1959, Brown Collection, carton 207, 3, 5–12.

63. Ibid., 41, 45–46, 48. As Davis clarified, his statement was not to be taken as an "admission of guilt" but as acknowledgement that such a line of argument would not succeed with the governor (41). Not surprisingly, during his presentation at the meeting the psychiatrist Isidore Ziferstein would likewise stress Chessman's rehabilitation. Ibid., 105–108.

64. Ibid., 68, 71, 75.

65. *Los Angeles Times,* October 16, 1959. Governor's Press Release, October 17, 1959, Brown Collection, carton 207.

66. Clemency hearing transcript, October, 14, 1959, 50; Governor's Press Release, October 17, 1959; Governor's Press Release, February 19, 1960; all in Brown Collection, carton 207.

67. Poole to Brown, October 14, 1959; McGee to Brown, October 8, 1959; both in Brown Collection, carton 207. One insider sympathetic to Chessman was Byron Eshelman, San Quentin's Protestant Chaplain. Writing to Brown in 1960, Eshelman referred to Wells, saying he "was known to a more obstreperous and violent person than Chessman, but who had not killed, and was commuted." Eshelman to Brown, February 15, 1960, Brown Collection, carton 207. In his death penalty memoirs, Brown concluded a chapter on the case by stating: "Chessman was a nasty, arrogant, unrepentant man, almost certainly guilty of the crimes he was convicted of, but I didn't think those crimes deserved the death penalty then, and I certainly don't think so now." See Brown, *Public Justice, Private Mercy,* 52.

68. Full text of Brown's reprieve in Duffy, *88 Men and 2 Women,* 136–137. Full telegram in ibid. "Punishment to Fit the Times?" *Newsweek* (February 29, 1960), 21. Sampling of press reaction in Duffy, 136–137. Leavy quoted in letter, Chessman to Brown, February 26, 1960, Brown Collection, carton 207.

69. Brown's reprieve in Duffy, *88 Men and 2 Women,* 136–137. *Newsweek* (February 29, 1960), 21–22. Frank Harper, "California's Death Penalty Fight," *Dissent* (Winter 1961), 101.

70. *San Francisco Examiner* (March 3, 1960); both poll results reported in *San Francisco Examiner* (March 4, 1960). Brown backs away from bill in *San Francisco Examiner* (March 5, 1960). Even with Democratic majorities in both houses, the Senate tally was 21 to 6 (13 no comment) and the Assembly was 55 to 11 (12 no comment) against Chessman. As for general abolition, numbers showed 27 to 11 against in the Senate, 45 to 25 opposed in the Assembly. In other words, even many of the death penalty opponents in the legislature would not openly back Chessman. On the eve of the hearings, San Francisco Assemblyman Phillip Burton led the pro-abolition side in a KQED TV debate; *San Francisco Examiner* (March 4, 1960). On Assembly leader Schell's appeal to the John Birch Society, see Carey McWilliams, "Has Success Spoiled Dick Nixon?" *The Nation* (June 2, 1962), 487–493.

71. California State Senate, *Report of the Senate Committee on Judiciary [Death Penalty Bill]* (Sacramento: California State Senate, 1960). Davis in ibid., 97–100. Parker in ibid., 160.

72. Leavy in *Report on Judiciary Hearing,* 168–173; on impact of Leavy's media splash, see Brown, *Public Justice, Private Mercy,* 47–48. *San Francisco Chronicle* (March 11, 1960). *San Francisco Examiner* (March 11, 1960).

73. Davis quoted in *San Francisco Examiner* (March 11, 1960). Harper, "California's Death Penalty Fight," 99–102. Loewenburg, "An Interview with Richard Drinnon," 76–81. Douglas granted the 1959 stay because he saw procedural problems, but he was not sympathetic to Chessman's overall claim of innocence; see Parker, *Caryl Chessman,* 4.

74. *The California Poll* (March 3, 1960). For a general review of national

and international trends in the postwar period, see Erskine, "The Polls: Capital Punishment."

75. Hardwick, "The Life and Death of Caryl Chessman," 506. Meister, "Who Hates Chessman," 275–277. On liberal disdain for mass opinion, see Ross, "Reading the Rosenberg Letters," 15–41; and Richard Pells, *The Liberal Mind in a Conservative Age: American Intellectuals in the 1940s and 1950s* (New York: Harper & Row, 1986), 117–183.

76. *Service Union Reporter* (March 1960), Brown Collection, carton 207. *California Eagle* (April 28, 1960). Wells, letter to the editor, *California Eagle* (October 20, 1960). Wells to Brown, February 3, 1963, CRC-SSRC. Though it is unclear whether Wells sent the February 3 letter, he says that his attorney Leo Branton had mentioned the case to Nat King Cole, who "volunteered to invite Gov. Brown over for dinner some evening and present the appeal to him informally." Further evidence of African American support for Chessman was reported by Assemblyman Carley Porter of Compton, who told a Brown aide that a local poll found ten-to-one support for commutation. Mickey Haggard to Brown, February 19, 1960, Brown Collection, carton 210.

77. Jones to Brown, November 16, 1959, Brown Collection, carton 210.

5. CHESSMAN'S GHOST (1960–1974)

1. *New York Times* (May 3, 1960). The Jansky letter quoted above is in the Brown Collection, carton 210; the Reagan quote is from Andrew Kopkind, "Running Wild: California's Political Rat Race," *New Republic* (October 30, 1966), 19.

2. *Los Angeles Times* (May 3, 1960).

3. "Conscience, Chessman, and Capital Punishment: The Case for Clemency," *Los Angeles Times* (April 27, 1960). Herb Caen, "As It Must to All Men," *San Francisco Chronicle* (May 1, 1960). Hundreds of letters written to Brown after the execution illustrated the national resonance of the case. David and Marlene Demarest of Manitowoc, Wisconsin, for example, wrote, "Your action was a national disgrace, an outrage to civilized men everywhere." Common, too, were the angry words of "Shamed American" from New Rochelle, New York: "When are *you* going to die, *murderer?*" David and Marlene Demarest to Brown, May 5, 1960; "Shamed American" to Brown, May 2, 1960; both in Brown Collection, carton 210.

4. March 1960 legislative address reprinted in Brown, "A Matter of Conviction." Brown, *Public Justice,* 52.

5. Michael Rossman, *The Wedding Within the War* (Garden City, N.Y.: Doubleday, 1971), 31. "Golly Gee, California Is a Strange State," *Ramparts* (October 1966), 11–33. Reagan quoted in Bill Boyarsky, *The Rise of Ronald Reagan* (New York: Random House, 1968), 195.

6. On white backlash, see Totton J. Anderson and Eugene C. Lee, "The 1966 Election in California," *The Western Political Quarterly* 20, no. 2 (June 1967): 544; Edmund G. Brown, *Reagan and Reality: The Two Californias* (New York: Praeger Publishers, 1970), esp. 14–28, 98–111; Michael P. Rogin and John L.

Shover, *Political Change in California: Critical Elections and Social Movements, 1890–1966* (Westport, Conn.: Greenwood Press, 1970), esp. 199–201; and Horne, *Fire This Time,* 301–302.

7. "The Chessman Affair," *Time* (March 21, 1960), 16–20. "Conscience, Chessman, and Capital Punishment: The Case for Clemency."

8. For the influence of Mills on the early New Left, see James Miller, *"Democracy Is in the Streets": From Port Huron to the Siege of Chicago* (New York: Anchor Books, 1987), 78–91, quote on 83. For a chronology of Bay Area student activism, see Dale L. Johnson, "On the Ideology of the Campus Revolution," *Studies on the Left* 2 (1961): 73–75. Michael Harrington, "The American Campus: 1962," *Dissent* (Winter 1962), 164–168. As Harrington further characterized the early New Left, "Its tone is moral, focusing on questions like peace, capital punishment and human equality, ignoring economic conflict and social planning" (ibid.).

9. Although they use a different descriptive label, Barbara and John Ehrenreich provide a similar explanation of the origins of the New Left in "The New Left: A Case Study in Professional-Managerial Class Radicalism," *Radical America* (May–June, 1977). For examples of common picket slogans, see *Time* (March 21, 1960), 16. For summary of San Quentin vigil, see *San Francisco News-Call Bulletin* (May 3, 1960). Stephen Bartholomew, "A Man Just Died Around the Bend," *San Francisco State Golden Gater* (May 4, 1960). *San Francisco Chronicle* (May 3, 1960). White to Governor Brown, May 4, 1960, Brown Collection, carton 210.

10. Dorothy McMinn to Brown, May 5, 1960, Brown Collection, carton 210; Sherina Friedlander to Brown, May 4, 1960, Brown Collection, carton 210; Rossman, *Wedding Within the War,* 34. Recalling his participation in the Chessman vigil—his first political protest, and one that would "mold [his] consciousness forever"—Abbie Hoffman said, "Around me people were in tears. Someone moaned, 'No! No!' as if he had been wounded." Cited in *Run Run Run: The Lives of Abbie Hoffman,* by Jack Hoffman and Daniel Simon (New York: Putnam, 1994). Meanwhile, in New York City on the day of the execution, Jay Jacobs wrote in *The Reporter,* "The streets were full of people who somehow looked a lot less innocent than they had that morning." Jay Jacobs, "A Clear Day in Central Park," *The Reporter* (May 10, 1960).

11. Paul Jacobs and Saul Landau, *The New Radicals: A Report with Documents* (New York: Random House, 1966), 13. Terry Southern, "Pellet of Nihilism," *The Nation* (May 21, 1960), 440. Gregory Corso, "On Chessman's Crime," *Yugen* 7 (1961): 29–30. Tuli Kupferberg, "Death and Love," *Kulchur* 3 (1961): 29–31. On Bay Area artists' depictions of Chessman, see Rebecca Solnit, *Secret Exhibition: Six California Artists of the Cold War Era* (San Francisco: City Light Books, 1990).

12. Paul Goodman, "The Fate of Dr. Reich's Books," *Kulchur* 2 (1960): 19–23. Paul Goodman, *The Society I Live in Is Mine* (New York: Horizon Press, 1962), 75–77.

13. Norman Mailer, "The White Negro," in *Advertisements for Myself* (New York: Putnam, 1981), 301–306. Norman Mailer, "Superman Comes to

the Supermarket," in Gerald Howard, ed., *The Sixties: The Art, Attitudes, Politics and Media of Our Most Explosive Decade* (New York: Washington Square Press, 1982), 150.

14. Ronald Berman, *America in the Sixties: An Intellectual History* (New York: Free Press, 1968), 122, 275–276.

15. Susan Brownmiller, *Against Our Will: Men, Women, and Rape* (New York: Simon & Schuster, 1975), 299–300. Cummins, *Rise and Fall of California's Radical Prison Movement*, 62. Berman, *America in the Sixties*, 282.

16. Michael Harrington, "The Mystical Militants," in Irving Howe, ed., *Beyond the New Left* (New York: McCall, 1970), 34–39.

17. "California Is a Strange State!" 22, 23–24, 33. Scheer's third and more immediate criticism concerned Brown's effort to dump Simon Cassady, the head of the California Democratic Council and vocal critic of Brown's support for LBJ's Vietnam escalation; ibid., 17–21. For left criticism of Scheer's position, see Healey and Isserman, *Dorothy Healey Remembers*, 199–204; and "'New Politics' in California," *The Nation* (October 17, 1966), 372–373.

18. Chessman letter, see *Call Bulletin* (May 3, 1960). Brown's "impeachment" statement cited in letter, J. Upmann to Brown, May 6, 1960, Brown Collection, carton 210. Chessman to Brown, February 26, 1960, Brown Collection, carton 207. Brown quoted in *Los Angeles Times* (May 3, 1960).

19. "Brown Has Lost 'Swing Voters,' Nixon Tells GOP," *San Francisco Chronicle* (March 19, 1961). Jackson Doyle, "Death Penalty a Campaign Issue," *San Francisco Chronicle* (August 12, 1962).

20. "Will It Be Brown or Nixon?" *Newsweek* (October 29, 1962), 19–23.

21. "The State as Hangman," *New York Times* (February 2, 1963). Brown quoted in *New York Times* (February 1, 1960). "The Campaign Against Death," *Look* (May 7, 1963), 29. Field Institute, *California Poll* (March 19, 1963). For the bill's defeat, see "Capital Punishment," *The New Republic* (June 8, 1963). Brown's moratorium included a number of exceptions: repeat murderers, double homicides, murders during kidnapping, murders of police officers, murders of prison guards. See *New York Times* (February 1, 1960).

22. On Brown's use of clemency, see Joseph A. Spangler, "California's Death Penalty Dilemma," *Crime and Delinquency* (January 1969), 142–148. "On the Way Out," *The Nation* (November 23, 1964), 367. On "logjam," see below. Field Institute, *California Poll* (April 29, 1965). *The Nation* (November 23, 1964). Overall, Brown commuted 23 sentences during his two terms, as compared to 35 executions; Earl Warren's ratio was 8 commutations to 82 executions, and Goodwin Knight commuted 6 out of 47. See Spangler, "California's Death Penalty Dilemma."

23. *The Nation* (November 23, 1964). Hugo Adam Bedau, "The 1964 Death Penalty Referendum in Oregon: Some Notes of a Participant-Observer," *Crime and Delinquency* (October 1980), 528–536. In 1958, the Delaware legislature ended the state's death penalty. During legislative hearings, Herbert Cobin, president of the state's Prisoner's Aid Society, submitted a report outlining nine reasons for abolition. Among Cobin's major arguments against the death penalty were its failure as a deterrent, its tendency to punish the poor, and its "demor-

alizing" effect on public officials, whose careers were dedicated to "rehabilitating offenders." Accordingly, the legislature's action prompted Delaware's Attorney General, Januar D. Bove, Jr., to declare, "We are proud that our State has abolished capital punishment and has taken this forward step in the field of criminology." In 1961, however, two widely publicized murder cases resulted in public outcry to restore the death penalty. Both murders involved black men who, while on parole, killed elderly white people in rural areas of the state. In response, the Delaware state legislature reinstated capital punishment later that same year. Delaware's experiment in the new criminology, in short, ended due to public outcry against black criminals specifically, and the larger premise of rehabilitation in general. Herbert L. Cobin, "Abolition and Restoration of the Death Penalty in Delaware," in Bedau, *Death Penalty in America*, 362–373. With legislative support and little media fanfare, New York Governor Nelson Rockefeller, a liberal Republican, signed legislation ending the death penalty for all but two offenses—killing police officers or prison guards—in June 1965. See *New York Times* (June 2, 1965).

24. Horne, *Fire This Time*, 263–326, 266, 281. Brown, *Reagan and Reality*, 14, 98–111, 123. Brown faced severe criticism within the Democratic Party, according to Anderson and Lee; party members "sensitive to capital punishment criticized Brown vigorously for his many attempts and ultimate failure to save convicted rapist-slayer [*sic*] Caryl Chessman from execution in 1960" ("The 1966 Election," 544).

25. "Reagan Announces He's a Candidate for Governor," *Los Angeles Times* (January 5, 1966). On Watts arrests and general crime rates, see Horne, *Fire This Time*, 239–240. Robison quoted in "Meaningless Statistics," *Time* (August 19, 1966). Brown, *Reagan and Reality*, 98–111. On opinion polls, see Anderson and Lee, "The 1966 Election," 543–544. Brown, *Reagan and Reality*, 123. On manipulation of FBI crime statistics by politicians during the period, see Jessica Mitford, *Kind and Usual Punishment: The Prison Business* (New York: Knopf, 1971), 64–86.

26. Tom Wicker, "Reagan Shuns Image of Goldwater in Coast Race," *New York Times* (June 1, 1966). Carey McWilliams, "How to Succeed with the Backlash," *The Nation* (October 31, 1966), 440–441. Field Institute, *California Poll* (September 22, 1966). On national Republican strategy, see Richard M. Nixon, "If Mob Rule Takes Hold in U.S.—A Warning from Richard M. Nixon," *U.S. News and World Report* (August 15, 1966), 64–65; and "G.O.P. Will Press Racial Disorders as Election Issue," *New York Times* (October 4, 1966). On race and Goldwaterism, see Irving Howe, "The Goldwater Movement," in *Steady Work* (New York: Harcourt, Brace, and World, 1966), 224–230. On race and the rise of New Right in California, see Rogin and Shover, *Political Change in California*, 153–201.

27. *New York Times* (December 24, 1966).

28. *New York Times* (December 29, 1966). The one-third number (nineteen of sixty) is calculated from a July 1967 NAACP lawsuit charging racial discrimination because seventeen of the fifty-eight on California's death row were black —the fates of the two others, Aaron Mitchell and Calvin Thomas, are discussed

below. On the lawsuit, see *Los Angeles Times* (July 6, 1967). Of the four Brown commutations, three were white, one was Chicano; see Wolfe, *Pileup on Death Row,* 48. Wolfe's book was dedicated to Chessman.

   29. "Reagan's Inaugural Talk," *Los Angeles Times* (January 6, 1967). Phil Kerby, "Revolt Against the Poor: The Reagan Backlash," *The Nation* (September 25, 1967), 262–267. As explained by Jessica Mitford, the prison budget was not included in Reagan's ten percent "across the board" cutback in state spending; instead it rose steadily during Reagan's first six years in office. See Mitford, *Kind and Usual Punishment,* 189–198.

   30. On California executions, see *Los Angeles Times* (April 16, 1967) and *San Francisco Chronicle* (July 6, 1967); for comparison to national trends, see Hugo Adam Bedau, "The Issue of Capital Punishment," *Current History* (August 1967), 82–87, 116. On the Lavergne case, see *Los Angeles Times* (March 14, 1967). Douglas's role is cited frequently in Michael Melstner, *Cruel and Unusual: The Supreme Court and Capital Punishment* (New York: Random House, 1973); Reagan quoted in ibid. Reagan's official announcement of Meese's appointment as clemency secretary stated that Meese was "a believer in capital punishment as a deterrent to crime"; see *New York Times* (December 24, 1966). Assemblyman Charles Warren, meanwhile, unsuccessfully proposed a moratorium on executions until a public referendum in the June 1968 primary; see Jack Donahue, "Capital Punishment—a Time for Honesty," *Los Angeles Times* (April 9, 1967).

   31. Jerry Le Blanc, "'Killing Me Solves Nothing' (Interview with Aaron Mitchell)," *Ebony* (June 1967), 122. For an overview of the case, see Wolfe, *Pileup on Death Row,* 3–76. On the clemency hearing, see *Los Angeles Times* (April 11, 1967). "Man of Conviction," *Newsweek* (April 24, 1967), 29. April 1967 also saw the California legislature debate a gun-control bill aimed at disarming the newly formed Black Panthers. Reagan's support for the bill became a focal point of the Panthers' dramatic armed march on the Capitol three weeks after Mitchell's execution. See Phillip Foner, *The Black Panthers Speak* (New York: J. B. Lippincott Co., 1971), 41–42.

   32. On the Thomas commutation, see *Los Angeles Times* (June 30, 1967); on the NAACP lawsuit, see *Los Angeles Times* (June 28 and June 30, 1967). Meese quoted in Boyarsky, *Rise of Ronald Reagan,* 211.

   33. Boyarsky, *Rise of Ronald Reagan,* 201. On California's prominence in the LDF's legal struggle, see Meltsner, *Cruel and Unusual,* 225 and passim. Reagan quoted in *San Francisco Chronicle* (July 7, 1967). Field Institute, *California Poll* (May 22, 1969). Reagan quoted in Boyarsky, *Rise of Ronald Reagan,* 195. The frequency of death penalty decisions awarded by California juries matched the political climate of the 1960s—only six from 1960 to 1962, eleven in 1963, four in 1964, ten in 1965, seventeen each in 1966 and 1967, twenty-one by late 1968. See Spangler, "California's Death Penalty Dilemma," 143.

   34. Reagan quoted in Boyarsky, *Rise of Ronald Reagan,* 202. For Reagan, the two categories of "mad dogs" overlapped. As Boyarsky notes, in a meeting with ACLU officials Reagan defended the death penalty by giving the "details of one of the most macabre cases from California criminal annals and then ask[ing] his visitors how they would treat the killers in that case without the death pen-

alty. One of those at the meeting recalled listening in surprised silence while the governor graphically described the crime, which involved the sexual mutilation of the male victim" (195–196).

35. Thorsten Sellin, "The Inevitable End of Capital Punishment," in Sellin, ed., *Capital Punishment* (New York: Harper & Row, 1967), 239–253. For the list of states, see Bedau, "The Issue of Capital Punishment," 82–87. The movement's shift from a political to a legal struggle is best outlined in Haines, *Against Capital Punishment*, 23–54.

36. "Justice, Georgia Style," *Commonweal* (October 21, 1961), 84. Sylvan M. Shane, "Window on a Gas Chamber," *The Nation* (March 10, 1962), 170–171. "Capital Punishment," *The New Republic* (June 8, 1963), 5. In his 1961 statement, Donal Macnamara placed discriminatory application as the fourth of ten reasons why the American League to Abolish Capital Punishment was opposed (the threat to rehabilitative penology was first). Donal E. J. Macnamara, "Statement Against Capital Punishment," in Bedau, *Death Penalty in America*, 188.

37. Goldberg's two other objections also bear relevance. Aside from the "standard of decency" argument, Goldberg said that the court should consider whether death is a disproportionate penalty for any crime in which no life is taken. Although it is difficult to gauge its direct impact on Goldberg's opinion, Chessman's case had brought this issue to national attention. Goldberg further argued that the death penalty for rape violated the Constitution if "the permissible aims of punishment (e.g. deterrence, isolation, rehabilitation) [can] be achieved as effectively by punishing rape less severely than by death (e.g. by life imprisonment)." Rehabilitative life imprisonment, in other words, served as Goldberg's substitute for the death penalty. See Haines, *Against Capital Punishment*, 26; and Bedau, *The Courts, the Constitution, and Capital Punishment* (Lexington, Mass.: Lexington Books, 1977), 12.

38. For LDF efforts, see Haines, *Against Capital Punishment*, 14–32; and Eric L. Muller, "The Legal Defense Fund's Capital Punishment Campaign: The Distorting Influence of Death," *Yale Law and Policy Review* 4 (1985): 158–187. The LDF's decision to defend poor whites, who, according to Muller, were often "culled from the most racist segment of society," caused some controversy within the organization itself (159, 177).

39. Haines, *Against Capital Punishment*, 42–45. Muller, "The Legal Defense Fund's Capital Punishment Campaign," 179.

40. All national death penalty poll results taken before 1970 can be found in Erskine, "The Polls." Harris Survey, "What Do Americans Think of the Death Penalty," in Bedau, *Death Penalty in America* (1967 ed.), 240–241. Among the findings of the various polls: in 1937, women favored the death penalty by a rate of 57 percent to 43 percent, but by 1966 were opposed 49 to 38 percent, and in 1969 45 to 44 percent. Catholics were in favor 52 to 38 percent in 1965, opposed 45 to 44 percent in 1966, and in favor 54 to 37 percent in 1969. Democrats were opposed 51 to 39 percent in 1966, but in favor 50 to 40 percent in 1969. Men remained supportive, by a rate of 58 to 33 percent in 1960, 47 to 45 percent in 1966, and 60 to 34 percent in 1969. White collar support remained steady at about 54 percent in the late 1960s, with 36 percent opposed. Blacks

averaged about 33 percent support (no exact anti–death penalty figures are given for 1960s). See Erskine, "The Polls." A 1972 Gallup Poll, however, recorded 64 percent opposition (versus 24 percent in favor) among nonwhites. See Neil Vidmar and Phoebe Ellsworth, "Public Opinion and the Death Penalty," *Stanford Law Review* (June 1974), 1254. In their analysis of pro–death penalty opinion, Vidmar and Ellsworth emphasize retribution over deterrence, linking the former to overall hostility toward racial integration (1255–1262).

41. A summary of abolitionist support can be found in Bedau, *The Courts, the Constitution,* 3–6. Early in his administration, Nixon called for the federal death penalty in response to politically motivated bombings; see Ramsay Clark, *Crime in America: Observations on Its Nature, Causes, Preventions and Control* (New York: Simon & Schuster, 1970), 332.

42. For general background on the prisoners' movement, see Cummins, *Rise and Fall,* 128–150. On racial hostilities during Warden Nelson's administration, see Robert Minton and Stephen Rice, "Using Racism at San Quentin," *Ramparts* (January 1970), 19–23.

43. Angela Y. Davis, "Political Prisoners, Prisons and Black Liberation," in Angela Y. Davis, ed., *If They Come in the Morning* (New York: Signet, 1971), 36–38. "The Folsom Prisoners Manifesto of Demands and Anti-Oppression Platform," in Davis, ibid., 74; Nelson quoted, 36. First on the list of twenty-nine demands by the Folsom Prisoners was representation at parole board hearings; fifth was an "immediate end to indeterminate [sentences] . . . to be replaced by fixed terms" (69–70).

44. Trevor Thomas, *This Life We Take: A Case Against the Death Penalty* (San Francisco: Friends Committee on Legislation, 1970), 10–15, 18, 32–34. At the end of the pamphlet, Thomas reiterated longstanding Friends arguments. Ultimately, he supported "a public philosophy which values rehabilitation and crime prevention more than revenge or punishment," and argued that "the death penalty is not consistent with that philosophy" (34).

45. American Friends Service Committee, *A Struggle for Justice* (New York: Hill & Wang, 1971), v–vi, 8. For recent evidence, the report most often cited "the California correctional system, which has pushed further toward full implementation of the rehabilitative ideal than any other prison system in the United States" (82).

46. AFSC, *A Struggle for Justice,* 107, 10. Specifically, the Friends called for fixed sentences, not based on "proof" of rehabilitation; the "uncertainty" of the "indeterminate sentence," they argued, "is one of the more exquisite forms of torture" (146–153, 29).

47. Mitford, *Kind and Unusual Punishment,* 323–324. Erik Olin Wright, *The Politics of Punishment: A Critical Analysis of Prisons in America* (New York: Harper & Row, 1973), 131. On racism in parole board decisions, see Wright, 106–120. Similar points about rehabilitative treatment were made by San Quentin prisoners taking college courses at the time. For a sampling, see *Inside: Prison American Style,* edited by Robert Minton, Jr. (New York: Random House, 1971).

48. Haines, *Against Capital Punishment,* 35–38. Although the majority of justices agreed that the death penalty violated the Eighth Amendment, signifi-

cant differences of opinion existed. Only Justices Brennan and Marshall declared that capital punishment was entirely unconstitutional. According to Haines, Brennan "concluded that [an] execution is uniquely degrading to human dignity and cannot be shown to serve any legitimate purpose better than incarceration." Marshall, meanwhile, felt that the Court's decision would have popular support if "the public [was] more knowledgeable of the actual facts of capital punishment." The positions taken by Douglas, Stewart, and White, however, focused directly on the procedural application of the death penalty. Douglas felt that "death-sentencing procedures were so discretionary that discrimination against minorities and the poor became inevitable." For White, the arbitrary application of the death penalty negated its deterrent effect. Unless a more coherent procedure was established, Stewart, like White, found the death penalty too "capricious" to be constitutional. Thus, "because only two of the justices had ruled that executions by their very nature violate the Constitution," Haines argues, "it was clear that some sort of 'improved' death penalty could rise again in the aftermath of *Furman*."

49. Nixon quoted in *New York Times* (June 30, 1972). Bedau summarizes the immediate reaction to *Furman* in *The Courts, the Constitution*, 93.

50. Mary Ellen Leary, "Voting Their Fears," *The Nation* (December 4, 1972), 548–549; and Leary, "California Views the Death Penalty," 55–59. Reagan's immediate reaction to the *Furman* decision was to encourage California voters to support Proposition 17. See *New York Times* (June 30, 1972).

51. Haines, *Against Capital Punishment*, 52–54. In March 1973, polls showed 63 percent support for the death penalty, a figure which reached 67 percent two years later. See Haines, 45.

52. On Mitchell protests, see Wolfe, *Pileup on Death Row*, 43–50.

53. "On the March Again: New York and San Francisco," *The Nation* (May 1, 1967), 550–553.

CONCLUSION: 1974 AND BEYOND

1. Wells's release summarized in Kevin Wallace, "Getting Out, in Style," *San Francisco Chronicle* (July 2, 1974); "Chauffeur Meets Con at Prison Door," *Sacramento Bee* (July 2, 1974); and "In Jail 46 Years, Man Wins Parole," *New York Times* (July 8, 1974). Wells particularly cited the help of Willie Brown in "Wells Says 'Power of the People' Freed Him," *The Black Panther* (July 13, 1974). Wells's "power to the people" explanation is noted in all of the above except *The Sacramento Bee*.

2. "About Charles Garry: Wesley Robert Wells," *The Black Panther* (June 21, 1969). "Welcome Home, Bob Wells," *The Black Panther* (August 3, 1974). Three-part Wells interview in *The Black Panther* (July 27, August 3, and August 10, 1974). Garry, *Streetfighter in the Courtroom*, 35. Garry's 1974 quote in "Wells Says 'Power of the People' Freed Him."

3. On Jerry Brown's 1960 influence, see Robert Pack, *Jerry Brown: The Philosopher Prince* (New York: Stein and Day, 1978), 135–140.

4. On the death penalty during the Brown years, see Tim Redmond and Alan Kay, "In Defense of Rose Bird," *San Francisco Bay Guardian* (September 3,

1986), 9–14. On the end of rehabilitation in California during the 1970s, see Pack, *Jerry Brown,* 135–140; Cummins, *Rise and Fall of California's Radical Prison Movement,* 252–253. On the national politics of rehabilitation in the 1970s, see Edgardo Rotman, *Beyond Punishment: A New View on the Rehabilitation of Criminal Offenders* (Westport, Conn.: Greenwood Press, 1990).

    5. Brown quoted in David Broder, "Candidate Brown—A Politician of the 70s?" *Los Angeles Times* (May 9, 1974). On Brown's antiliberal fiscal policy, see Davis, *City of Quartz,* 180–182. Brown vetoed the 1977 Deukmejian bill, only to be overridden by legislative veto (a 1977 Field Poll recorded 71 percent support for the death penalty in California, versus 23 percent opposition). At the same time, however, Brown passed more anticrime legislation in first two years in office than Reagan had in eight. See Pack, *Jerry Brown,* 135–140.

    6. Caryl Chessman, "A Letter from Death Row," *Psychology Today* (February 1969), 39–41.

    7. On the racialized politics of the New Right in California and elsewhere since the 1960s, see Howard Winant, "Behind Blue Eyes: Whiteness and Contemporary US Racial Politics," *New Left Review* (September/October 1997): 73–88. On the recent politics of crime, see John Irwin, James Austin, and Chris Baird, "Fanning the Flames of Fear," *Crime and Delinquency* (January 1998): 32–47. On California's prison population, see Mark G. Koetting and Vincent Schiraldi, "Singapore West: The Incarceration of 200,000 Californians," *Social Justice* 24, no. 1 (1997): 40–53. For a recent, comprehensive statement against the death penalty, see Marvin E. Wolfgang, "We Do Not Deserve to Kill," *Crime and Delinquency* (January 1998), 19–31.

    8. Christian Parenti, *Lockdown America: Police and Prisons in the Age of Crisis* (New York: Verso, 1999), 243. For a sampling of abolitionist arguments favoring life without parole, see Richard C. Deiter, "Sentencing for Life: Americans Embrace Alternatives to the Death Penalty," in Bedau, *Death Penalty in America,* 116–134.

    9. Mareva Brown, "Beyond Death Row: A Second Chance at Life," *Sacramento Bee* (November 12, 13, and 14, 1995).

    10. On Massie's earlier position, see Truman Capote, "Today, I Was Scheduled to Die," *Esquire* (October 1968), 194–196; and Robert L. Massie, "Death by Degrees," *Esquire* (April 1971), 179–180. On his actions while on parole, see Mareva Brown, "Trusted to Go Straight, He Killed for 2nd Time," *Sacramento Bee* (November 13, 1995).

    11. On Lavergne's life after parole, see Brown, "Beyond Death Row" (November 12 and 13, 1995).

Index

Composition:	G & S Typesetters, Inc.
Text:	10/13 Sabon
Display:	Sabon
Printing and binding:	Thomson-Shore, Inc.